Motivational Interviewing

Theory, Practice and Applications with Children and Young People

Edited by Dr Eddie McNamara

Positive Behaviour Management

PBM
7 Quinton Close
Ainsdale
Merseyside PR8 2TD

www.positivebehaviourmanagement.co.uk

D1438606

First published 2009 by Positive Behaviour Management (PBM)
7 Quinton Close
Ainsdale
Merseyside
PR8 2TD

ISBN 978-0-9562918-0-6

Acknowledgements

I would like to take the opportunity to thank Dr. Henck van Bilsen for introducing me to Motivational Interviewing at the 1988 Behaviour Therapy World Congress conference held in Edinburgh. Further attendance at an extended MI training course and a "booster" session both run by him consolidated my grounding in MI.

Thanks too to my wife Joan without whose unqualified support I would not have been able to have had such a fulfilling career.

Contents

Contributors

Eddie McNamara

Eddie McNamara works as an Independent Educational Psychologist. He has written extensively in the areas of the prevention and management of problem behaviour, changing behaviour through changing how young people think about their behaviour and eliciting motivation to change from children and young people. Eddie has written books, chapters and articles of a very practical nature in these areas. He is also a sort after trainer in the area of MI and an accomplished speaker.

Cathy Atkinson

Cathy Atkinson is an Educational Psychologist working for Bury Council and Academic and Professional tutor on the Doctorate in Educational and Child Psychology course at the University of Manchester. She has used MI extensively in work with primary and secondary aged pupils and has undertaken research into the effectiveness of MI as an intervention. She runs Facilitating Change, an organisation which promotes the use of MI in helping young people to understand and challenge their behaviour and which offers resources, training and support for practitioners wishing to use MI.

Clive Edmunds

Clive Edmunds has worked in the field of drug and alcohol treatment for 17 year as counsellor, trainer, programme developer, consultant, tutor and course designer. Currently he is Registered Manager of a detox and stabilisation unit in the west country. He has also worked in community drug services with adults and young people as well as working as a freelance trainer attached to the local drugs services education and training team. Clive has been running training courses on Motivational Interviewing since the late 1990s. He trained with Steve Rollnick and Jeff Allison and went on to train as an MI trainer with Miller and Rollnick.

Abbey Rice

Abbey has an MA Psychotherapy and Counselling and is Parenting Coordination Manager for Portsmouth City Council - with a focus on coordinating the development and delivery of a comprehensive range of support and guidance sevices for all Portsmouths parents. She has a particular interest in the application of Motivational Interviewing to working with 'hard to reach' pre-contemplative parents. Abbey also heads up a Youth Consultancy operating as a Social Enterprise. Young people have been trained and supported to deliver as 'Young Consultants' accredited Self Development and Training Skills courses to other youngsters (age 11-25yrs).

Vanessa Wood

Vanessa is an Educational Psychologist working with West Sussex Educational psychology Service. She is one of three educational psychologists seconded to the West Sussex Youth Offending Service parenting project. She has an MSc in Experimental Psychology and an MSc in Educational Psychology. Vanessa has a particular interest in the behaviour of children and young people, both at home and at school.

Mawuli Amesu

Mawuli is a Qualified Social Work Manager, Trainer and an experienced practitioner using the solution focused brief therapy Motivational Interviewing approach. Mawuli has over 14 year experience working with children, young people and their families in a variety of settings, including Social Care, Education and Health. Mawuli is currently working in Education as a Behaviour Improvement Programme Consultant, and previously managed two Multi-agency teams consisting of Educational Psychologists, Teachers, Family Workers, Behaviour Support Workers, and Education Welfare Officers. As a Solution Focused Motivational Interviewing Practitioner/Trainer, Mawuli's skills are a valued resource for Social Care in their preventative work with children and their families to prevent breakdown and with YOT's (Youth Offending Team) to prevent recidivism. He regularly works in Education providing training in behaviour management and group work to improve behaviour and attainment.

Vicky Booth

Vicky is an Educational Psychologist in Doctoral Training, currently undertaking the professional training course at The University of Sheffield and working for Wigan Educational Psychology Service. She has a particular interest in exploring the views of young people who are refugees/asylum seekers - through narrative, in order to build on the strengths and resiliencies of these young people. A strengths-based perspective has permeated her work, including teaching for five years and working as an Assistant Educational Psychologist in Sheffield. Vicky sees Motivational Interviewing as being a positive approach for including young people in facilitating change for themselves and the settings they learn in.

Martin Hughes

Martin is a Senior Educational Psychologist for Sheffield City Council's Children and Young People's Directorate and an Associate and Professional tutor to the Doctoral training programme for Educational Psychologists in the School of Education, Sheffield University. He has worked in three educational psychology services in the UK and was a Senior Educational Psychologist with the Ministry of Education in Singapore. Martin is interested in using Q methodology in order to explore the viewpoints of children, so as to understand better, how practitioners might engage more effectively as helpers and how appropriate approaches might be located within a suitable model of change. Martin believes that if professionals had a better understanding of a young person's view of their own behaviour, potential help and possibilities for change, then interventions might be targeted more effectively. Martin also does occasional work as an expert witness.

Stuart Duckworth

Stuart is currently undertaking a Doctorate in Educational Psychology at Manchester University focussing on Narrative approaches to working with adolescents. Stuart's current focus of work is the 'Social Inclusion' of children with SEBD and/or at risk of permanent exclusion. His further areas of interest are the application of psychology in the wider community and with other agencies within Children's Services. Areas of Psychology of particular interest include Motivational Theory, SFBT & Solution Oriented approaches, Narrative Therapy, Resilience, Positive Psychology - and other areas that emphasise and utilise people's strengths/resources. Stuart is a member of Sefton EPS.

Patricia Davison

Patricia is employed by the Belfast Library and Educational Board (BELB) Educational Psychology Service. She worked as a main grade psychologist until her promotion to specialist senior with the Behaviour Support Team (BST) in 2004.

The work with the Behaviour Support Team involves promoting positive behaviour management and inclusion in schools. Patricia provides training and consultation on issues regarding social, emotional and behavioural difficulties, and works preventatively and systemically with schools. Other areas of interest within psychology include promoting mental health in schools.

Joe Duffy

Joe has been working as a Psychologist since 1990. Since 1998 he has been working as a Senior (Specialist) Educational Psychologist in the South Eastern Education & Library Board's Behaviour Support Team.

The primary aim of the Team is to encourage the promotion of positive behaviour in schools. This involves providing INSET, supporting and advising/consulting with staff and working with children and young people who have emotional and behavioural difficulties.

In September 2007 Joe became a Professional & Academic Tutor, on the Doctorate in Educational, Child and Adolescent Psychology Course, School of Psychology, Queen's University Belfast.

Jonathan Middleton

Jonathan began his teaching career in 1987 and worked in a specialist Social Services Unit. Jonathan qualified, as an EP in 1995, became a senior EP (Behaviour and Inclusion) and was then made Principal EP. Jonathan's doctorate involved investigating the perceptions of young people in SEBD provision. His continuing interest is focused upon young people and their families who are described as experiencing social, emotional and behavioural difficulties.

Patricia Lunt

Tricia Lunt was originally a Primary school teacher and an early years Advisory Teacher. She now works as an Educational Psychologist for St Helens Local Authority. Tricia believes education can be transformed for the better by listening to the views of children, young people, their parents and carers. Her interests are in therapeutic interventions, social, emotional and behavioural difficulties, counselling and autism.

Beth Williams

Beth Williams is a registered Chartered Psychologist in private practice. Beth previously worked for Tameside Metropolitan Borough Council. Whilst working in Tameside Beth used motivational interviewing as part of her generic EP work, trained others, including secondary school learning support unit and pastoral staff, teachers within the Home and Hospital Service and the PRU to use MI. She used MI extensively in her work as lead psychologist with BEST (Behaviour Educational Support Team).

Preface

Eddie McNamara

Working with children and young people is an exciting and rewarding occupation. Significant numbers of young people grow up experiencing emotional, behavioural and social difficulties (EBSD) which, if not successfully addressed in their pre-adult years, often result in dysfunctional adults. This dysfunctionality may find expression in the person evidencing mental health problems – causing distress and problems to themselves, their families and sometimes the wider community.

The incidence of behavioural and/or mental health problems in both youth and adult populations is difficult to quantify, not least because of issues surrounding definitions and problems with regard to collecting data. However, the incidence is sufficiently high for the UK Government to give a high priority to the expansion and development of mental health services for children and young people.

Such an emphasis on early intervention has significant face validity – for successful early intervention has the potential to reduce the incidence of mental health problems in adulthood. Further, it is also intuitively reasonable to assume that the earlier problems are addressed the greater the likelihood of success – for 'problem behaviour' is less rigidly entrenched in the individual's behavioural repertoire.

Up to The 1960's psychoanalytic methods were the favoured approach.

These methods were somewhat exclusive to the extent that they could only be used by professionals with many years training and experience – and therefore reached but a small proportion of the population that needed help. Consequently, behavioural approaches, based on learning theory, very quickly replaced such methodology in the 1970's and onwards – particularly in educational settings.

Behavioural approaches are based on the assumption that behaviour is learnt: and so tackling inappropriate behaviour became an exercise in teaching the young person to learn appropriate behaviour which replaces the inappropriate behaviour.

Such a rationale has had, and continues to have, a major positive impact on the methods used by the helping professions when engaged with 'disturbed' or 'disturbing' young people.

However, over recent years, it has become accepted that behavioural approaches can be somewhat limited with regard to tackling effectively the complexity of the problems that are addressed. Why? The answer to this question is as follows. Children and young people function within three modalities, thinking, feeling and behaving. Consequently some problems presented by children require the intervention to address feelings and thinking as opposed to merely addressing behaviour – for sometimes addressing behaviour alone is insufficient - see McNamara (2004).

The methodologies that are currently being developed and used to redress the shortcomings of the behavioural approach are referred to as 'cognitive-behavioural approaches'. It has been accepted that i) how people think can effect how they behave and ii) sometimes the focus of intervention should be on changing the way people think in order to effect change in their behaviour.

There are a number of principles that underpin cognitive-behavioural approaches. Perhaps the most important of these is that the intervention should be seen as a collaborative endeavour between the 'helper' and the 'helped'.

For such a principal to find expression in reality requires that the person, young person in our case, wants to be helped ie is motivated to change.

When such is not the case, then attempts can be made to elicit motivation by using the techniques of motivational interviewing (McNamara, E. 1998). However, some young people present as particularly resistant to the idea of change, be they drug addicts, pupils engaging in serious disruptive behaviour or other groups. Such groups are often referred to as 'hard to reach'.

This book addresses the problem of hard to reach children and young people.

Chapter 1 describes the theory and practice of Motivational Interviewing (MI). For if the powerful positive effects of Cognitive–Behavioural approaches are to be harnessed then a necessary pre-requisite for them to effect change is for the person to be helped to actually want to be helped ie to be motivated to change. In many situations such is not the case – and then the initial 'problem' facing the helper is to elicit motivation to change. The first chapter of this book describes how this can be achieved.

When the person to be helped is very resistant to the notion of change, some common sense approaches that people might use can actually have the opposite effect to that intended ie they might consolidate resistance. These approaches are referred to as "roadblocks to change" (Gordon, 1970). This is such an important issue that a chapter has been devoted to how one can respond effectively to resistance on the part of the young person. The strategies used deliberately do not confront the resistance head on but accommodate it to a degree – to the extent that it is recognised as being valid and may even be partially agreed with. However, such recognition and partial agreement is accompanied by an alternative perspective or a reframing of the words of the young person – a response which may encourage the young person to look at their situation from a different and potentially more productive perspective. These techniques are termed "rolling with resistance" and are addressed in *Chapter 2.*

In *Chapter 3,* Cathy Atkinson describes her work with children and young people in educational settings. She describes how MI can be used to help 'nudge' initially reluctant young people through the stages of change by facilitating them to explore and challenge their own ideas and beliefs about behaviour which is of concern to others and sometimes to themselves.

In *Chapter 4* Clive Edmunds shares his experience of using MI when working with adults in a residential setting and describes his gradual move to working in a community setting for a young peoples service. Clive describes two case studies, identifying those aspects that seemed to be successful and those that did not.

Government legislation in recent years has resulted in parents being referred to help agencies. Such parents include those given Parenting Orders, those having children referred to Youth Offending Teams and so on. Some, perhaps many, of these parents are reluctant to engage with the professional members of these teams. In *Chapter 5* Vanessa Wood and Abbey Rice describe how they engage with such parents. They include in this chapter four illustrative case studies of working respectively with reluctant, resigned, rationalising and hostile parents.

Mawuli Amesu, in *Chapter 6,* brings our attention to the similarities between the theory and practice of MI and Solution Focused Counselling (SFC). He then goes on to illustrate ways in which techniques from MI and SFBT (Solution Focused Brief Therapy) can be combined to help children, young people and their families work through the process of change.

When working within the MI paradigm, judgements are made by the counsellor as to which stage of change the client is at. Such judgements are substantially made on the basis of what the client says and how they say it, although client non verbal behaviour is also of account. Sometimes children and young people find it hard to put into words their thoughts, feelings, beliefs and judgements. Vanessa Wood and Abbey Rice describe how they have circumvented such problems by developing a Questionnaire approach to this aspect of MI. They describe their work in *Section 1* of *Chapter 7.*

In *Section 2* of this chapter Martin Hughes and Vicky Booth describe how they have addressed the same problem by developing card sorting assessment strategies derived from Q-Sort Methodology.

The contents of *Chapters 8 and 9* are novel in that the focus of the three contributions moves away from a focus on the clinical application of MI in therapeutic settings.

In *Section 1* of *Chapter 8* Jonathan Middleton and Patricia Lunt report on a retrospective evaluation of a Project to facilitate the staff of a school for SEBD (Social, Emotional and Behaviourally Disturbed) pupils acquiring and using MI skills.

In *Section 2* Stuart Duckworth describes how he utilised the stages of Change Model to facilitate a school staff self assess where they where as individuals and also as a staff group with regard to five priority areas identified for staff development.

In *Chapter 9*, Joe Duffy and Patricia Davison describe the way in which they have integrated MI strategies into a consultation model within the context of school-based behaviour management teams.

References

Gordon T. (1970) Parent Effectiveness Training, New York : Plume

McNamara, E (1998) Motivational Interviewing : The Theory and Practice of Eliciting Pupil Motivation. PBM publications, Ainsdale, Merseyside UK.

McNamara, E (2004) When All Else Fails. Special Children Jan/Feb, 17 - 20

Part 1

The Theory and Practice of Motivational Interviewing

Chapter 1

The Theory and Practice of MI

Eddie McNamara

In the current educational climate everyone is encouraged to promote active pupil learning, empower pupils, engage in cooperative learning and develop non coercive pupil management skills. These are admiral aims but to a large extent their achievement depends on a commitment from the pupils to share the aspirations and goals of their teachers. In other words pupils have to feel motivated.

This chapter is concerned with strategies that can be used to elicit commitment to change from pupils ie elicit intrinsic motivation. The counselling approach which incorporates these strategies is known as "motivational interviewing". If such commitment can be elicited, then internal regulation of behaviour can be fostered so that the teacher-learner interaction is one of cooperative learning, not imposed learning. While the emphasis of this chapter is on school related problems, the description of the theory and practice of motivational interviewing has applicability to a wide range of counselling situations.

Motivation

Motivation is a very important concept because of its central role in facilitating pupil endeavour. Although the concept of motivation may appear elusive, at the practical level teachers and psychologists have addressed the many factors that influence pupil behaviour in order to facilitate pupil learning.

Covington (1992) identified three sources of motivation: they are:

i) emotion – feelings can arouse and inhibit action

ii) cognition – thoughts can trigger, sustain and inhibit action

iii) physiology – heightened levels of adrenalin can produce fight or flight responses

These *internal* motivational factors contrast with the *external* motivational factors, usually rewards and sanctions, that are often incorporated into teachers' whole class and individual pupil management strategies.

Rewards/punishments can be considered aspects of motivation in that behaviour tends to occur more frequently when it is rewarded and less frequently when it is punished. As rewards and punishments are environmental consequences of behaviour they are considered to be external motivators.

However, individuals may wish to behave in some ways but not in other ways regardless of external consequences. For example, on one occasion a student may wish to go to a discotheque and have "a good time" and on another occasion the student may forego the visit to the discotheque in order to study – consequently not experiencing the "good time".

In this latter situation the environmental determinant of behaviour (discotheque attendance and associated "good time") is over-ridden by internal controls or *internal motivators.*

In other words at any given time behaviour is governed by the interaction of internal and external motivational factors.

The *self regulation* of behaviour can be viewed as the degree of control an individual exercises over the environmental influences on behaviour.

In educational situations learning experiences are designed to facilitate student learning. Teachers attempt to make the experiences interesting so that the students will persist at the tasks in the face of difficulty ie be *motivated*. This scenario constitutes an example of the teacher setting up a learning situation to elicit *internal motivation*.

In addition to making the learning activity interesting the teacher also gives the student feedback both during and after task completion. This feedback, when positive, is reinforcing and encourages the student to continue to apply him/herself to academic task demands. Such teacher behaviour praise, feedback and encouragement – constitutes *external motivation*.

Teachers may not always succeed in making the academic task demands interesting. Consequently external motivational systems are often developed to reward pupils ie motivate them. These systems may include social reinforcement (praise and attention), stars, stickers, team points, certificates or free choice of activity.

External motivational systems are very effective in the Primary school sector and can also be effective in the Secondary school sector. However the use of "crude" external motivational systems such as stars, stickers, house/team points and so on is less age appropriate in the secondary educational sector – to the extent that there is an expectation that as pupils grows older so they will become less reliant on external motivational systems and will become more self-motivating.

Self-Motivation

The concept of self motivation is complex – for the internal self-regulatory system is influenced by many factors e.g. aspirations and feelings of competency. Learning in a school context is not always pleasant and interesting. It usually requires a lot of effort and persistence from the learner. Some learning activities may even create discomfort and tension and therefore be resisted by the student. When there is resistance to learning the institution of an external motivational system has to overcome this resistance. Even when successful, this external regulation of behaviour is really only a temporary solution, for it is important that pupils learn to regulate their own behaviour and do not come to rely solely on external forms of regulation.

In summary, there are both internal and external regulatory systems that determine how students behave. The external regulatory system is made up of the environmental factors that influence behaviour. The internal regulatory system is more complex and is made up of such things as the student's aspirations and feelings of competency.

Conclusion

Thus it can be concluded that motivation is not a unitary construct but is a term used to summarise the net effect of all the internal and external factors that influence behaviour.

Pupil Motivation

Boekaerts (1994) has described three different levels at which motivation can be studied in educational situations. They are the *superordinate level*, the *middle level* and the *momentary* level.

Superordinate level   This refers to the student's general inclination towards learning.

Middle level   This refers to the student's inclination and attitude towards different areas of learning e.g. science, languages or music.

Momentary level   This refers to the student's commitment to specific curricular tasks.

When students do not show an inclination towards learning at either the superordinate and middle levels and spasmodic or negligible inclination at the momentary level then they are variously described as *disaffected, disillusioned, alienated, passive* and *reluctant* learners. If such personal dispositions find expression in behaviours which unduly interfere with the learning and teaching processes in classroom situations the pupils are referred to as *disruptive*.

The above array of labels used to describe pupils communicates a pessimistic outlook with respect to educational and social achievement. Firstly, the pupils do not share a commitment to the goals and aspirations of their educational institution and teachers. Secondly, inherent in these descriptions of the students is the assumption that the pupils concerned are not motivated to change and therefore their situation is permanent and unchangeable.

This is a rather pessimistic scenario given the increasing concern about the growing numbers of disaffected pupils.

Fortunately pupil management techniques have been developed to effect change in pupil behaviour. These techniques have been described in the literature e.g. McNamara, 1996(a) and 1996(b). However the pupil management techniques described aim to bring the pupil behaviour under teacher control. This "control state" is something of a halfway house for ideally the control state aimed for should be self-control ie the pupil should be in control of his/her own learning. There can of course be degrees of self-control. This concept is best illustrated by viewing the locus of control as being somewhere along a continuum the poles of which are teacher control and pupil self-control. This concept is illustrated in Figure 1.1

Figure 1.1: (The Continuum of Control (Jolly and McNamara, 1994)

The concept of a continuum allows for the proposition that pupil behaviour may be partially under teacher control ie externally regulated, and partially under pupil self-control ie internally regulated. Thus there can be degrees of self-control.

The external regulation of pupil behaviour can be viewed as an external motivational system. However it may be the case that pupils do not wish to behave in pro social and pro academic ways, in which case the institution of an external motivational system has to overcome this resistance. Attempts to institute external motivational systems to address disaffection have usually focused on changing pupil behaviour, specifically at changing academic behaviour. However this may be too narrow a focus of intervention for disaffection is more than negative academically orientated behaviour.

Disaffection

This consists of an integrated set of negative attitudes, beliefs and behaviours with respect to the demands of school life generally and with respect to academic demands in particular.

Given these characteristics of disaffection it is difficult to identify, construct and implement an external pupil management programme that will achieve all the necessary change. This difficulty is becoming increasingly recognised and responded to.

Tackling Disaffection

Human activity takes place in three modalities – *thinking, feeling* and *behaving*. There is a relationship and a degree of interdependency between how people think, feel and behave and this relationship can be presented in diagrammatic form – see Figure 1.2.

This model illustrates why attempts to effect change in human behaviour solely through the modality of *behaviour* are unnecessarily restrictive – for it ignores the possibility of effecting change through the modalities of thinking and feeling. In addition, if the behavioural difficulties are a consequence of faulty thinking then to address the behavioural difficulty without addressing the faulty thinking may be ineffective ie if *dysfunctional thinking* results in *dysfunctional behaviour* then the dysfunctional thinking should be addressed.

Self Change

When an individual engages in inappropriate behaviour the movement to engaging in appropriate behaviour involves two stages. The *first* stage involves the individual deciding that he/she wants to change ie becomes motivated to change. The *second* stage involves translating the commitment into successful action: it is important to remember that wishing for change does not mean that it will be achieved for striving for change can be hampered by lack of the skills necessary to achieve the change.

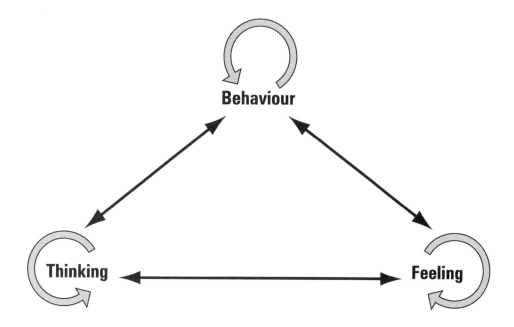

Figure 1.2: The interactional relationship between thinking, feeling and behaving

Stage one is probably best achieved by counselling techniques ie talking therapies. Stage two is more likely to be achieved by behavioural and/or cognitive behavioural strategies.

Behavioural strategies have been described extensively in the literature e.g. McNamara (1996a),(1996b) as to have cognitive behavioural strategies e.g. Fox (2001), Squires (2002).

This chapter is concerned with stage one – strategies for eliciting commitment to change. The counselling approach that incorporates these strategies is known as motivational interviewing. If such commitment can be elicited then internal regulation of behaviour can be fostered so that the teacher-learner interaction is that of *cooperative learning*, not *imposed learning*.

Motivational Interviewing

This counselling approach enables counsellors, teachers and other professionals to address the problem of lack of motivation to change in a structured and positive manner. Motivational Interviewing (MI) has proved successful with clients presenting with addictive behaviours e.g. to heroin, alcohol. By "proved successful" is meant that clients who may have been coerced into treatment have become motivated and actively committed themselves to the treatment programmes (Miller and Rollnick, 1991).

In educational situations some pupils do not want to be in school and do not share the goals and aspirations of their teachers. By analogy it seems appropriate to address the problems of these pupils using the counselling approach of motivational interviewing.

There is an extensive literature on the effectiveness of self-management programmes e.g. Kanfer and Spates (1977). The use of any self-management programme is dependent on the commitment of the pupil to change his/her own behaviour. There must be commitment to both the behaviour change and to the self-change programme. Thus, eliciting pupil commitment to behaviour change is a necessary pre-requisite for pupils to engage in self-management programmes. Lack of commitment to change is an obstacle to change particularly pertinent to the situations of the pupils who qualify for the various descriptors used previously to describe some pupils ie alienated, reluctant, passive, poorly motivated, disaffected.

The counselling approach described as *motivational interviewing* is an effective way of eliciting pupil commitment to behaviour change – change that is necessary if the pupil is to access and implement self-management programmes. Apart from designated staff with significant pastoral responsibilities, it is unlikely that many teachers will engage in motivational interviewing in counselling situations – but most teachers with a knowledge of the theory and techniques of motivational interviewing can incorporate some of the techniques into their day to day conversations with pupils ie engage in motivational conversations.

A description of MI follows. The structure is as follows:-

i)   The model of the Stages of Change

       The *theory* and *goals* of MI – goals that facilitate movement from the stage in which the pupil does not accept that a problem exists (precontemplative) to the decision to change stage (determinism) in which the pupil has accepted that a problem exists and has decided to do something about it.

ii)   The strategies and techniques used in MI.

The Model of the Stages of Change

In 1982 Prochaska and DiClemente published one of the most influential articles to appear in the psychological literature – "Transtheoretical Therapy: Towards a More Integrative Model of Change". They reported that over 200 psychological therapies had been identified. Such a range of potential psychotherapeutic interventions is a source of potential difficulty for the Psychotherapist who seeks to identify the most appropriate intervention for a particular psychological difficulty.

Prochaska and Di Clemente (op.cit.) asked the pertinent question "Are there over 200 unique processes of change for each of the forms of therapy identified?" They did not find separate change processes unique to each system of therapy. But a comparative analysis of 18 leading systems of therapy led them to the conclusion that there were 5 central processes of change. This conclusion led to the development of the stages of change model. This is referred to as the transtheoretical model (TTM) as it reflects the path of therapeutic change regardless of the type or nature of the therapeutic process engage in.

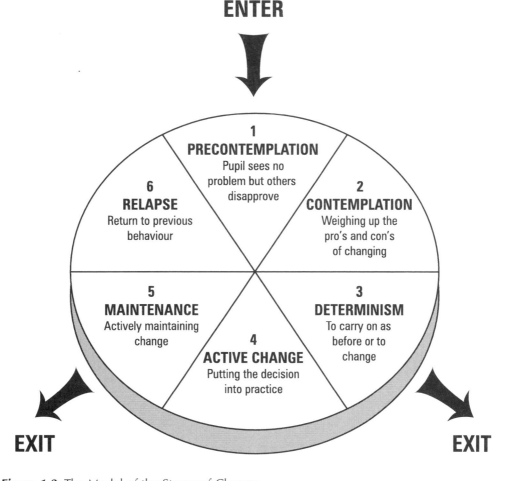

Figure 1.3: The Model of the Stages of Change

The TTM is not part of MI but essential to it: for MI strategies aim to facilitate a client to move from a situation in which they have no inclination to change their 'problem' behaviour through a series of stages to a situation in which successful client self-change of behaviour has been achieved. The TTM is the means by which the therapist can 'calibrate' where the client is with respect to readiness to change and hence identify the next stage to facilitate client movement to. MI is the means by which the therapist facilitates such movement.

The TTM has been described as consisting of 5 or 6 stages – depending on whether or not the 'decision to change' is viewed as a distinct stage.

The model of the stages of change is illustrated in Figure 1.3.

Stage 1

Precontemplative

In this stage the client* does not acknowledge that a problem exists. The client may not be conscious or aware that a problem exists or may not accept that the situation is problematic. In this stage it is not the client who thinks that he/she has a problem, but rather significant others e.g. parents, teachers, counsellors, society. The disaffected pupil is in the precontemplative phase. There are many reasons to be in precontemplation. Miller and Rollnick (1991) summarise these reasons under the headings i) reluctance ii) resignation iii) rationalisation and iv) rebellion.

1. **Reluctant** precontemplators	2. **Resigned** precontemplators
3. **Rationalising** precontemplators	4. **Rebellious** precontemplators

Reluctant precontemplators

These are people who through lack of knowledge or inertia do not want to consider change. This phase is characterised by a lack of explicit awareness either about the impact of the problem or sometimes even an awareness of the facts about the problem. Reluctant precontemplators are characterised by a reluctance to change rather than a resistance to change. The counselling strategy to address reluctant contemplators aims to raise knowledge, awareness and concern about the problem.

---

* When general statements about the use of MI are made the terms "client" and "counsellor" are used. When statements about the use of MI are made with reference to children and young people then the term "pupil" or "student" is used and the terms "counsellor" and "teacher" are used inter changeably.

Resigned precontemplators

These are people who appear to have given up on the possibility of change and who are resigned to the status quo. They sometimes feel overwhelmed by their problem and either don't want to even think about it or feel that it is too late to do anything about it. They may well have tried unsuccessfully in the past to tackle the problem. The counselling strategy to address resigned precontemplators aims to both instill hope – by promoting feelings of *self-efficacy* and *internal attribution* – and to explore the barriers to change.

Rationalising precontemplators

These are people who can readily identify reasons why the problem is not a problem or why it may be a problem for other people but not for themselves. The rationalising precontemplator often feels that he/she has all the answers – in contrast to the resigned precontemplator who feel that he/she has none of the answers. The rationalising precontemplator can be differentiated from the rebellious precontemplator in that the resistance of the former is more in the *thinking* whereas the resistance of the latter is more in the *emotions*.

Empathy and reflection are the counselling techniques of particular use, particularly double sided reflection.

Rebellious precontemplators

These are people who usually present as hostile and resistant to change. Rebellious precontemplators often exhibit low self-esteem incorporating external attributions and low feelings of self-efficacy.

Some observations on the precontemplative stage

1) It may be particularly difficult to move a client on from the precontemplative stage: it is therefore important for the counsellor to have as the initial goal movement towards the comtemplative phase – and not to a decision to either change or not change – for if the contemplative phase is underemphasised the client may well decide on the status quo. However, it must also be recognised that the client may wish to exercise informed choice and carry on for the present with what others consider a problematic behaviour. At the least the counsellor tries to ensure that this is an informed choice by eliciting and bringing into full consciousness i) information about the behavour and ii) the impact and consequences of the behaviour.

2) "The problem" may not mean the same thing to the client as it does for the counsellor. For example, a student may be referred to a school counsellor for persistently copying another student's homework. The student may see the problem as "getting caught" rather than one of copying per se.

3) We cannot make precontemplators change their behaviour – and it is usually counter-productive to try to do so. *See Chapter 2*

Stage 2

Contemplative

In this phase the client is willing to consider the problem and the possibility that change may be desirable and beneficial. Many clients with problems present themselves to the counsellor at the contemplative rather than the precontemplative stage - for the contemplative stage is a stage of ambivalence. For example, many smokers do consider that smoking may be a problem but they do not give up smoking. What the counsellor has to facilitate is a move from the contemplative stage to the decision stage ie determination to take action to give up smoking. Motivational interviewing strategies aim to assist in the movement to decision making. These strategies include eliciting information about i) the negative consequences of the problem and ii) the positive consequences of change. Eliciting personal information from the client is far more powerful than the counsellor providing information at a more general level. It is important during the contemplative stage that the pros and cons of the change are considered as well as the pros and cons of the *problem behaviour*. For example, the problem behaviour may be disruptive classroom behaviour. The pros of this from the pupil's perspective may be that i) the teachers focus on social behaviour and let poor quality academic behaviour go without comment and ii) the pupil may gain peer group esteem. The cons are that the pupil will i) not do well academically ii) be subject to disciplinary consequences and iii) have reports of unsatisfactory behaviour sent to parents.

The pros and cons of change could be as follows. Pros – i) academic progress is more likely ii) sanctions will be avoided and iii) parental approval will be forthcoming. The cons might be i) peer group ridicule for changing from oppositional to compliant behaviour and ii) the perception that changing behaviour from oppositional to cooperative was synonymous with the teachers "winning" and the self "losing".

Some observations on the contemplative stage

1) It may be possible to anticipate some of the possible cons of changing and plan to minimise their effect: sometimes the cons of change may have been identified because of previous unsuccessful attempts to change e.g.

    Pupil   *"When I did my homework on Tuesday I had to miss training (football) and so they put me on the bench"*

    Teacher   *"So you want to do your homework on Tuesday night but you also want to go to football training"*

2) Contemplation is not a commitment to change. This is an important distinction to make as failure to engage a client in a treatment programme may be a consequence of misinterpreting interest in changing ie contemplation, with a decision to change. For example, during health campaigns in the workplace it is not uncommon for between 70% to 80% of the smokers in the workforce to express an interest in giving up smoking. When programmes are developed and offered the take up rate is often less than 5%. This is strong empirical

evidence that interest is not synonymous with commitment to change. The "missing link" in such health promotional activities is a motivational strategy to facilitate a move from contemplation to determination and readiness to take action. In educational situations scenarios which reflect the above contemplation /decision to change "missing link" are not uncommon. When pupils are referred to the form tutor because of misdemeanors it is not uncommon for the pupil to:-

i)   agree to change his/her behaviour

but

ii)   within days be re-referred for similar behaviour

On the basis of this the pupil may be described as insincere, expedient, lacking self control, lacking appropriate social skills and so on. Any of these conclusions may be accurate, but it may also be the case that in the counselling situation the pastoral teacher either:-

i)   concluded the interview when the pupil was in the contemplative stage and misinterpreted this as a decision to change on the part of the pupil

or

ii)   concluded *for the pupil* that the pupil would change his/her behaviour.

The techniques of motivational interviewing, particularly that of *eliciting concern*, facilitate client movement from contemplation to decision to change

3) Sometimes the client will have made previous unsuccessful attempts to change his/her behaviour ie overcome the problem(s). Analysis of these attempts can:

i)   help identify obstacles to effective change

and

ii) identify "limited success" – and build on this, using the technique of *positive restructuring,* to promote feelings of self-efficacy and hence the probability of commitment to change.

Stage 3

Determinism – Commitment to Action

This stage is characterised by the decision to take action to cease engaging in problematic behaviour and/or engage in positive behaviour. The client appears ready for and committed to action. This stage, while characterised by the decision to take action, also includes preparing and planning for change. Later developments of the model change the semantics of Stage 3 from 'Determinism' (decision to change or not change) to 'Preparation' –the stage in which planning and commitment are secured.

When a client is identified to be in the determinism phase it is important not to conclude that this is a stable state – for there exists the possibility that the client may revert to the contemplative phase: ie it is usually the case that all ambivalence has not been fully resolved. During the "planning for change" activities it is important to respond to all the opportunities available to consolidate the move from precontemplation through contemplation to determinism ie to reflect back the client utterances indicative of increased knowledge, concern, internal attribution and self-efficacy.

The planning stage involves:

i)   deciding what the client will actually do

and

ii) identifying possible pitfalls and obstacles and appropriate responses to them.

Commitment and enthusiasm for change cannot make up for lack of skills. Therefore the planning strategy to address both i) and ii) involves problem solving strategies ie eliciting from the client possible responses and facilitating wise choices. It should always be remembered that strong commitment alone does not guarantee change.

Stage 4

Action – Implementing the Plan

The plan to achieve change is implemented by the client between the end of the session at which the plan was agreed and the beginning of the first session of the action phase. The action phase sessions serve a variety of purposes for the pupil. They are:-

i)   an opportunity to make a *public commitment* to change

ii) an opportunity to receive *confirmation and support* for the plan

iii) an opportunity to receive *external feedback* on progress of plan

iv) an opportunity to receive *positive reinforcement* for programme success

v)   an opportunity to receive *positive feedback* after verbalising feelings and thoughts of self-efficacy and internal attributions and

vi) as a result of v) *increase in sense of self-efficacy* and *internal attribution*

Stage 5

Maintenance

The length of time the client is involved in the action stage is variable. During the action stage the new pattern of behaviour is built up and consolidated. In the maintenance phase the specific active support of the counsellor and of the programme strategies e.g. graphing of record of successful behaviour change, is withdrawn. In a sense the maintenance phase is a "test" of the success of the intervention programme – for ideally the behaviour change achieved by the intervention will carry on when the programme is phased out.

Stage 6

Relapse

This phase completes the Stages of Change model. In a sense it can be considered a stage that gives added validity to the model in that it reflects the reality that even when change is achieved and sustained there always exists the possibility that relapse may occur.

A knowledge of the phases of change model facilitates the counsellor supporting the client to re-enter the cycle at the appropriate stage. If the relapse is recognised and referred to the counsellor early enough then the re-entry may be at the action phase: if referral is delayed then the re-entry may be at the contemplative phase.

A major strength of the model is the inclusion of the relapse phase since this is an explicit recognition that clients may relapse and it constitutes a positive and optimistic message that relapse should not be interpreted as "the problem cannot be overcome" but the message that "sometimes a tough problem is not completely overcome at the first attempt".

The Goals of Motivational Interviewing

To	**increase**	**Knowledge**
To	**increase**	**Concern**
To	**promote**	**Self-efficacy**
To	**promote**	**Internal Attribution**
To	**promote**	**Self-Esteem**

Figure 1.4: The Goals of Motivational Interviewing

There are five specific goals of MI. Two of the goals are directed at facilitating client movement from the precontemplative stage to the contemplative stage and two goals are directed at facilitating client movement from the contemplative stage to the determination stage ie to a position where the client decides to change.

The goals of MI are to promote *knowledge* of the problem situation and *concern about* the problem situation. If these two goals are achieved then client movement is facilitated away from the precontemplative stage and towards the contemplative stage.

In parallel with these two goals are the aims of promoting client feelings and beliefs of *self-efficacy* and an *internal attribution* of "the causes" of the problem.

In the counselling situation these objectives are not striven for in a sequential linear fashion ie first elicit knowledge about the problem situation, then elicit concern, then promote feelings of an internal attributional disposition and self-efficacy.

The counselling situation is dynamic and interactive: the skill of the counsellor lies in identifying opportunities to move towards the goals and respond to them effectively using the strategies of MI.

The four goals of MI described above are of particular importance as their relationship to client movement within the model of the Stages of Change is central to the practice of MI – see Figure 1.5.

There is a fifth goal of MI – *promoting self-esteem*. Everybody has a picture of themselves, their self image. People can evaluate their self-image either positively or negatively. If people self-evaluate themselves positively they are said to have high self-esteem whereas if they self-evaluate negatively they are said to have low self-esteem.

This is perhaps an oversimplistic notion of self-esteem, for peoples' evaluation of themselves can vary according to the frame of reference used. For example, a pupil may have low self-esteem in the academic domain – evaluating him/herself as academically less able – whereas in the sporting domain the same pupil may evaluate him/herself as a high achiever.

High self-esteem facilitates movement both from the precontemplative stage to the contemplative stage and from the contemplative stage to the determination (decision to change) stage.

If a client is low in self-esteem then the likelihood that the client will *generate* and *accept negative information* about his/her situation is reduced: for to accept such negative feedback might further diminish the client's self-esteem. However a client with high self-esteem will be more likely to accept and respond constructively to negative feedback. The client low in self-esteem is therefore less likely to accept negative feedback and more likely to engage in *denial or projection:* projection, a tendency to blame others or attribute the cause of the problem to external factors, is particularly obstructive to client movement through the stages of change as it is indicative of an external attribution style ie the client's analysis of the problem can be reduced to the proposition:-

> *"the causes of the problem are other people and/or environmental factors: therefore it's not my problem . . . and in any event there's nothing I can do about it".*

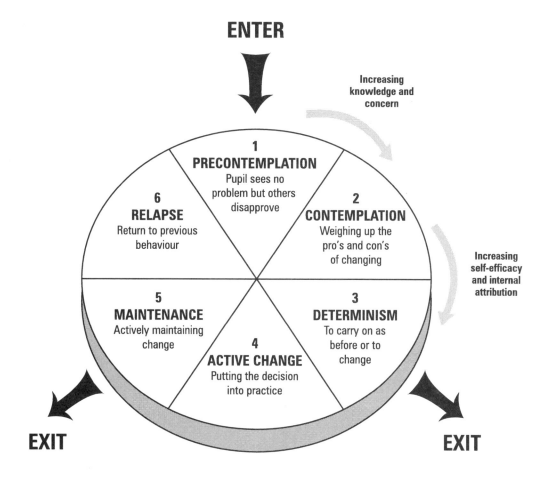

ENTER

Increasing knowledge and concern

1 PRECONTEMPLATION
Pupil sees no problem but others disapprove

6 RELAPSE
Return to previous behaviour

2 CONTEMPLATION
Weighing up the pro's and con's of changing

Increasing self-efficacy and internal attribution

5 MAINTENANCE
Actively maintaining change

3 DETERMINISM
To carry on as before or to change

4 ACTIVE CHANGE
Putting the decision into practice

EXIT   **EXIT**

Figure 1.5: Facilitating Movement through the Stages of Change

The techniques of MI aim to help the client move away from this position to one in which the client acknowledges a problem, decides to do something about it and feels that he/she can succeed with the chosen strategy.

The objectives and rationale of MI are summarised in Figure 1 6.

CONCEPT	OBJECTIVE	REASON
Knowledge	Promote	Increase the probability of movement from the precontemplative to contemplative stage.
Concern	Promote	Increase the probability of movement from the precontemplative to contemplative stage **and** thence to determination ie a decision to change
Self-esteem	Promote	Negative feedback will be more readily accepted and likelihood of denial, rejection and projection reduced
Internal Attribution	Promote	i) Increases belief that causes or attribution of "the problem" can be influenced and ii) increases the probability that 'failure' will be attributed to lack of effort not to external factors
Self-Efficacy	Promote	Facilitates the belief that change is achievable and increases i) persistence when the task proves difficult and ii) continued commitment when initial efforts result in failure.

Figure 1.6: Within person variables: therapeutic objectives and rationale to elicit/facilitate client motivation.

If a pupil is entered on the special needs register of a school then the pupil is entitled to an individual educational programme (IEP). When the IEP targets the behaviour of a pupil it is often referred to as an individual behaviour plan (IBP). The IBP has maximum chance of success if the pupil i) agrees the need for it, and ii) commits him/herself to it. This proposition is illustrated in Figure 1.7.

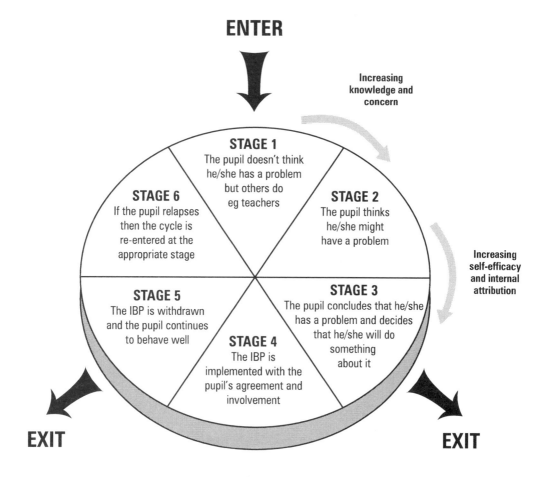

Figure 1.7: Individual Behaviour Plans and the Stages of Change

Motivational Interviewing Techniques

The techniques of MI can be considered an amalgam of humanistic, Rogerian and behavioural counselling.

The *humanistic* component is an unconditional positive regard for the client – value judgments about the client as a person are not made.

The *Rogerian* component takes the form of non directive counselling. The Rogerian method in its pure form takes the form of totally non directive counselling ie the counsellor follows the direction of the client. By reflecting back to the client the client's own utterances the counsellor uses the client's statements, observations and feelings to elicit further statements, observations and feelings. Thus the counsellor joins the client on the client's "journey".

The *behavioural* component of MI is used to modify the Rogerian component so that the *non directive* approach becomes a *guided* approach. This is achieved by the use of *selective active listening*. Before describing the characteristics of selective active listening, active listening – a core component of most counselling approaches – is described.

Active listening

Active listening has both non verbal and verbal dimensions. Active listening involves communicating to the client that what he/she says is of interest, relevance, importance and worth listening to ie is valued.

The *non verbal* behaviours that communicate this value include eye contact, facial expression and posture. For example, if the counsellor sits back, arms folded and intermittently looks at the clock on the office wall then this would not constitute active listening: active listening would include eye contact, leaning towards the client and nodding to give the client non verbal feedback that the therapist is following, understanding and sympathetic to what the client is saying.

The *verbal* manifestations of active listening include *reflecting, summarising* and *structuring* the client's utterances.

Reflecting

This can consist of parroting/repeating, rewording and paraphrasing.

   i)   **parroting/repeating** This involves simply repeating the exact words
        used by the client e.g.

Pupil   *"I nearly always do my homework"*

Counsellor   *"You nearly always do your homework"*

It is important that this reflection is not received by the client as a question – for the client may then respond with a "yes" or a "no", consequently closing down rather than opening up the exploration of a problem area. The counsellor guards against allowing a reflection slipping into a question by slightly lowering rather than slightly highering the tone of voice at the end of the reflection. This technique should not be over used as repetitious use may irritate the client.

At this point the counsellor might be tempted to ask *direct questions* to elicit information e.g. about the specifics of homework completion and non completion e.g.

   *"tell me the homework you get each night and tell me which homeworks
   you usually do and those you don't?"*

This temptation should be resisted: the time to ask direct questions is at the determination stage ie after the client has made a decision to change: the client can then be asked direct questions as part of the collaborative procedure to agree a self-change programme. The use of selective active listening is the strategy used at this early stage to elicit further information and some concern about the problem

At this early point in the counselling process direct questions should be kept to a minimum. Direct questions may:-

a)   allow the client to reply with a *"yes"* or a *"no"* and consequently close down the area of enquiry

b)   elicit resistance from the client as personal disclosures at an early stage of the procedure may be threatening to the client and not supportive of moves towards the four key objectives of motivational interviewing.

ii) **Rewording** This involves restating the client's utterances using different words and synonyms: this is particularly useful when the client uses colloquial terms e.g.

Pupil   *"I threw a rubber at the teacher and it hit him on the side of the head . . . it was wicked"*

Teacher   *"you hit the teacher on the head with a rubber and you now realise that it was a bad thing to do"* nb statement not question.

Pupil   *"No . . . it was great . . . it was a good laugh . . . everyone was laughing their heads off"*

In this case the pupil was not using the dictionary meaning of the word "wicked" but a colloquial meaning indicating "enjoyable and amusing". This is the main purpose of using rewording – for it helps to establish that the client and counsellor both *mean/understand the same things* by the words used.

The use of rewording also avoids the potential of irritating the client by the over use of parroting.

iii) **Paraphrasing** This counsellor's reflective response moves a little away from merely attempting to reflect back exactly what is said (parroting) and establishing agreement about the *content* of what is said (rewording). The counsellor attempts to establish the *intention* and *underlying meaning* of the client's words. In a sense it can be seen as a hypothesis testing reflective response e.g.

Pupil   *"Everyone knows I'm hard . . ."*

Teacher   *"You think that the other pupils see you as the toughest pupil in this school"*

Pupil   *"Yeah; they're all scared of me . . . the teachers too"*

Summarising

This strategy consists of the counsellor drawing together utterances of the client into a neat, succinct summary: this summary serves to allow the client to agree, disagree, modify or correct the counselor's accuracy of summary e.g. after five or six client-counsellor interactions the counsellor might summarise as follows.

Teacher *"As I understand it, you have been excluded from school on three occasions. If you are excluded again it will be a permanent exclusion. At first when I asked you how you felt about this you said 'I'm not arsed'. Now you said you are worried about it because it is unlikely that you will get a place in another school".*

    Pupil   *"yes"*

A summary can be used by the counsellor as a stimulus to elicit further *information, concern* and possibly *commitment* to action from the client e.g.

    Teacher   *"Not following teacher's instructions in class and then arguing with the teacher when asked to leave the classroom has led to you being excluded three times and the next exclusion may be permanent...and you do not want to be permanently excluded... what conclusion do you draw from this?"*

    Pupil   *"I suppose I'd better make sure I don't get into an argument with the teacher again"*

Structuring

Frequently in a counselling situation the client responds to the counsellor's prompts with information that can provide the counsellor with opportunities to further help the client volunteer more information about his/her situation. This in turn may provide the counsellor with opportunities to promote the development of client concern about his/her situation. However information that has the potential when reflected back to promote concern in the client, might need structuring to enhance its potential to do this.

For example

    Teacher   *"Tell me more"*

    Pupil   *"I'm not going to apologise to that dickhead"*

    Teacher   *"You are not going to apologise to the headteacher"*

    Pupil   *"No, even if I'm out of school for another 2 weeks"*

    Teacher   *"You're not concerned about missing school"* *

    Pupil   *"My GCSE exams start in three weeks and he's (the headteacher) not letting me back in for revision lessons"*

    Teacher   *"You're worried about missing your revision lessons"* *

    Pupil   *"Yes . . . You need 5 C-level GCSE's to get into the Sixth Form College"*

    Teacher   *"Let's see if I've got it right. You want to go to the Sixth Form College and you need at least 5 C-level GCSE's to get there. If you don't resolve your difficulty with the headmaster you will be unable to attend revision lessons. If you don't go to revision lessons there's less chance of you getting 5 C-level GCSE's".*

*This is an example of an advance of technique, the reflection of concern.

Pupil   *"Yes"*

Teacher   *"What conclusion do you draw from my summary of what you've said?"*

Pupil   *"I don't know really . . . well I suppose I'd better try and get back into school for the revision lessons"*

Selective Active Listening

The behavioural component of MI is the crucial strategy used to facilitate client movement from the precontemplative stage through the contemplative stage to the determination (decision to change) stage. The phrase "active listening" is prefaced by the descriptor "selective" because the counsellor *selectively* reflects back to the client that content of the client's verbalisations which facilitates the primary goals of MI being achieved ie verbalisations that are indicative of:

i) specific information about the problem being made explicit

ii) concern about the problem being expressed

iii) feelings of enhanced self-efficacy

iv) indications of internal attribution

Examples of Selective Active Listening

i)   specific information about the problem being made explicit thus enhancing the clients knowledge.

Pupil   *"Michael's always messing around that's why I hit him"*

Teacher *"You hit Michael"*

Pupil   *"He's always getting on my nerves so I punched him"*

Teacher *"You punched Michael"*

Pupil   *"Yes, and now I'm suspended"*

The teacher only reflected back to the pupil those parts of the pupil's utterances that were leading to the nature of the pupil's unacceptable behaviour being made explicit. Consequently the parts of the utterances that did not facilitate this were ignored ie *"Michael's always messing around . . ."* and *"He's always getting on my nerves"*. Thus by being selective in what was reflected back to the pupil the teacher elicited the nature of the problem behaviour from the pupil.

ii) concern about the problem being elicited

Pupil   *"Yes, and now I'm suspended"*

Teacher *"You punched Michael and as a result you have been suspended"*

Pupil   *"Yes, I shouldn't have lost my temper"*

Teacher *"You lost your temper"*

Pupil   *"I try to control it but sometimes I can't"*

Teacher *"Sometimes you can't control your temper"*

Pupil   *"Yes, that's what gets me into trouble"*

In this continuation of the MI interview the client is led from a description of a specific incident (punching Michael) to i) the identification of a more general problem, losing his temper, and to ii) an expression of concern about this general problem. The technique of selective active listening is seen in the teacher reflecting back *"you lost your temper"* but not *"I shouldn't have"* and reflecting back *"Sometimes you can't control your temper"* but not *"I try to control it"*.

iii) feelings of enhanced self-efficacy being promoted

Pupil   *"I've always done awful in all my exams except for science"*

Teacher *"You've done well in science"*

Pupil   *"Only because I like science and I revised"*

Teacher *"So when you revise you can do well in exams"*

The teacher's first response *"You've done well in science"* is a selective reflection which emphasises a positive pupil achievement and therefore promotes feelings of self-efficacy: *"I've always done awful in exams"*, the negative component of the pupil's utterance, is ignored.

iv) promoting an internal attribution bias

The above teacher-pupil interaction continued as follows:

Pupil   *"Only because I like science and I revised"*

Teacher *"So when you revise you can do well in exams"*

The teachers second response, *"when you revise you can do well in exams"* is a selective reflection that supports the development of an internal attributional style.

The Techniques of Motivational Interviewing – a Summary

Rogerian counselling is non directive: the counsellor "follows" the client's thoughts and feelings by reflecting back to the client the client's own verbalisations – which act as the eliciting stimuli or triggers for further client verbalisations which in turn further develop the previous thoughts and feelings.

In contrast to Rogerian counselling, behavioural counselling is directive: the counsellor selectively reflects back to the client. The reflections emphasise the contents of the client's verbalisations which are most likely to act as eliciting stimuli or triggers to lead or guide the client to further develop his/her verbalisations about his/her behaviour, thoughts and feelings in a direction which results in increased knowledge (information) and concern, promotes self-esteem and enhances feelings of self-efficacy and an internal attributional tendency. Conversely the counsellor either plays down or completely ignores the contents of the client's utterances that do not promote these aims of MI. This is therefore a behavioural counselling strategy as the counsellor is *reinforcing* client utterances consistent with the goals of MI and *extinguishing* client utterances that are obstructive to these goals.

MI can be viewed as a synthesis of Rogerian and behavioural counselling to the extent that none directive strategies are used to elicit a ranges of client utterances and then these utterances are responded to using *behavioural counselling strategies* to facilitate the client moving in the direction of the goals of MI.

Motivational Interviewing – Advanced Techniques

The four main advanced techniques are:

i) positive restructuring

ii) special reflections

iii) provoking

iv) Columbo technique

Positive Restructuring

This involves feeding back with a positive interpretation information given by the client with a negative interpretation e.g.

Pupil   *"I missed four homeworks last week"*

Teacher *"You did six homeworks last week"*

The aim of positive restructuring is to encourage a more positive self-image on the part of the pupil and to promote feelings of self-efficacy. Positive restructuring also strengthens the teacher-pupil relationship.

Special Reflections

At the simple level reflections take the form of repeating, rewording or paraphrasing the client's statements. The aims are i) to ensure that the therapist understands what the client is saying and to communicate this to the client and ii) to elicit self-motivational statements. Special reflections are extensions of simple reflections; there are four types.

1 *Reflections of feelings*

In this technique the counsellor attempts to reflect the feelings underlying the client's spoken words: it is to a degree a hypothesis testing approach for the counsellor has to make judgments about the client's feelings from his/her demeanour and tone of voice e.g.

Pupil   *"I went to all my lessons except Mr Smith's"*

Teacher *"You don't like Mr Smith . . . or Chemistry"*

Pupil   *"I used to like Chemistry but I hate Mr Smith"*

Teacher *"You hate Mr Smith"*

Accurate feeling reflections can both develop and consolidate client-therapist rapport and elicit further "feeling statements" from the client.

2 *Reflections of conflict*

The reflection of conflict is important as it indicates that the client is in the ambivalent contemplative stage – a necessary prerequisite for a client to move on to decision to change. e.g.

Pupil   *"I know I won't get to college if I don't pass my exams, but if I work my mates will take the piss out of me"*

Teacher *"You really want to work but you are worried about what your friends will say"*

The aim of reflecting conflict is to elicit from the client a consideration of the pros and cons of changing ie to consolidate the contemplative stage and then facilitate a move to the determination stage.

3 *Overshooting*

With this type of reflection the counsellor reflects a client's statement but exaggerates it e.g.

Pupil   *"I don't like English, French, Maths, Science or RE"*

Teacher *"You don't like any subjects"*

Pupil   *"Oh yes, I do, I like . . ."*

The aim of overshooting is to elicit from the client either confirmation of the "overshoot", positive restructuring, qualification, modification or any other observation that expands on the client's response.

4 *Undershooting*

This is the opposite to overshooting. The counsellor reflects the client's utterances but plays down the contents e.g.

Pupil   *"I can't stand some lessons"*

Teacher *"You're not keen on some lessons"*

Pupil   *"I f***ing hate chemistry and physics"*

The aims of undershooting are to elicit an expression of intensity of feeling about aspects of the problem and to elicit specificity of feeling.

5 *Provoking*

With this technique the counsellor reflects to the client that he/she has no problems. The aim is to elicit from the client that he/she actually does have problems e.g.

Teacher *"You seem to be saying that you don't have a problem"*

Pupil   *"Well I wouldn't say that"*

Teacher *"You do have a problem"*

Pupil *"I suppose I could behave better in class"*

Teacher *"You misbehave in class"*

Pupil *"Only really in French and Music"*

Provoking can be considered an extreme form of undershooting.

6 *Columbo Technique*

Some clients feel threatened in the counsellor-client situation as they like to be in control: they resist what they perceive to be a counsellor dominant, client submissive relationship. This perception can sometimes be utilised to good effect. The counsellor feigns incompetence and thereby is not seen as a threat by the client. In fact the counsellor's "inadequacy" may elicit a "helping" response from the client e.g.

Teacher *"I know I'm supposed to know how to help you but I'm not sure I know what to suggest"*

Pupil *"Well John Smith's been using one of those self-assessment diaries and he hasn't been in trouble for ages"*

Dr Henck Van Bilsen (1991) named this technique after the television series detective Columbo (Peter Falk). The Columbo technique can be a powerful facilitator of movement from the precontemplative stage to the contemplative stage and then to the determination stage.

Examples

Increasing knowledge and concern which leads to movement from the precontemplative stage to the contemplative stage with the opportunity to further progress to the determination stage.

Example i)

Pupil *"I nearly always do my homework...."*

Teacher *"Nearly always . . ."* a **reflection** that elicits the specific **information** that sometimes the pupil did not do his/her homework.

Pupil *"Well sometimes I don't"*

Teacher *"Sometimes you don't do your homework . . ."* a reflection that elicits further detailed information about none homework completion.

Pupil *"Well, on Tuesday I have football and I'm pushed for time . . ."*

Teacher	*"On Tuesday you usually don't do your homework because you go to football practice"*	**summarising,** which elicits an **expression of concern**
Pupil	*"Yes, it's a pain"*	
Teacher	*"It's a pain"*	a **reflection of concern** which elicits further **information** – information about the negative consequences of non homework completion
Pupil	*"Yes, I usually get lines or a detention"*	
Teacher	*"You get lines or detention because you don't do your home-work and you don't do your homework because you go to football practice . . . how do you feel about that?"*	**summarising** followed by a **Socratic question** (see next section). This elicited **concern** and an observation indicating **lack of feelings of self-efficacy**
Pupil	*"I don't like it . . . but there's nothing I can do about it"*	
Teacher	*"You want to do something about not doing your homework on Tuesday night?"*	reflecting a conflict and eliciting reiteration of **feelings of lack of self-efficacy**
Pupil	*"Yes, but I can't"*	
Teacher	*"Would you like to explore with me if there's anything you can do that you haven't thought of?"*	a **question** aimed at eliciting a response indicating that the pupil is in the **contemplative stage** with an "open door" to the **determination stage**
Pupil	*"yes"*	

Example ii)

Pupil	*"I got a 'U', an unclassified for maths"*	
Teacher	*"You got an unclassified for maths"*	a **reflection** that elicits a response indicating feelings of **low self-efficacy** and **internal attribution**
Pupil	*"Yes I'm stupid . . . I didn't work hard or revise"*	

Teacher	*"You didn't work hard or revise"*	**selective active listening -** reflecting the internal attribution content: but the pupil focuses on external factors
Pupil	*"No, I was knocking around with my mates . . . they've left school"*	
Teacher	*"You were spending time with your friends"*	**selective active listening -** reflecting the aspect of the pupil's utterance that was incompatible with spending time revising. This reflection elicited an indication of **conflict.**
Pupil	*"Yes, and they take the piss out of me if I say I'm staying in to revise"*	
Teacher	*"You wanted to stay in and revise but you didn't because your friends would make fun of you"*	**a summary of the conflict** makes it explicit and elicits a positive conflict resolution statement from the pupil ie movement the **determination stage**
Pupil	*"Yes, I'm going to take no notice of them in the future"*	
Teacher	*"Have you got a plan of what you will do?"*	a question aimed at facilitating movement from the **determination stage** to the **active change stage**
Pupil	*"I'm not sure . . ."*	
Teacher	*"Would you like some help?"*	a question eliciting confirmtion that the pupil has moved to the **active change stage**
Pupil	*"Yes"*	

Example iii)

Eliciting concern and promoting feelings of self-efficacy and internal attribution facilitates movement from the precontemplation stage to the determination stage

Pupil	*"I hardly did any of my homeworks last week"*	
Teacher	*"You did some homework last week"*	positive restructuring – which promotes a positive self image **(higher self-esteem)** and encourages feelings of **self-efficacy: specific information** is also elicited
Pupil	*"yes . . . English and er, er, Geography"*	
Teacher	*"You didn't get into trouble with the English and Georgraphy teachers"*	**summarising** and **structuring** elicits pupil concern about getting into trouble for not completing homework
Pupil	*"No, thank goodness"*	
Teacher	*"You don't like getting into trouble for not doing homeworks. You did your English and Geography homeworks and so didn't get into trouble with the English and Georgraphy teachers"*	further **summarising** and **structuring** incorporating the concern elicited creates the opportunity to ask a Socratic question which facilitates movement from the **contemplative stage** towards the **determination stage**
	"What conclusion do you draw from that?"	
Pupil	*"I should do all my homeworks because if I do my homework I won't get into trouble"*	
Teacher	*"Would you like me to show you some homework time management programmes?"*	a **direct question** seeking confirmation that the pupil is at the **determination stage** and is ready to prepare to enter the **active change** stage
Pupil	*"Yes"*	

The examples illustrate that potentially the client can "travel" in many different directions: the counsellors role is to guide/facilitate the client travelling in directions which increase knowledge and concern and feelings of self-efficacy and an internal attributional style. In doing so the counsellor is facilitating movement from the precontemplative stage, through the contemplative and determination stages to the active change stage.

The Use of Questions

The basic strategy of Motivational Interviewing is the use of active listening and selective active listening techniques.

Newcomers to counselling often express surprise that direct questioning is not a part of active listening: in addition newcomers also experience initial difficulty in not asking questions when engaging with clients.

Direct questioning is not a part of active listening because the purpose of active listening is to facilitate the client discovering, analyzing and clarifying problems and then going on to formulate personal responses and direct questioning is obstructive to this process. For example, if the counsellor asks a direct question and the client answers "yes" or "no" then this response can "close down" the client's exploration of his/her situation. In addition, if the counsellor asks questions relevant to a problem perceived by others but not the client, the client's resistance to the possibility that a problem exists might be consolidated e.g.

Example I

Pupil   *"I'm excluded (from school) and it's not fair . . ."*

Teacher *"How many times have you been excluded from school?"*

Pupil   *"Two, and I still think it's not fair"*

This limited client response can be compared with the more productive progress made by the client when the counsellor used reflective techniques rather than a direct question e.g.

Example 2

Pupil   *"I'm excluded (from school) and it's not fair . . ."*

Teacher *"You're excluded"*

Pupil   *"Yes, once more and it's permanent"*

Teacher *"Permanent"*

Pupil   *"Yes, if you get three exclusions you can't come back"*

Teacher *"How does that make you feel?"*

Pupil   *"Worried"*

Teacher *"You're worried that if you get excluded from school once more the exclusion will be permanent"*

Pupil   *"Yes, I won't be able to get into another school so I won't be able to take my GCSE's"*

The direct question posed in example 1 elicited the information desired but also provided the pupil with the opportunity to consolidate resistance to change and deny the problem. In contrast, the reflective listening strategy described in example 2 elicited the same information as the direct question in example I but also created the opportunity for pupil concern to be elicited – a necessary pre requisite for moving to the contemplative and determination stages.

Socratic questioning

Re-examination of the counsellor's role in example 2 reveals that a question was asked, namely *"How does that make you feel?"* This was not a question which could elicit a response that could "close down" the interview but an open ended Socratic question. Socratic questioning is used to a degree during Motivational Interviewing to facilitate "guided discovery" ie to facilitate the client "discovering" and verbalizing concerns about his/her situation. While Socratic questioning should be used sparingly it can nonetheless be a powerful facilitator of movement from the precontemplative stage to the contemplative stage and then to the determination stage. Its main advantages are that it:-

i) draws the client's *attention* to information and/or feelings which are relevant to the "problem" situation but which are outside the client's current focus.

ii) facilitates the client using the "new" information or "discovered" feelings to either *re-evaluate* a previous conclusion or construct a *new idea*.

iii) tends to move the client from the *concrete to the more abstract*.

iv) formulates the question so that the client is *able* to respond.

Examples of these four characteristics of Socratic questioning are to be found in example 2 above vis:

i) direct attention to feelings: *"How does that make you feel?"*

ii) discover feelings: *"Worried"*

iii) moves from concrete to more abstract: *pupil moves on from fact of suspension to consequence/implication of suspension*

iv) formulates the question so that pupil is able to answer: in example 2 the pupil was able to answer the question *"How does that make you feel?"* However in some circumstances it may be inappropriate to ask this question as the client may be unaware of his emotions. For example, if the pupil is offering information about his/her father who had deserted the family he/she might not be able to respond to the question *"How does that make you feel?"* but the pupil might be able to respond to the question *"Are you aware of any tension or discomfort when we talk about your father?"*

Motivational Interviewing is a collaborative endeavor and it breaches collaboration to ask questions that the client can't answer.

Assessment of Pupil motivation to change

The pupil's motivation to change can be assessed during the pupil interview/ counselling session on the basis of the pupil's statements about the "problem situation". Undue weight should not be put on a single pupil statement; it should also be remembered that a pupil may be at different phases of the change model for different behaviours and that the pupil's assessment of his/her situation may vary at different moments or during different interview sessions ie the pupil may be at the **contemplative stage**. Bearing these two provisos in mind, a number of pupil statements are listed with an indication of where in the model of phases of change the pupil might be located.

Pupil Statement	Phase of Change	Comment
1. I didn't swear at teacher	Precontemplation	Disagrees with feedback of own behaviour (denial)
2. I'm not disruptive	Precontemplation	Disagrees with teacher's "diagnosis" (denial)
3. Stop bugging me	Precontemplation	Expresses no need/desire for help (projection)
4. I'm quite happy	Precontemplation	Appears undistressed about the situation
5. I forgot etc.	Precontemplation	When failed to keep appointment with teacher
6. It's not me it's ...	Precontemplation	External attribution of cause of the problem
7. All teachers are d***heads	Precontemplation	External attribution of cause of the problem
8. Yes I do misbehave but so does everybody else	Precontemplation/ Contemplation	Acknowledgement of the act but not of the problem
9. Everybody messes about	Precontemplation	I'm no different from everybody else
10. If they (teachers) leave me alone I won't bother them	Precontemplation	External attribution of the problem
11. I haven't got any problems	Precontemplation	Denial of the problem situation
12. It's the teachers, they pick on me	Precontemplation	External attribution
13. Sometimes I'm disruptive	Contemplation	Accepts feed back about own behaviour

Pupil Statement	Phase of Change	Comment
14. I don't like getting in trouble	Contemplation	Concern expressed about the situation
15. Can I remain in school if I behave myself?	Contemplation	An example of "envisioning"
16. Sometimes I behave myself	Contemplation	Implicit acknowledgement that pupil sometimes misbehaves
17. Sometimes I do mess about	Contemplation	Differs from 9 above as uses the "I" self-reference pronoun – "I" statements should be encouraged
18. Perhaps I could behave better	Contemplation	Acknowledging a problem may exist
19. What can I do?	Contemplation/ Determinism	A wish to do something about the problem. The pupil is ready to consider moving into active change.
20. Yes, I would like to keep out of trouble	Contemplation/ Determinism	Acknowledgement of the problem situation and a desire for change; falls short of a statement of intent to do something about the problem but this may be implicit
21. I counted to ten when I felt like swearing	Determinism	An example of the pupil experimenting with self-change strategies
22. What can I do?	Determinism	The decision for active change has been taken
23. I don't care if they kick me out of school	Determinism	Has expressed a reluctance to change and will accept the consequences
24. Keeping this diary makes me think about changing my behaviour. I don't misbehave as much	Active Change	Self-change programme on-going

Pupil Statement	Phase of Change	Comment
25. I'm aiming for good reports	Active Change	Self-motivated change target set
26. I think I've got worse since I stopped keeping the diary	Relapse	The gains made during active change my have been lost

Assessment: An Exercise

The following exercise was devised by the author over 15 years ago when he began engaging in MI training. Fifteen student statements were listed and presented as in Figure 1.8. The intent was that each of the statements in Figure 1.8 was to be representative of a particular stage of the stages of change model. The intended task was for the trainees to allocate each statement to a stage and indicate their judgement by placing a tick in one of the boxes, numbered 1 to 6, at the right hand side of the statement. However, early trainee feedback revealed that some of the statements that were listed could legitimately be placed in more than one stage. Nonetheless, these statements were left in the list for the following reason. The exercise consisted of two parts. Firstly, it was carried out as an individual exercise and then as a group exercise. After each trainee had allocated the statement to a particular stage of the stages of change model the trainees were asked to compare their responses with those of other group members and to discuss discrepancies. This turned out to be a powerful learning experience for the trainees – particularly the discussions about student statements that could be located at more than one stage.

This exercise allowed the trainees to discover, as apposed to being told, that while some statements categorically indicate the stage of the stages of change model that the client is at, for other of the statements such was not the case.

Readers are asked to carry out this exercise and then consider their responses in the context of the following observations.

What can I do ?

The intend of the inclusion of this question was to provide an example of a student statement which would indicate that the student was at the determinism stage and ready to move into the active change stage i.e. was ready to embark on the process of change.

However, feedback from trainees revealed, correctly, that the statement could indicate that the student could be at the contemplation or relapse stage. The justification for the assessment being that the student was at the contemplation stage was that the student may have been seeking information about what would be required of him if he engaged in change ie as part of the exercise of "weighing up the pros and cons of changing".

A further possibility was that the student had actually passed through the stages of change but had relapsed. In this case the student's mindset might have been "what else can I do ?" - indicating that they felt that nothing they could do would achieve sustained change.

STAGES OF CHANGE

| 1. Pre-contemplation | 2. Contemplation | 3. Decision |
| 4. Active Change | 5. Maintenance | 6. Relapse |

		1	2	3	4	5	6
1.	What can I do?						
2.	Sometimes I behave well.						
3.	All teachers are d~~~heads.						
4.	I don't care if they kick me out.						
5.	I think I have got worse since I stopped keeping a diary.						
6.	Keeping this diary makes me think about my behaviour - I don't misbehave as much.						
7.	I'm aiming for good reports in all lessons this week.						
8.	Yes, I would like to keep out of trouble.						
9.	Yes, I do (misbehave), but so does everyone else.						
10.	Everybody messes about.						
11.	Sometimes I mess about						
12.	Perhaps I could do better.						
13.	If they (the teachers) leave me alone I won't bother them.						
14.	I haven't got any problems.						
15.	It's the teachers, they pick on me.						

Figure 1.8: Stages of Change Exercise.

Sometimes I behave well

the importance part of this student statement is the part of the statement that has not been verbally articulated: for Implicit in this student statement is the message "and sometimes I don't behave well". This student statement places the student at the contemplation stage of the stages of change model. The aim of the counsellor in this situation is to facilitate the student verbalising this implicit message. A simple reflection such as "Sometimes you behave well" may facilitate the student going on to describe situations in which they don't behave well ie bring into the dialogue information about problem situations. This in turn may provide the counsellor with opportunities to elicit concern about the behaviour.

All teachers are dickheads

this statement places the student in the pre-contemplation stage – attributing any problems that are in evidence to teachers ie not excepting a personal contribution to the problem situations.

I don't care if they kick me out

this statement indicates that the student is at the determinism stage i.e. having weighed the pros and cons of change has made the decision to accept the consequences of "no change". However, a case could also be made that the statement places the student in the relapse phase i.e. having achieved change for a period of time has relapsed and decided that sustained change is not possible or perhaps not even desirable. A further possibility is that the student is at the pre contemplative stage ie has not considered the pro's and cons of change.

I think I have got worse since I stopped keeping a diary

this statement places the student in the relapse stage, or at least in the segment of the stages of change model which indicates movement from maintenance to relapse.

Keeping this diary makes me think about my behaviour -- I don't misbehave as much

This statement places the student at the active change stage.

I'm aiming for good reports in all lessons this week

This statement too places the student at the active change stage

Yes I would like to keep out of trouble

This statement is difficult to place categorically at one stage of the stages of change model. It Indicates acknowledgment of a problem ie "trouble", and also of concern. Consequently the student could be considered to be moving from the contemplation stage into the determinism stage or to have "just moved into" the determinism stage. With statements of this nature care should be taken not to precipitously move on to planning for change before one has consolidated the student's desire for change.

Yes I do misbehave but so does everybody else

This statement places in the student in the contemplation stage -- for it is an acknowledgment on the student's part that he misbehaves. However, concern is not explicitly or implicitly part of the message of the student statement -- as indicated by the corollary "but so does everybody else".

In a sense it could be considered that the student has just moved into the contemplation stage. The task of the counsellor in this case is to facilitate the student moving on from general statements about the situation to specific statements regarding himself. For example, the counsellor might respond using selective active listening ie "you mess about"- dropping the voice at the end of the response to ensure that it comes across to the student as a statement, not as a question.

Sometimes I mess about

this statement places the student At the contemplation stage -- for the student unequivocally volunteered the information that a potential problem exists ie mess about. The goal of the counsellor in this case is to this is to facilitate the student "unpacking" the description "mess about" In order for the specific behaviours engaged in by the student to be identified.

Perhaps I could do better

This statement too places the student at the contemplation stage - for it is an acknowledgment that the student's behaviour may fall short of that which is required. A goal for the counsellor in this case is to facilitate the student identifying and describing specifically in what way his, the student's, behaviour could improve.

If they, the teachers, leave me alone I won't bother them

When drawing up this training exercise, this student statement was intended to be an example of a student at the pre-contemplative stage i.e. a student who had no desire to change and has an external attributional style ie blamed the teachers for any problem situations he became involved in. However, the second part of the sentence, "I won't bother them", is an acknowledgment that the student in question realises that he does "bother" the teachers. Hence it could be concluded that this student statement is at the interface of the pre-contemplative and contemplative stages or even in the contemplative stage. A selective active listening response such as "you bother the teachers" would be appropriate.

I haven't got any problems

This student statement was designed to be a statement which categorically placed the student at the pre-contemplative stage. However, this statement could also be a summary of the student's views after he had passed through the stages of change and had been in the maintenance stage for some time.

It's the teachers, they pick on me

Again, this student statement was designed to be a statement which categorically placed the student at the pre-contemplative stage. It was meant to indicate that the student was pre-contemplative and had an external attributional of style. Can you, the reader, think of an alternative interpretation of this student statement which would place the student at a stage other than pre-contemplative?

This exercise has been included by the author when engaged with other professionals in a training capacity - whether the objective of the training has been to raise awareness of MI and impart knowledge or to engage trainees in more substantial training with the aim of skill acquisition.

The most important teaching aim achieved by the use of this exercise is to illustrate that while some student statements can be "easily" interpreted as indicating that the student is at a specific stage of the stages of change model, for other student statements such is not the case. For these "other" statements, context, intonation and knowledge of the student's history are necessary additional pointers as to how the student statement should be interpreted.

Further, when trainees have engaged in this exercise, it is useful to point out that i) care should be taken not to "over-interpret" a single student utterance ii) students may be at different stages of the change model with regard to different problems and iii) in the course of an interview, a students position with regard to a given problem may vary. Consequent to the latter, when engaged in the collaborative planning of a student self-management strategy, it is therefore important to consolidate when the opportunities arise the student's concern and belief that they can succeed.

Concluding Comments

Engaging clients in programmes to improve their situation requires that the client wants to change ie is motivated. In many life contexts, including schools, clients are not motivated to change. Consequently if change is necessary either change has to be imposed, which may be a very difficult task, or else clients have to be provided with an opportunity to become motivated – and motivational interviewing allows the "helper" to make available that opportunity.

Motivational interviewing is an optimistic approach to helping people change because it rejects the view that motivation is an aspect of personality and therefore substantially resistant to change. Rather it views motivation in a practical manner and describes the concept in a manner which is useful. In other words an individual's commitment or non commitment to change in a problem area of functioning e.g. alcohol or drug abuse, is viewed as the individual's motivation or non motivation to change. Further, if the individual is helped to develop a desire for change then the individual can be said to have been helped to acquire motivation.

Motivational interviewing is being used in an increasing number of situations in which counselling help is offered. Apart from designated staff with significant pastoral responsibilities, it is unlikely that many teachers will engage in motivational interviewing in counselling situations – but most teachers with a knowledge of the theory and techniques of motivational interviewing can incorporate some of the techniques into their day to day conversations with pupils.

With training it may well be that in the future the behaviours that make up "motivational interviewing" will become part and parcel of "normal" teacher behaviour and thus contribute to an even more positive motivational milieu in our schools.

References

Boekaerts. M. (1994) Motivation in Education. The Fourteenth Vernon-Wall Lecture delivered at the Annual Conference of the Education Section of the British Psychological Society.

Covington, M.V. (1992) Making the Grade: a Self-Worth Perspective on Motivation and School Reform. Cambridge University press.

DiClemente, C.C. (1981) Self Efficacy and Smoking Cessation Maintenance: A Preliminary Report. Cognitive Therapy and Research, 5, 175 - 187

Fox, M. (2001) Cognitive-Behavioural Management Posive Behaviour Management (PBM), 7 Quinton Close,Ainsdale, Merseyside PR8 2TD

Jolly, M. and McNamara, E. Towards Better Behaviour. Posive Behaviour Management (PBM), 7 Quinton Close, Ainsdale, Merseyside PR8 2TD

Kanfer, F.H. and Spates, C.R. (1977) Self-Monitoring, Self-Evaluation and Self-Reinforcement in Children's Learning: A Test of a Multi-stage Model. Behaviour Therapy, 8, 17 - 23.

McNamara, E. (1996a) The Theory and Practice of Behaviour Contracts Positive Behaviour Management (PBM), 7 Quinton Close, Ainsdale, Merseyside PR8 2TD

McNamara, E. (1996b) The Theory and Practice of Classroom Management Positive Behaviour Management (PBM), 7 Quinton Close, Ainsdale, Merseyside PR8 2TD

Miller, W.R. and Rollnick, S. (Eds) Motivational Interviewing: Preparing People to Change Addictive Behaviours. The Guilford Press (1991)

Miller, W.R. and Rollnick, S. (Eds) Motivational Interviewing: Preparing People for Change The Guilford Press (2002)

Prchaska, J.O. and DiClemente, C.C. (1982) The Transtheoretical Approach: Crossing Traditional Boundaries of Therapy Homewood. IL: Dowe Jones/Irwin.

Van Bilsen, H. (1991) Motivational Interviewing: Perspectives from the Netherlands. In Motivational Interviewing: Preparing People to Change Addictive Behaviours. The Guilford Press (1991)

Squires, G (2002) Changing Thinking and Feeling to Change Behaviour: Cognitive Interventions Positive Behaviour Management (PBM), 7 Quinton Close, Ainsdale, Merseyside PR8 2TD

Chapter 2

Rolling with Resistance

Eddie McNamara

The Government drive for social inclusion is being reflected in schools by the drive for educational inclusion. In particular there is a special drive to reduce the number of pupils excluded from school. About a decade ago the Government recommended the setting-up of Pupil Learning Support Centres in schools. It was recommended that such Centres – targeting pupils at risk of exclusion - should offer anger management training, social skills training and counselling.

However, there is a problem, or at least a potential problem, with implementing this strategy, a problem which may account for the lack of success of some, if not many, Centres. Namely, the pupils attending the Centres may not wish to engage in any of these three activities.

In order to be in a position to benefit from this specialised Curriculum the pupils need to be motivated: when they are not, motivation has to be elicited.

It is in addressing the problem of *lack of motivation* that motivational interviewing (MI) has increasingly become a strategy of choice across many areas in which professionals attempt to engage "reluctant clients". MI evolved from the work of two psychologists, Bill Miller and Steve Rollnick, and developed at about the same time as the Transtheoretical Model of Change (Prochaska & DiClemente, 1984)). This model proposed a six stage process in which clients progress from an initial stage at which the client did not accept that a problem situation existed – and therefore did not feel a need to address it i.e. *engage in a process of change* - to a fifth stage at which change had been achieved, i.e. *the problem addressed successfully* and at which the client exited the model. The sixth stage, relapse, was included to accommodate the reality that not infrequently clients do not succeed at their first attempt to change.

The methods used to help children and young people presenting as 'problems' to others or who experience problems themselves have changed significantly over the years - see Preface.

This chapter addresses the problem of hard to reach pupils. The first section describes some approaches that are used in an attempt to overcome resistance to change, approaches that can inadvertently consolidate resistance. These approaches have been referred to as 'roadblocks to change' (Gordon,1970). The second section describes some strategies for 'rolling with resistance' (Miller & Rollnick 1991) – one of the principles of motivational interviewing.

Section 1: Roadblocks to Change

Sometimes, perhaps often when the pupil is truly disaffected, attempts to engage the pupil in conversation are met with no response or the response *"don't know", "don't care"* or *"leave me alone".*

Alternatively, the pupil might engage in conversation but be evasive or defensive. For example, a teacher may be intent on discussing with the pupil the problem of homework completion. However, the pupil may focus his contribution to the conversation around his view that too much homework is given, not enough support is given or too little time is given for completion of homework.

When resistance is apparent, teacher response to this may actually produce more resistance on the part of the pupil, whereas it is necessary to reduce it if the pupil is to move forward to change.

When a teacher tries to instruct, argue or plead with a pupil in order to put across a particular view the approach can be seen as confrontational by the pupil.

These adult responses are examples of "roadblocks" to change identified by Gordon (1970). Gordon (op. cit.) listed twelve types of parental responses which constitute "roadblocks" to change - although the intent of the parents is to facilitate change. Teachers too often respond to pupils with the response style shown by parents.

Teachers seeking to reduce resistance will need to avoid this style of communication in their dealings with pupils.

"Roadblocks" to Change

1. Ordering, Directing, Commanding

The general aim of these approaches is, by exercising one's authority, to insist that the pupil *changes his behaviour.*

Examples of this response category include:

"Don't you dare talk to me in that tone of voice".

"Just get back to Mr. Smith's class and apologise to him immediately".

"Stop trying to make excuses and make sure that you go to detention this evening".

2. Warning, Admonishing, Threatening

The general aim of these approaches is, by emphasising punitive consequences, to *stop the pupil* behaving in a certain manner.

Examples of this response category include:

"Keep going on like that and you'll end up suspended".

"You better make sure you don't say something that you'll regret".

"You're going to end up in big trouble if you go on like that"

3. Exhorting, Moralising, Preaching

The general aim of these approaches is to help the pupil *change his behaviour* or *act in a certain way* by appealing to his better nature or sense of responsibility.

These responses are characterised by the adult telling the pupil what they should or ought to do. Examples of this response category include:

"You ought to apologise to Michael as soon as you see him".

"Year 8 pupils shouldn't behave like that".

"You must always be polite to your teachers".

4. Advising, Giving Solutions or Suggestions

The general aim of these approaches is to provide solutions for the pupil which will involve *behaving in a certain way,* i.e. the adult is thinking for the pupil.

These teacher behaviours consist of the teacher telling the pupil how to solve a problem, providing answers or solutions, or suggesting courses of action. Examples of this response category include:

"Why don't you join the homework club and do your homework in the library before you go home?"

"You need to apologise to Miss Jones and then you might be allowed back in her lessons."

"I suggest that you see the careers officer and discuss your options with him".

5. Lecturing, Teaching, Giving Logical Arguments

The general aim of these approaches is to elicit behaviour change from the pupil again by the reasoning for the pupil.

These strategies involve trying to convince the pupil with facts, logical information, arguments and personal opinions. Examples of this response category include:

"You'll realise when you're older that I'm right."

"Work out what jobs you can get if you're got GCSE maths".

"You must put the time in studying if you want to pass five GCSE's".

6. Judging, Criticising, Disagreeing, Blaming

The general aim of these approaches is to make the pupil *feel bad* about themselves and consequently change their behaviour.

These responses have in common that they are negative adult behaviours that involve criticising and/or blaming the pupil. Examples of this response category include:

"You're definitely wrong about that."

"That's a very selfish way of looking at the situation."

"You're wrong you know."

"It's your fault you're in this bother, isn't it?"

7. Praising, Agreeing

The general aim of these approaches is to encourage the pupil to *change his behaviour* because it would be natural and appropriate for them to do so.

Many people will find it strange that for some pupils being positive about them and their judgements/opinions can constitute a road block to change. The reason that this might be so is that the pupil sees such adult behaviour as an attempt to control their ie the pupil's behaviour, and they are not wiling to concede control.

Examples of this response category include:

"I think you have the ability to do well."

"You seem pretty popular to me."

"I think you're right."

"I completely agree with you."

Whilst providing affirmation of positive behaviours is important, giving praise can also be perceived as patronising, particularly with when the tutor precedes the remark with *"I"* statements, e.g. *"I think.."* *"In my opinion.."* Here the praise can be interpreted by the pupil as conditional on his having behaved in such a way that was acceptable to the tutor.

To counter the possibility of 'praise' being counterproductive, MI practitioners distinguish *affirmation* from *praise* and utilise affirmation not praise. Praise is usually distinguished by the use of 'I' statements whereas affirmation is characterised by third person statements e.g. "You have done well".

8. Interpreting, Analysing, Diagnosing

The general aim of these approaches is to help the pupil to *provide insight for the pupil* which will lead to behaviour change.

These behaviours communicate to the pupil your belief that you perhaps know him better than he knows himself. The adult might think that he has interpreted the pupil's behaviour, identified a motive or 'diagnosed' a problem.

Examples of this response category include:

"You're doing that to get your own back."

"You're saying that to make me feel sorry for you."

"You're self-esteem is pretty low, isn't it?"

9. Reassuring, Sympathising, Consoling, Supporting

The general aim of these approaches is to help the pupil to *feel better.*

"I'm sure that you'll get through this ok."

"It is a worry."

"Don't worry, things can only get better."

"I know some lessons can be very boring."

Whilst the tutor wishes to retain a sense of optimism, such approaches can stop the pupil from exploring his concerns further.

10. Probing, Questioning, Interrogating

The general aim of these approaches is to *find out more information* about the pupil's situation.

Asking questions may be very helpful when the pupil is motivated to collaborate with the adult to strive for change: but to ask the pupil to share information before they are ready is usually counter-productive, ie elicits resistance. The pupil needs to feel safe in the environment before he can feel sufficiently confident to respond to questions.

Examples of this response category include

"Why do you hate school?"

"When did you start feeling this way?"

"How many times have you bunked school this term?"

"What do you think will help?"

11. Withdrawing, Distracting, Humouring, Diverting

The general aim of these approaches is to encourage the pupil to think about something other than about the problem or what is worrying them.

Examples of this response category include

"Let's talk about this another time."

"By the way, what did your dad say when you told him that you scored the winning goal?"

"I bet you felt like hitting him one!"

"How did you enjoy on the field trip last week?"

12. Name Calling, Ridiculing, Shaming, Sarcasm

The aim of these approaches is to demean the pupil: to "put down" the pupil and elicit guilt and embarrassment.

Examples of this response category include

"Even pigs don't soil their own sty!"

"You behaved like a right prat!"

"I'm going to make an example of you at tomorrow morning's assembly!"

"Apply for Uni? You must be joking

All twelve categories of teacher behaviour described above, although intended to be helpful, can be unhelpful when attempting to engage a reluctant pupil in conversation. However, in different circumstances perhaps some of the approaches will be reasonable and some even effective. Many of the responses may be interpreted as the tutor trying to be corrective and set the pupil right – what can be termed the "righting reflex" (Rollnick et. al 2008). The tutor wants the best for the pupil and tries to find ways to cajole the pupil to change.

Roadblock 12, however, is the exception. Name calling, ridiculing, shaming and sarcasm are all totally unacceptable ways of talking to pupils.

At the pragmatic level, it is known that such adult behaviours can often either result in the pupil leaving the situation or elicit a verbally or even physically aggressive response from the pupil.

At the level of principle, such adult behaviours infringe the pupil's right to be treated with fairness, dignity and respect.

In the context of counselling, or indeed any "helping" situation in which adults are interacting with young people, e.g. parenting or teaching, unconditional positive regard for the young person is a basic requirement and a duty on the part of the adult. It is the inappropriate behaviour which is unacceptable and rejected, not the young person engaging in the behaviour.

Section 2: Responding to Resistance

Within motivational interviewing resistance can be viewed as speech that fails to engage in discussion of behaviour change. It is useful to consider that speech or non-verbal signals by a pupil which may be viewed as "resistance" indicate a dissonance in the relationship between pupil and tutor ie a lack of agreement. The feeling of the tutor may be that (s)he is in a combative verbal struggle with the pupil.

What behaviours may be classed as resistance? These could include instances where the pupil is arguing against change, negating tutor comments, blaming others for their situation or denying that there are any behavioural issues to resolve. It could also include the pupil refusing to engage with the tutor or indicating boredom by facial expression, body language and gestures. The pupil may also engage in a pretence of agreeing with the tutor by smiling, nodding and "playing the game". The preceding section contains a comprehensive list of adult verbal behaviour that can elicit or consolidate such pupil behaviours.

When the pupil is displaying resistant behaviour the tutor may attempt to demonstrate his power within the relationship by claiming pre-eminence or assuming the expert role e.g. "Don't argue with me because I know what is best for you". Alternatively, a tutor may elegantly articulate the case for change by providing stark feedback on the disadvantages of the pupil's current patterns of behaviour. Tutor advocacy of this nature may lead to a "point/counter-point" dialogue which results in an adversarial conversation between the two parties. This approach is not within the spirit of motivational interviewing.

Resistance can be viewed as the opposite of change talk. Within change talk the pupil may use language which indicates that he is preparing for change. For example, he may verbalise his/her desire for change, ability to change and reasons for and need to change current behaviours. The pupil may also use language which expresses a commitment to change and begin to discuss taking steps towards such change. This is a sequential process. Preparatory language in itself may not be indicative of future behaviour change but may indicate commitment language . The strength of commitment language e.g. "I will get better grades this term", has been found to be an indicator of subsequent behaviour change. (Amrhein et. al 2003).

Alternatively the pupil may use *sustain talk* – talk in which (s)he verbalises justification for sustaining the current behaviour. Such talk may include language expressing a desire to continue with current behaviour, an inability to change and reasons and need for continuing with the status quo. At a more extreme level the pupil can be openly hostile towards tutor intervention and use argument, blaming of others, interruptions and disengagement from the dialogue to avoid discussion of behaviour change.

Thus, within the dialogue certain pupil responses, specifically *change talk,* and *resistance,* signify consonance or dissonance in the tutor/pupil relationship. They are useful predictors of subsequent behaviour change.

Within motivational interviewing the tutor responds to change talk in order to increase it, and to sustain talk and resistance in order to reduce it.

The challenges for the tutor in minimising dissonance and maximising consonance in the relationship are demonstrated in Figure 2.1 below:

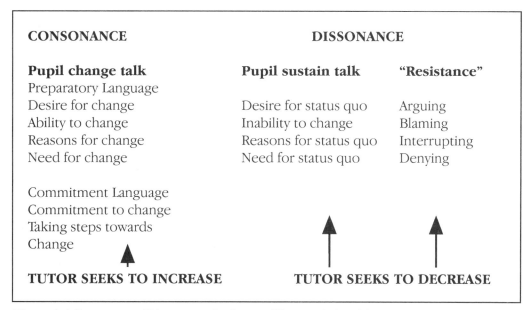

Figure 2.1 Consonance/Dissonance in the pupil/tutor relationship.

It is important to accept that a pupil who has been instructed to attend an interview may, quite naturally, object to being coerced to discuss their situation. This is normal. Indeed it would be strange for a pupil to look forward to such an interaction where the agenda was discussion of problematic behaviour. For the pupil may not be aware that current behaviours are an issue or they may be unwilling to change current behaviours.

Pupils who enter a dialogue unaware of need for change, or unwilling to change, can be viewed as not contemplating change ie they are at the pre-contemplative stage within the Prochaska & DiClemente model.

Alternatively the pupil may be prepared to consider change at some stage in the future or may be ambivalent about change. The tutor who begins a dialogue by setting out an agenda for change is working from an entirely different perspective than the pupil. The tutor is assuming some degree of readiness for change. It is likely that, in any resulting dialogue, dissonance in the relationship will develop.

Pupils who are the subjects of administrative systems designed to improve the quality of inputs, processes and outcomes within the learning environment may be cynical about the reasons for engaging in dialogues designed to promote behaviour change. Thus pupils may, some might say quite healthily, respond with behaviours which we then label as resistant but which are in fact natural responses to coercion.

When confronted with resistance the most effective tutor response is to *"roll with the resistance"*, i.e. to 'flow' with what the pupil verbalises - but offer a new perspective on the pupil's issue or reframe the words of the pupil in a way which allows him or her to explore his or her ideas more fully.

Rolling with resistance is one of the principles of motivational interviewing but is a challenging concept for many tutors whose natural tendency may be to directly confront or challenge pupil views or advocate specific courses of action. It involves respect for the pupil as an autonomous young adult and acknowledging and accepting his or her point of view. Resistance occurs when the pupil is not engaging in talk which considers change. There may be a variety of underlying thoughts and feelings which manifest as verbal resistance.

People not contemplating change may be classified as resigned, rationalising, rebellious or reluctant to change (DiClemente & Velasquez 2002). This classification is considered below.

Some pupils may be resigned to their current behaviour patterns. A pupil may feel he is "rubbish at maths" and that there is no point in his trying harder at coursework. Those who are resigned to continuing the status quo may lack hope. The role of the tutor is to maintain a sense of optimism but without directly arguing the opposite viewpoint i.e. that the pupil could succeed if he tried harder. The latter response may increase pupil resistance and promote the feeling of hopelessness in the pupil.

Some pupils may rationalise their current behaviours by a process of logical justification. An example is the pupil who comments that it is futile to work harder in maths because he "can't get a Grade C on his current syllabus so there's no point in trying for the difference between a D and an E grade." A tutor who attempts to reel off a list of reasons why, despite this fact, the pupil should work harder may increase the level of resistance and ultimately this may result in a win-lose argument between tutor and pupil.

Pupils may have a very heavy investment in the current behaviour and rebel against any attempts at curtailment. A pupil who does not enjoy lessons and behaves disruptively as "class clown" may have a need to retain that behaviour as it is crucial to his identity in the classroom environment. The tutor who appears critical of the behaviour or who tells the pupil that "all the others will get on in life but you" may be met by an emotional response such as anger or tears. The tutor role may then move towards calming or placating the pupil. The subject of behaviour change then becomes secondary to protection of the pupil's self-image.

Pupils may be reluctant to consider change because it takes too much effort to move out of their current "comfort zone" of behaviour. They may be fearful of the consequences of trying to change their behaviour. Acknowledgement that there is a problem requires the pupil to accept that, in one area of his or her life, behaviour is out of personal control - and loss of esteem may result from trying to change but failing. A tutor who exhorts this pupil to try harder may engender resistance in the form of the learner becoming more entrenched in his or her viewpoint. Such a pupil may deny there is a problem or blame others. Adolescents who have not taken responsibility for their own lives can be happy to enter a dialogue but may be keen to change the behaviour of others rather than their own behaviour.

We have noted that Motivational Interviewing sees "resistance" as symptomatic of dissonance in the relationship between tutor and pupil. Accordingly we can view pupil resistance as a "stop sign" which gives the tutor a cue to change style. It can be a signal that the pupil is not comfortable with the dialogue. The tutor needs to take a step back, understand the reasons for pupil resistance and address these. It is how the tutor responds to resistance that makes the difference. If the tutor is to positively discuss behaviour change with the pupil, the pupil must feel that he is in a safe environment and can comfortably explore the possibilities of such change.

So, what tutor responses are appropriate and likely to reduce pupil resistance?

Miller and Rollnick (2002) highlight a number of categories of responses which enable the interviewer to roll with resistance and avoid argument. Crucial to all responses is empathic listening and acceptance of the individual

The first category comprises variations on reflective listening responses.

A **simple reflection** can often pleasantly surprise a pupil who may expect to hear a counter perspective.

e.g. *Pupil:*   *"I'm rubbish at maths and hate going to the classes".*

  Tutor: *"You don't feel very competent when you are in the class and it puts you off going in there".*

An **amplified reflection** may emphasise in more extreme terms what the pupil has said. It is important that the tutor amplifies the reflection genuinely and without a sarcastic tone or facial expression indicating cynicism or incredulity. An amplified reflection allows the pupil to analyze their original statement and reconsider the intensity of it.

e.g. *Pupil:*   *"There is no point in trying...I haven't done any work this*
                   term so it's too late now".

      Tutor: *"You have completed absolutely no coursework at all*
                   this term".

The pupil can consider the objective truth of his initial statement and may
            respond:

      Pupil: *"Well, I did that assignment on history and passed that but*
                   not much else"

      Tutor: *"So, you've done one complete piece of quality coursework and*
                   there are a few pieces outstanding".

A **double-sided reflection** is useful to highlight ambivalence and allow the pupil
to relax in knowing that his/her ambivalence is acknowledged. The use of "and"
rather than "but" enables the tutor to highlight that the pupil is experiencing
conflicting thoughts or feelings.

e.g. *Pupil;*   *"Ok, so you shouldn't smoke weed in school but I only do the*
                   same as all the Year 11's do and what's wrong with smoking the
                   odd spliff?"

      Tutor: *"Sure and that's confusing. - On the one hand you know it is*
                   not 'on' to be using drugs and on the other hand it is no more
                   than what your friends do".

In the example above the tutor could usefully follow the dialogue by allowing
the pupil to consider the reasons why the school has rules banning drug use.
Often the pupil may then detail the reasons for the rules and the consequences
of taking drugs.

Other responses to resistance described by Miller and Rollnick include shifting
focus, reframing, agreement with a twist, emphasising personal choice and
control and coming alongside the pupil. These are outlined below.

We noted above that pupils may be very skilled at rationalising their current
behaviour and putting up strong arguments for maintaining the status quo.
Dialogue can become "stuck" on a certain point. Rather than engender resistance
the tutor can **shift focus** to another point.

e.g. *Pupil:*   *"OK I may have some problems with attendance but I am not a*
                   persistent truant. I have been in most weeks..."

      Tutor: *"I don't think that is the main issue at this point. I am concerned*
                   about some of the other things that are going on with you at the
                   moment. Tell me about what is happening for you in school
                   generally...".

In this way the tutor avoids getting stuck in an argument about the exact details
of attendance. The conversation may well return to absence patterns later in the
dialogue when there is consonance in the relationship.

Another useful technique is **reflection with a twist.** The tutor can offer initial agreement with the pupil but may slightly change or "twist" the direction of the dialogue in his/her response.

e.g. Pupil: *"Why are you teachers always banging on about coursework. What about the problems in this place? You'd get fed up if you had to put up with all the building works going on!"*

Tutor: *"Sure you make a relevant point there and that is important. We need to take account of the constraints you are all working under. Let's look at where you are in relation to school life in general"*

Similarly the technique of **reframing** acknowledges the truth of the pupil's statement but offers a new meaning or interpretation of it.

e.g. Pupil: *"My English tutor is always nagging me about my spelling and grammar when I do course work and she picks on me all the time"*

Tutor: *"It is making you angry that you feel singled out by your tutor who wants the best for you. Perhaps we could explore ways of communicating with your tutor that are more useful?"*

The spirit of motivational interviewing recognises the dialogue as a collaborative, problem solving approach which emphasises the autonomy and freedom of the individual to make informed choice. If people feel that their freedom to decide their own behaviour is being threatened they react by asserting their liberty. It is important to reassure the pupil that they alone decide their future levels of **control** over their behaviour.

e.g. Pupil: *"Everyone is on my case - to do this, to be like that, to act differently. I feel like a puppet in here"*

Tutor: *"Nobody can force you to change anything. You are a young adult and you're the expert on yourself. you know what changes you may choose to make and the decisions are all yours ultimately".*

A final strategy is **coming alongside** the pupil. This is an extreme form of amplified reflection or may be used as a summary. In effect it is accepting the pupil's expressed desire, reasons and needs to maintain the status quo and acknowledging that the pupil may not be ready for change. It is not a technique to be used as a manipulative ploy to encourage the pupil to argue for change nor should it be used in a manner which indicates that the tutor is giving up on the pupil. It is useful where the pupil has identified a number of reasons for continuing their behaviour.

e.g. Pupil: *I don't think anything is going to change me and this is just hopeless.*

Tutor: *"It may be that no support will change the way things are and you are best sticking with the way things are. What is your inclination?*

Paradoxically the pupil may then volunteer some reasons for change. Often at this point the pupil may generate an idea for change and place a condition on the change process.

In the example above the pupil may comment

Pupil;   *"Well, perhaps it might be OK if I could just get away from my current mates because I get sucked in"*

The techniques above can often feel to the tutor that they are giving up control of the dialogue and that the pupil is not being sufficiently challenged or confronted about his or her behaviour. It is important to remember the collaborative nature of the dialogue which treats the individual as an autonomous young adult. Within the spirit of motivational interviewing the tutor's role is to evoke the pupils own ideas about behaviour change and empower the pupil to achieve desired changes.

In summary, motivational interviewing seeks to encourage change talk by the pupil, and the interviewer's role is to use strategies to minimise dissonance in the relationship and focus on the target behaviour. Ultimately it is for the pupil to confront their own behaviours and explore and resolve their ambivalence about behaviour change.

References

Amrhein, P.C., Miller, W.R., Yahne, C.E., Palmer, M. and Fulcher, L. Client Commitment Language during motivational interviewing predicts drug use outcomes, Journal of Consulting and Clinical Psychology. Vol 71(5) October 2003, pp. 862-878

DiClemente, C.C. and Velasquez, M.M., (2002) Motivational Interviewing and the Stages of Change in *Miller W.R. and Rollnick, S Motivational Interviewing: Preparing People for Change,* New York, The Guilford Press

Gordon, T (1970)   Parental Effectiveness Training. New York: Wyden

McNamara, E (2004)   When All Else Fails. Special Children Jan/Feb, 17 – 20

Miller, W. R. and Rollnick, S. (1991) Preparing People to Change Addictive Behaviour New York, The Guilford Press

Miller, W. R. and Rollnick, S. (2002) Motivational Interviewing: Preparing People for Change. New York. The Guilford Press .

Prochaska, J.O. and DiClemente, C.C. (1984) The Transtheoretical Approach: Crossing Traditional Boundaries of Therapy. Homewood.Il., Dowe Jones/Irwin

Part 2

Applications of MI with Children, Young People, their Teachers and Families

Chapter 3

MI in Educational Settings: Using MI with children and young people

Cathy Atkinson

Using MI within educational settings

In adult counselling interactions, the impetus for behavioural change is often precipitated by worries about the impact of a particular behaviour (e.g. drinking or smoking). However, concerns about behaviour in schools are often expressed by a third party, such as a teacher or parent, rather than a young person. Atkinson and Woods (2003) identify MI as a useful approach for professionals working in schools, because in such circumstances the young person may be ambivalent about changing their behaviour. Furthermore, there are often reasons why the young person wants to maintain a particular pattern of behaviour, such as peer status or task avoidance (Atkinson and Amesu, 2007).

MI can be used to facilitate the movement of young people through the stages of change by encouraging them to explore and challenge their own ideas and beliefs about a particular behaviour. McNamara (1998) advocates the Model of Stages of Change (Prochaska and DiClemente, 1982; 1998) as a useful framework for assessing the young person's motivation to change. Statements that young people make about 'problem behaviours' will be indicative of their readiness for change and will help professionals identify the most appropriate strategies for supporting young people. Different techniques and strategies are likely to be more successful at different stages of change. For example, a behavioural contract may well be an unsuccessful intervention for a young person who is ambivalent about change. Some of the possible strategies which may be useful at each stage of change are identified in Figure 3.1.

When using an MI approach it is important to encapsulate what Miller and Rollnick (2002) refer to as the 'Spirit of MI'. There are three aspects to this.

1. Collaboration – *'That the method of motivational interviewing involves exploration more than exhortation, and support rather than persuasion or argument'* (page 34).

2. Evocation – That MI requires finding intrinsic motivation for change from within the person and evoking it. Resources and motivation for change are presumed to lie within the young person.

3. Autonomy – In the spirit of MI, responsibility for change should be given to the young person and it is the young person, rather than the supporting adult, who should ultimately present arguments for change. The professional should support the young person's capacity for self-direction and facilitate informed choice.

The difficulty with this philosophy for professionals working with young people in school is that behavioural support may be aimed at achieving some sort of 'social control', rather than helping the young person to address his or her needs (Atkinson and Woods, 2003). The rationale for this may of course be to protect the needs of the individual e.g. to prevent exclusion. However, Miller and Rollnick (2002) note that direct persuasion for behavioural change can be counterproductive, because not only is the ambivalent person unlikely to be persuaded, but direct argument may actually press the person in the opposite direction as they attempt to justify their behaviour.

6. RELAPSE	1. PRECONTEMPLATION	2. CONTEMPLATION
Emphasise positives – solution focused approaches **Revisit** commitment to change **Acknowledge** circumstances that may make maintenance difficult and consider additional support **Explore additional factors** that may have led to relapse (e.g. change in family circumstances, physical wellbeing) Explore resources – what has kept you from doing this **Appreciate change takes time** - most people will relapse at some time **Don't panic!!!**	Consciousness Raising – e.g. Cognitive Behavioural Therapy, Personal Construct Psychology, Solution Focused Brief Therapy **Increase Knowledge** - e.g. careers, learning opportunities **Support others -** Reframing, Empowering, Training, Referral to other agencies **Gather information about barriers** - e.g. family difficulties, peer group pressures, learning difficulties, mental health issues **Open up options** – e.g. social, leisure, learning and vocational, options for young people.	Strategies from Precontemplation plus: **Raise awareness** and consider options open to the pupil **Reframe problem** with the pupil **Offer support** in a non directive way (give choices) **Maintain contact** or identify key person who can support change when the pupil is ready **Map choices** **Develop understanding** of the psychology of change

5. MAINTENANCE	4. ACTIVE CHANGE	3. PREPARATION
Continued Pupil Self Management **Reward** **Countering** **Helping relationships** **Preparation for/rehearsal of difficult situations** where the pupil may relapse **Ongoing opportunities** to talk about feelings and progress made **Share positives** with parents/carers, peers, teachers.	**Pupil Self Management** with staff support (e.g. co joint monitoring) **Pupil owns plan** **Parent/carer involvement** **Self monitoring and review** **Environmental controls** e.g. change of class **Reward** **Countering** - providing alternative strategies (e.g. working on computer to become calmer) **Helping relationships**	**Prepare** young person and supporting adults for change (and relapse) **Agree** a plan with clear goals **Identify** who needs to support **Share** commitment and plan for change with others

Figure 3.1: Strategies that can be used at each of the stages of change

I have tried to use MI In my casework practice in an eclectic and needs focussed way, which takes account of the young person's situation and the context they are working within. The vignettes below detail some of the strategies and techniques I have used within an MI framework and will provide examples of how the approach might be used with young people.

Case Study 1 - Anthony – 'Working to Rule'

It's too late as far as I'm concerned. I can't change it now... I just can't be bothered.

Anthony, aged 13 years, was referred because of a generally negative attitude to school work, perceived low self esteem and difficulties in forming friendships. A bright and capable pupil, school were concerned about his lack of motivation and his problems relating to members of staff. Despite attending a school in an affluent area, Anthony lived on a large council estate with a high level of social disadvantage. He had been physically bullied as younger pupil.

When we first met, I used some Personal Construct work (for examples, see Beaver, 1996; Fransella, 2005) to allow Anthony to describe himself in the third person and in relation to other people. I also used an adaptation of the *typical day* technique from a brief motivational interviewing approach devised by Rollnick, Heather and Bell (1992) to identify lessons in which problems did and did not exist. It was evident from our discussions that Anthony was at the Precontemplative stage of change (Prochaska and DiClemente, 1998). Of the four types of category of precontemplator defined by McNamara (1998), Anthony would be best defined as a *rebellious contemplator* in that he appeared to be making an active choice to maintain behaviours that were perceived by school as being problematic.

Anthony told me that because he did not like school he had *"...stopped doing hardly anything. I just do as much as I've got to do."* Further discussions revealed that Anthony felt very angry at the way school had dealt with instances of bullying in Year 7 and felt that by taking this approach he would be making life uncomfortable for the adults working with him.

I attempted to increase concern in Anthony about his behaviour. I suggested that his behaviour seemed a bit like what people did in the workplace when they were dissatisfied with their job situation, which was *'work to rule'*. Anthony was happy with this concept. I tried to explore the *good things and the less good things* about working to rule, using the brief motivational interviewing approach (Rollnick et al, 1992). I also used Solution Focused questioning to try and help Anthony think about how school could be more enjoyable and to identify how he would know if he was enjoying school more. However, Anthony's objective was to make the school look bad by making it apparent that while he had not achieved his full potential when at school, he would do so at College.

> *"I'm going to stick with it till I finish school. Then I'm going to go to College and prove I can do it and that it's just the school. I'm just going to get better once I've left the school so [the school] won't look good."*

Continuing with the idea of increasing concern (McNamara, 1998) I asked Anthony to consider this position from two perspectives. Firstly, from the point of view of a busy Head of Year, looking over the GCSE results of 300 school leavers and secondly from his own viewpoint and how it would impact on his life chances. I asked him to explore two different pathways - the first in which he continued to 'work to rule' and the second in which he modified his attitude towards his schoolwork. His proposal is shown in Figure 3.2.

This diagram provided Anthony with a very clear picture of the impact his 'work to rule' stance could have on his future and a frame of reference for his behaviour. I was able to refer to this diagram in subsequent discussions with Anthony and with members of staff who were supporting him. The diagram enabled us to talk about him moving from the right hand to the left hand side – and how that might affect his future.

Despite this, Anthony still felt that change was not really feasible. His comments included, *"It's too late to do anything about it," "I can't get in higher sets now"* and *"You can't change the system"*. When I suggested a three-way meeting with his Head of Year, Anthony was reticent and pessimistic about what this might achieve. However, the empathic response and active listening strategies (see McNamara, 1998) used by the Head of Year in this meeting meant that Anthony felt heard and that his difficulties were appreciated, for example:

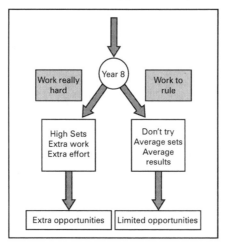

Figure 3.2 Anthony's projected outcomes of 'working to rule' and 'working really hard.'

> **Anthony:** *I don't like Geography because I don't like the person I sit next to. He's a bit of a snob and he keeps going "you [i.e. your family] don't drive a car and you don't get anything, do you?"*
>
> **Head of Year:** *So that's a bit like bullying then really isn't it?*
>
> **Anthony:** *Yes*

Once rapport had been established between Anthony and his Head of Year, he was happy to discuss how the Head of Year could support him in moving to the left hand side of the diagram. The idea of helping relationships is described by Prochaska, Norcross and DiClemente (1994) and is an important feature of MI in schools. Three way meetings can be one way in which the young person can verbalise a public commitment to change, an important feature of strengthening change possibilities (Miller and Rollnick, 2002). They can also be useful as a means of agreeing how school-based professionals, who have daily contact with young people, can help support intentions of change.

Following the intervention, the school SENCO reported that Anthony's subject teachers noted a more positive approach to his work and greater confidence in lessons. He had approached the SENCO (Special Educational Needs Coordinator) on one occasion to highlight difficulties in a particular subject (with a teacher) when in the past he had reportedly tended to avoid raising such issues. Although first indications were promising, Anthony required ongoing contact from key staff to ensure that he was able to maintain these positive changes and continue to move towards the left hand side of the diagram (Figure 3.2).

Case study 2 - Jamie – Change within a Context

McNamara (2001) describes a positive systemic intervention in a residential school for pupils experiencing emotional and behavioural difficulties (EBD) where staff worked collaboratively with a young man to reframe some of his negative core beliefs. Such an intervention can be powerful and effective. However, where support is directed less cohesively, attitudes held by staff and contextual pressures and demands can provide barriers to change and this needs to be an additional consideration when using MI is schools.

I was asked to work with Jamie, an 11 year old Year 6 pupil. The school's concerns centred on aspects of Jamie's behaviour, including non compliance, acting out in class, refusal to work and aggression during unstructured periods. Jamie was taught within a small group of ten children identified as having Special Educational Needs (SEN), separate from the rest of his Year 6 cohort.

Keen to ascertain how learning difficulties might be contributing to Jamie's perceived problems, I undertook some brief literacy and numeracy assessment and was surprised to find that all of his attainment scores fell within the average range. Furthermore, Jamie seemed bright and articulate, remorseful of his behavioural difficulties and the impact they were having at primary school. He stated that he was keen to make a fresh start at secondary school. In order to try and raise concern about the impact of his behaviour we discussed what his future years might look like if the behaviour difficulties persisted or ceased and we worked together to plot this into a diagram (see Figure 3.3 below).

One significant observation was that Jamie felt that if his behaviour improved he would be "Brainy...like other people in my class." I wondered if this related to his educational placement amongst children who had greater difficulties with learning. Jamie's identification of the problems associated with his behavioural difficulties suggested that he was at the Preparation stage and ready, with support, to make positive changes in readiness for his transfer to High School. Atkinson and Amesu (2007) suggest how adults can use questioning techniques to help the young person identify practical ways to achieve and maintain future change at this stage.

However, when I discussed suggested systemic interventions with his class teacher, including the possibility that a change of class might be more appropriate to meet Jamie's educational needs, it was evident that change within this particular context was likely to be difficult for him.

Jamie had clearly gained something of a reputation and with the impending Standard Attainment Tests (SATs) exams, the classteacher was reluctant to move Jamie from the group of children with SEN because of fears about the potential negative impact of his behaviour on that of the other pupils in the mainstream class. Furthermore, she felt that there was little that the school could do and cited problematic home circumstances as the reasons for Jamie's continuing difficulties. Jamie's parents had supported the referral, but did not attend school-based meetings to discuss support for Jamie.

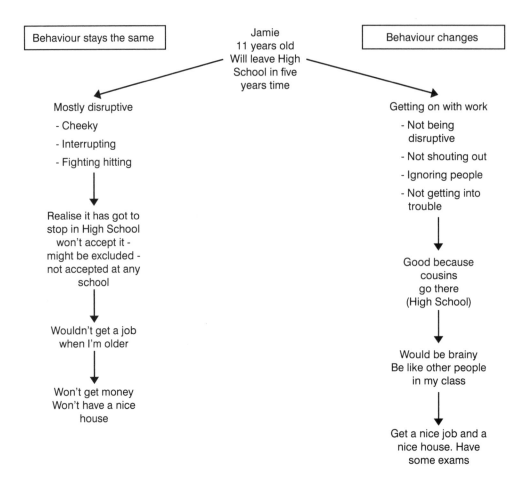

Figure 3.3 Life pathways for behaviour changing or staying the same.

In considering a positive intervention for Jamie, it was necessary to look at where the 'helping relationships' (Prochaska et al, 1994) lay within this particular context. This was necessary in order to achieve the best possible outcome for Jamie which I felt would be a successful High School transition. Following discussions with the school SENCO, it was agreed that Jamie would work with a teacher from the outreach behavioural support service, who fulfilled a parallel role at Jamie's future High School. Jamie responded well to this support and although he remained in the SEN class, his attitude was reportedly more positive. On transition to High School, the behaviour support teacher noted that he had settled well and was placed in teaching groups commensurate with his level of ability.

In the event that Jamie might return to previous behaviour, (the Relapse stage), the EP for his High School was alerted and allocated appropriate contingency time within the first term for offering additional support or consultation. It is important for practitioners working from an MI perspective to anticipate relapse. Rollnick et al (1992) note that resolutions to change often break down and it is important that the young person does not avoid contact if things go wrong.

Figure 3.4 below provides a visual representation of where some of the different stakeholders may have been in relation to the Model of Stages of Change. The school in question had undergone quite substantial recent upheaval and was under the scrutiny of Ofsted and it was easy to understand the pressures contributing to the seeming inflexibility of Jamie's classteacher. In other situations I have encountered, the young person has expressed a desire to change their behaviour, but other systemic, familial or community factors have constituted barriers to change. Obtaining the most sophisticated picture of why change is not occurring can help the practitioner to identify the most appropriate approach to intervention.

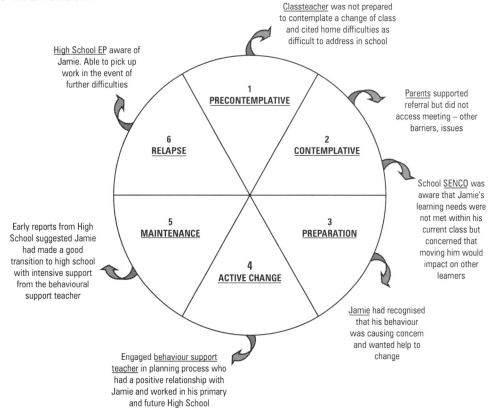

Figure 3.4 Systemic influences and perceptions of stakeholders' positions on the Model of Stages of Change

Case Study 3 – Robbie – How MI can help identify difficulties

Robbie, 15, was on the verge of exclusion from his mainstream secondary school when I was asked to see him. Consultation with the Assistant Head revealed great frustration about Robbie's behaviour. Although he was a high achiever and in all the top sets, Robbie was described as aggressive and manipulative. He reportedly felt himself to 'rule the roost' and to be 'beyond reproach.'

By the time I met with Robbie, he had already been permanently excluded but was allowed back to school specifically to see me. He was to attend an exclusions appeal and desperately wanted to return to school. I saw this as positive and hypothesised that he was at the Preparation stage, ready to work perhaps towards negotiating a behavioural contract (McNamara, 1996) with staff which would help him manage his behaviour. However, when we came to discuss the incident that led to the exclusion (persistent verbal aggression towards a member of staff), it was clear that Robbie was not willing to accept any responsibility for his behaviour. Robbie attributed events leading to his exclusion to the behaviour and actions of teachers and other pupils.

One of the goals of MI defined by McNamara (1998) is to promote internal attribution. With this in mind, we charted the incident that had ultimately led to his exclusion, to enable Robbie to examine his role in the pattern of events. Robbie had had a mobile phone with him in class, but the ring tone had not been switched on. When, on receiving a message, he looked at the phone, he was reprimanded by his teacher who told him phones were not allowed. Robbie said that the phone was not on and the situation escalated and consequently he was asked to leave the room. At this point he became verbally aggressive towards the member of staff.

When I asked Robbie to look at the sequence of events and identify whether anything could have happened differently, his only response was that the teacher should not have shouted. Even when asked about the phone, Robbie genuinely did not appear to understand how he might have been in the wrong. As far as he was concerned, he was adhering to the school rule which stated that phones should be switched off in class.

I found Robbie's responses significant. There seemed to be a contradiction between his desire to return to school (indicating he might be at the Preparation stage) and his reluctance to accept responsibility for his actions (which rooted him at the Precontemplative stage). Although it was possible that he was a *rationalising precontemplator*, attributing problems to other people rather than himself (McNamara, 1998), his apparent lack of insight stimulated me to gather some more information.

With Robbie's agreement, I visited his mother at home. She was desperate for him to return to school and extremely concerned about the impact of his exclusion on his education. When I shared the findings of my MI session, she was unsurprised and said that he had always had difficulties with rules. She cited one recent example when Robbie had become exasperated with a teacher who had written that he had been *'spitting in the bin'* while he maintained that he had, *"only done it once"*. Furthermore, he justified this behaviour saying, *"I needed to clear my throat"*. Although Robbie's social communication skills had superficially seemed strong, there was a possibility that he might have a difficulty understanding and appreciating non literal language. Discussions with subject teachers about Robbie's ability to empathise and introspect also suggested difficulties in these areas.

I agreed with Robbie to do some assessment work. Assessment of his thinking and reasoning skills revealed a large and highly significant discrepancy between his verbal and non verbal skills in favour of the latter which suggested a language disorder. I indicated to school and to his parents the possibility of a specific difficulty and explained to Robbie that this meant that there were certain things that he found difficult which might cause him great frustration. I used the 'mobile phone' example to explore how things were often not 'black and white' but that they were often grey areas. I summarised my findings to Robbie in the form of a solution focused letter, detailing the issues that had been covered and solutions for resolving these (Johal-Smith and Stephenson, 2000), cited in Atkinson and Woods, 2003). An excerpt is provided in Figure 3.5.

We also talked about 'black and white thinking'. This means that you like to have a very clear idea about how things should be. However, this is not always how things are in life and as we discussed, there are lots of 'grey areas'.

Do you remember we talked about the incident in school when the teacher shouted at you after you had looked at your phone and you shouted back:

- You told me that the rule was that you couldn't have your phone on in lessons **(clear rule/black and white thinking)**

- But your phone was on even though it wouldn't have made a noise **(unclear rule/grey area)**

- You told me that the teacher knew that phones were allowed in lessons as long as they were not on **(clear rule/black and white thinking)**

- But you also told me that this teacher did not like mobile phones and so might be much more strict than other teachers **(unclear rule/grey area)**

Often there are rules in life which not everyone sticks to exactly.

I think that it is possible that you have a specific difficulty with explaining and with black and white thinking. A specific difficulty means that you have a difficulty in these areas, but not in others.

This means that you sometimes feel angry when people don't stick to the rules, but that you find it difficult to explain this, so sometimes you do things instead that get you into trouble. The good news is that I think that you can understand this clearly and I think that your teachers will be able to help you with these skills and that this will help you avoid getting into trouble, which I know is what you want.

Figure 3.5 Extract from a letter to Robbie explaining his difficulties

Although Robbie was reinstated on appeal in light of this new information, he was subsequently permanently excluded again following a fight with another pupil. He was frustrated about this because he felt his behaviour had improved (which it had) and that he had been in fights before. He again found it difficult to identify that the behavioural expectations had changed and that fighting was no longer acceptable if he was to maintain his placement. When he moved to a Pupil Referral Unit (PRU), detailed information was provided to his new provision about his strengths and difficulties to try and alleviate the risk of similar problems recurring and to ensure appropriate support for his difficulties. It was important to discuss with staff the inherent problems in providing inflexible behavioural management strategies and that to work effectively to achieve change, planning would need to take account of his additional and different needs and to involve Robbie and his parents as partners.

Summary

I hope that these three case studies serve to exemplify the way that MI and the Model of Stages of Change can be used flexibly when working with children and young people of different ages and with different needs. As noted in Figure 3.1, there is a whole range of skills and strategies which can be incorporated into an eclectic intervention to reflect the needs of the individual. It also means that skills practitioners bring from a range of paradigms e.g. solution focused therapy, anger management, multi-agency working, can be incorporated according to the practitioner's particular strengths and competencies (Atkinson and Woods, 2003). Where the facilitator is to able to create an ethos based on the principles of MI, demonstrating understanding and empathy with the young person, they will be able to develop an appropriate and tailor-made support package. This should reflect the needs of the young person, acknowledge their stage of readiness to change and engage supportive adults in ongoing consultation.

References

Atkinson, C. and Amesu, M. (2007) Using Solution-Focused Approaches in Motivational Interviewing with Young People. *Pastoral Care in Education, June,* 31-37.

Atkinson, C. and Woods, K. (2003) Motivational Interviewing Strategies for Disaffected Secondary School Students: a case example. *Educational Psychology in Practice 19* (1), 49-64.

Beaver, R. (1996) *Educational Psychology Casework: A Practical Guide.* London: Jessica Kingsley Publications.

Fransella, F. (2005) *The Essential Practitioner's Handbook of Personal Construct Psychology.* Chichester: John Wiley & Sons Ltd.

Johal-Smith, H. and Stephenson, M. (2000) Psychology for the millennium: global challenges, local solutions: discovering the expert. *Paper presented at the British Psychological Society Division of Educational and Child Psychology Annual Conference,* 5-7 January 2000. Kent: Kent Psychological Service.

McNamara, E. (1996) *The Theory and Practice of Behaviour Contracts.* Positive Behaviour Management. Ainsdale, Merseyside

McNamara, E. (1998) *The Theory and Practice of Eliciting Pupil Motivation: Motivational Interviewing - A Form Teacher's Manual and Guide for Students, Parents, Psychologists, Health Visitors and Counsellors.* Positive Behaviour Management. Ainsdale, Merseyside

McNamara, E. (2001) Motivational interviewing and cognitive intervention *in* Gray, P. (Ed) *Working with Emotions: Responding to the Challenge of Difficult Pupil Behaviour in Schools.* London: RoutledgeFalmer.

Miller, W. R. and Rollnick, S. (2002) *Motivational Interviewing: Preparing People for Change.* New York: Guildford Press

Prochaska, J. O. and DiClemente, C. C. (1982) Transtheoretical Therapy: Toward a More Integrative Model of Change. *Psychotherapy: Theory Research and Practice, 19,* 3, 276-288.

Prochaska, J. O. and DiClemente, C. C. (1998) Comments, criteria and creating better models: In response to Davidson, in Miller, W. and Heather, N. (Eds) *Treating Addictive Behaviours,* 2nd edition. New York: Plenum Press.

Prochaska, J. O., Norcross, J. C. and DiClemente, C. C. (1994) *Changing for Good: A Revolutionary Six-Stage Program for Overcoming Bad Habits and Moving Your Life Positively Forward.* New York: Quill.

Rollnick, S., Heather, N. and Bell, A. (1992) Negotiating behaviour change in medical settings. The development of brief motivational interviewing. *Journal of Mental Health,* 1, 25-37.

Chapter 4

Substance Abuse: Using MI in Community Settings with Young People - A Personal Perspective

Clive Edmunds

I first encountered Motivational Interviewing (MI) when I worked with adults in a residential drug and alcohol treatment unit.

My clients were in effect a captive audience. A captive audience who had already made some significant changes in their lives - for they had removed themselves from the environment in which their drug use took place. It could be argued that they were well on the way to change, and in some cases had already achieved change, for they had placed themselves in a situation in which they were exposed to the rigour and routine of a residential treatment programme.

In reality, whilst many had the appearance of people in the 'action phase', the action taken was often under duress and could be considered a 'temporary sabbatical' from drug or alcohol use in order to satisfy someone else's wishes. The need to continue addressing motivational issues was paramount.

Nonetheless, as opposed to working in a community setting, I did have the opportunity to work with the client group on a daily basis. This proved helpful to me as a Practitioner as I have long been of the belief that MI is at its most effective when used a little and often. Having the opportunity to spend sometimes as little as 10 minutes each day with the client, specifically focusing on motivational issues, ensured that my own introduction to using this approach was a reasonably positive one.

When I began working with clients in community settings I did not have the 'luxury' of working with them on a daily basis. I quickly realized that the meetings I had with clients were going to be less frequent and would be interspersed with non-attendance - and were not infrequently characterized by what for me was the novel experience of them being intoxicated. Further, I quickly realised that many of the clients that were referred to me to work appeared to be firmly entrenched in a pre-contemplative state.

After a number of years developing my own MI skills I became an MI trainer. In this capacity I came into a contact with practitioners working in a broad range of settings, all of whom were involved in some way with the task of facilitating behaviour change in clients. A recurring question raised by practitioners on training courses was "will MI be a useful addition to my practice?" Of particular relevance to this chapter was the increasingly asked question "Will it work with my clients, I work with young people?". Indeed, some of the training course participants articulated the view "MI will not work with my clients. I work with young people".

Sometimes I tend to think that those of us who spend our lives trying to help people who do not always appear to want our help, need to believe that our particular group of clients are tougher, more intransigent, more resistance and more challenging than anyone else's. Whatever the reality is, it is my experience that it is hard work trying to encourage workers that the sullen, disinterested juveniles referred, unwillingly, to their service, would respond to an approach which they sometimes summarized as " American clap trap".

In my early days as a trainer, when I hadn't worked personally with young people, my response was to highlight studies, all of which supported the use of Motivational Interviewing with young people.

For example , I quoted Lawendowski (1997). He found that one session of Motivational Interviewing with 77 adolescents entering out-patient treatment in the USA, for substance abuse resulted in i) significantly higher subsequent attendance and ii) at follow-up three months post-discharge those having received MI reported significantly higher levels of total abstinence and significantly less days of illicit drug use vis

> *"Participants receiving the MI feedback showed significantly*
> *better treatment engagement and outcome as well as*
> *significant decreases in substance use".*

I also quoted McCambridge and Strang (2004). They provided one MI session to Further Education students in Inner London who were involved in use of alcohol, tobacco and illicit drugs. They reported

> *"....... the first substantial evidence of non-treatment*
> *benefit to be derived among young people involved*
> *in illegal drug use is receipt of motivational interviewing"*

The findings generated by studies such as are quoted above suggests that MI is an intervention worthy of consideration for use with substance misusing young people. However, trainees on my courses not infrequently questioned the veracity and validity of the studies reported, queried what sort of young people featured in such trials and often indicated that they mistrusted such reports. I was unable to counter such observations from personal experience at that time as I hadn't worked with young people using MI.

Subsequently I took up a position as a Tier 3 drugs-worker, in a young people's drug service. This service accepted referrals from many sources, most commonly Youth Justice Teams, generic Youth Support Services and schools. The Service provided support to those under the age of 18 experiencing drug and alcohol problems in their life. Prior to commencing the role, I expected a scaled down version of the adult drug use I was familiar with - but characterised by youthful experimentation and an emergence of associated problems.

This expectation was soon dispelled. Often the only difference was that these clients were physically smaller and hadn't been using drugs for quite as long as their adult counterparts. Their use of heroin, alcohol and ecstasy, the accompanying offending behaviour, the destruction of family life and the damage to educational and career aspirations was just the same.

Thus I was able to discover for myself whether MI *'works'* with young people. In short, my answer to the question *"Does MI work with young people?"* is *"yes"* - although the answer does rather depends on what you are expecting to achieve i.e. what *"works"* means.

Of relevance to working with young people is the following quotation from Slesnick, Meyers, Meade and Segelken (2000) –

> *"Few youths identify their risk behaviour as a problem in need of treatment or other services. Motivational Interviewing, with its non-judgmental and non-confrontational style, may be a useful approach for outreach or initial engagement".*

The first part of the sentence above encapsulates the main difficulty encountered when trying to engage meaningfully with young people in order to work with them to try to address their substance use, for many of the young people have yet to see it as "a problem". Metaphorically speaking, many of them are at the beginning of a journey, which in many cases will run for many more years, through many traumas. For many of these young people "using" is still fun - even when there is compelling evidence to the contrary. Indeed, from their perspective, the only thing that stops it from being fun is the intrusion of people like myself.

Almost without exception, I found that the client group that I was trying to engage with were aware of the statistics with regard to the prognosis for substance abusers, had been exposed to the *"just say 'no'"* message, knew what they were doing, had experienced school exclusion, had been involved with the Youth Justice system and knew the risks - yet they still found 'using' attractive.

This almost total lack of preparedness and willingness on the part of the young person to even acknowledge a problem behaviour meant that I had to review the way in which I used MI.

Engaging with a client who demonstrates a high degree of ambivalence and is still firmly attached to "problem behaviour" was not new to me.

What was new was a client group who, in most cases, had never previously contemplated the problem using presented, and had never considered doing something about it. Whilst I don't believe I stopped using certain strategies, or avoided techniques, I believe I became far more cautious and far more circumspect about what I said and when I said it. I also believe that I became even more acutely aware of the importance of paying attention to Stages of Change, recognising that if I assumed a client was more (or less) ready than they actually were, I was likely to meet with complete shut-down and an end to co-operation.

My own experience has been that the potential pitfalls that beset my work with any age group feel more pronounced and more liable to be fallen into with young people. The whole relationship feels more fragile, requiring of a gentler hand.

Further, I had to reconsider what I considered to be achievable using MI in a community setting.

Having now worked in a variety of settings in which MI has been my predominant approach, while not necessarily being in a position to offer definitive advice, I feel that I am in a position to share my own opinions, experiences and findings.

The Spirit of MI

In my opinion, it is working within the spirit of MI that matters far more than using any particular combination of strategies. Those who are relatively new to MI may find it difficult to fully understand what exactly "working within the spirit of MI" means. This was certainly true for myself - as initially when engaging, or attempting to engage, in MI practice, my attempts often consisted of 99% "strategy".

While the spirit of MI is collaborative, evocative and honouring the client's autonomy, for me the key to actively working within the spirit of MI is undoubtedly to use skilful reflective listening. "Unskilful" reflective listening tends to feel awkward and unnatural, creating a disjointed interaction. An observation occasionally made by trainees in training sessions has been that young people don't respond well to reflective listening, at times often mistaking the reflection for a definitive statement made by the Practitioner. While this may sometimes be the case, I believe it to be far less so when the reflective statements are artful, appropriate and well considered. In my opinion, the best advice that can be given to a professional intending to engage in any kind of client orientated work is to put in some reflective listening practice –and when they have done this to do it again, and again, and again!

Ensuring Meeting with the Client

When attempting to work with clients in the community setting it is necessary that they show up for appointments. This is a statement of the obvious, but it is important not to underestimate how much of an achievement this can be for clients who do so. Some Practitioners may not give client attendance the value that I do - feeling that the client's attendance often has more to do with a response to some enticement e.g. the maintenance of a script, or because to not attend would be a potential breach of a court-imposed order of some sort. However, I believe that for any individual likely to be engaged in a chaotic and unpredictable way of life, keeping appointments of any sort is to be celebrated and affirmed. Of course it is important to ensure that the affirmation is appropriate and ideally something that has meaning to the client.

Affirmation

I have found that the impact on the client of affirmation is enhanced if

- It is *'meant'* - by this I mean that what you are affirming is something that you genuinely feel is a positive. An appreciation of a client's social circumstances and an understanding of the lengths to which they may have gone to attend, greatly assist this process.

- It is not perceived as *'patronising'* - but on the other hand does not *underplay* the achievement. It is important to remember that affirmation has more to it than simply praising somebody -- for the latter is easily perceived as patronising by the client.

- It is *consistent.* If you affirm something one time, make sure you do so the next time. Clients notice these things.

Often, just *acknowledging* that you are aware of someone's struggle is enough.

Another key to increasing client attendance is to recognize that it is unlikely that the Practitioner is offering anything that many clients want. Assuming that any client will automatically want to come and sit with you, the Practitioner, and allow their life to be scrutinized is a misguided assumption.

What's in it for the client?

This may sound like a slightly mercenary question but it is realistic. People modify behaviour for a reason and generally the change is made because the change brings about an improvement for themselves. Later on in a collaborative working relationship with the client it may be the case that the supportive relationship that you have helped to create may be reward enough but initially this is not necessarily going to be so.

I do not advocate practices such as buying lunch for all my clients, and I've never made a habit of it. But nonetheless the Practitioner who goes out of his way to reduce inconvenience for the client with regard to attending an appointment, an appointment which holds no tangible reward, is more likely to enhance engagement with the client -- which is preferable to sitting in a consulting room for hours on end waiting for a client who does not appear.

Examples of such accommodations include switching venues, seeing the client at their home, picking them up and bringing them to the meeting venue and so on.

Strategies that 'Work'

There was a time when I felt that I was getting close to listing the strategies that work and those strategies that do not. I no longer feel this to be true. As with reflective listening and affirmation, skilful and well thought out use of strategies is far more important than which particular strategy one uses.

Nonetheless, two particular strategies require careful consideration when working with children and young people. These are i) *looking back/forward* and ii) *coming alongside.*

Looking Back/Forward

Looking back, for example, may be inappropriate for the 14 year old client who is sitting on the 10th floor of a tower block having -

- negotiated burnt out stair wells and empty lift shafts to get there
- lived with an alcoholic mother for most of their life
- a brother in prison
- a father not known to them

With such a client looking back to time when things were better is extremely difficult.

Highlighting this is not to say that looking back is never a good idea, but more to impress the vital importance of ensuring that use of any strategy must always be appropriate to the client.

Coming Alongside

This is always a potentially risky strategy. Joining the client in their hopelessness doesn't always have the desired effect of getting them to verbalize arguments in favour of change.

For example, on one occasion an angry relative of an alcoholic client of mine rang me up and asked why I had told his sister to keep drinking. Now I didn't actually tell her to keep drinking, but neither did I bombard her with an arsenal of reasons why she should stop. I acknowledge her right as an adult to ultimately choose her own path and determine her own actions. I voiced my understanding of the role that alcohol played in her life, how empty she felt without it and my acceptance that at that moment in time it might not be the right time in her life when she was ready to stop drinking.

Working with Children and Young People

In a sense working with children and young people is different. For example, the United Nations Convention on the Rights of Children (1989) states that

"children need special care and protection".

It is important that, when working with children and young people, as well as when working with adults, that the intrinsic spirit of MI, the *"affirmation of a client's freedom of choice",* and the recognition of the clients right to make decisions for themselves, is emphasized.

Some adults would argue that children are too young, too inexperienced and too ignorant to know what is best for them. Some such adults would then go on to argue that it is debatable that children should have the right to make their own decisions.

However, the United Nations Convention on the Rights of Children is protective of children in adult - child decision-making situations. The Convention makes explicit the children's rights vis -

> *"the right to say what you think should happen when adults*
> *are making decisions that affect you and you have the*
> *right to have your opinion taking into account".* Article 12

> *"The government should provide ways of protecting*
> *you from dangerous drugs"* Article 33

and

> *"You (children) should be protected from any activities that*
> *could harm your development".* Article 36

Thus, when working with children and young people, a fine balance has to be reached with regard to emphasizing the children's freedom to choose on the one hand and defining the limits of this on the other.

One easy way of engaging with children and young people is to be nice to them. But then, buying them a burger occasionally does not amount to helping them address problem issues - other than hunger !

When working with children and young people it is necessary to be always upbeat, friendly and forgiving when they do not show up to appointments.

However, when the objective is to engage meaningfully with this client group, being the 'good guy' alone will not suffice. While I believe that my interactions with this client group are characterized by a natural, easy-going relaxed approach, nonetheless in parallel I am quite persistent in pursuing a specific agenda. This agenda is almost always about behaviour change. This is not a soft approach, for it is easier for the client to sit and tune out whilst the irate Practitioner berates them, than to be expected to take part, to think about their life and find words to describe their struggle.

Max

Max was 14 years of age and already had several years experience of living outside of a family unit. His family of origin, though large, was dispersed to various parts of the country and Max had taken to "sofa surfing".

Max was referred to me by a Criminal Justice worker. Before I had even met with Max I had a fair idea of the exasperation that the Criminal Justice worker who referred him had experienced. "He's 'a dear' but f***ing useless" was her succinct description of Max.

My own thoughts on meeting Max were indeed that he was "a dear".....and good-natured...... and polite...... and guarded...... and homeless...... and vulnerable..... and exploited..... and naïve..... and broke......and lacking in hope - but hardly "f***ing useless".

My mantra when working with people of any age has become

> *"If you treat an individual as he is he will stay as he is.*
> *But if you treat him as if he were what he ought to be*
> *and could be, he will become what he ought to be*
> *and could be".*
> Johann Wolfgang von Goethe (1634-1719)

My first objective with Max was to get him to turn up for appointments. Towards the end of our first meeting –

- which was brief

- took place in my car

- followed a considerable drive through city streets trying to pick out a young man wearing a Bolton Wonderers shirt

I produce my diary and proceeded to identify an appropriate slot for an appointment in a week's time.

<u>Me</u>   *"Next Wednesday, at 2 pm at the team office, Max, that suit you?"*.

<u>Max</u>   *"Yes, great, see you then"* said Max as he hopped out of the car and was gone.

Max didn't see me the next week or the following week. Each failure to show was eventually followed by an apology and a grin and usually following appointments which he failed ended up with me driving around the streets trying to spot that white football shirt.

Clearly I was less confrontational and critical of Max than many of the adults he had come into contact with. But beyond this I was of no use or interest to him. He'd been told by his Worker that he needed to see this chap i.e. me, as a condition of not being placed in a \residential Establishment, so he did, as long as 'this chap' could find him.

Every time we met up the interaction was pretty much the same. Max was always polite, offered almost no detail of his life and took no responsibility for anything, including the appointment.

After several weeks of the same pattern of behaviour I decided to try something different. Some may call it bribery and some may call it other things. I told Max that if he turned up at the office for his appointment I would take him for a burger. He was on time for this appointment! For the first time he seemed to be prepared to talk. As we sat over burger and coffee he told me about his family, how he missed them, about some of the abuse he had received at the hands of older 'using' acquaintances and about his hopes and aspirations. Despite the 'miracle' brought about by a simple burger I was concerned about what would happen the following week. The next week, although this is not always the case, I did not buy him a burger nor at any time in the future did I. Nonetheless, Max did not miss another appointment.

I felt that for Max I came to represent the one person in the world he could talk to about how hard things were - how much he felt an innocent child living and functioning in an extremely frightening part of the world. The very last time I saw Max he rang me and asked if I could go and meet him. This was outside our usual meeting time and the first time he had ever initiated contact. I picked him up and as he sat in my car he told me how frightened he was as he owed people money and that they were threatening "to do him damage". He had an offer from his sister to go and live with her and her family in Bolton, so he was going.

So what did I, or more specifically MI, do for Max? I believe that if I had worked in a more prescriptive fashion and had been more direct, telling him what to do, then the initial signs may have been more encouraging. I might not have had to drive around so much looking for him if I'd been more censorious when he missed an appointment. But for me the whole point of seeing someone like Max was not to be yet another adult setting boundaries and limitations, but to provide him with the opportunity to engage meaningfully, to invite him to tell me what was wrong with his life. Max lived on sofas, was regularly beaten up by older people, was lonely and often took to wandering the streets as he had no money and nothing better to do. He really didn't need telling that his life on drugs was a problem so I didn't tell him. But on the occasions that I did meet with Max he slowly and painstakingly began to tell me that his substance abuse was problematic. In so doing, the articulation of his difficulties had more meaning and ultimately far more impact on him than had I attempted to emphasize this to him myself.

So if rules one, two three, four and five are *"get better at reflective listening"*, then the rest of the top 10 rules would be *"be patient, be patient, be patient, be patient and be patient"*.

Max was an example of the ultimate challenge that can face anyone wanting to use reflective listening. For one of the necessary essential components of effective reflective listening is that the client gives you something to reflect. This is usually a verbal statement but can occasionally be non-verbal. Max's response to most things, regardless of whether he had been asked a question on not, was "I don't know". Thus a worst case scenario for a non-productive reflective listening interaction would be a successive use of responses such as –

"So you don't know"
"So you really don't know"
"So you haven't a clue"
"So you just can't think of anything"
"So if you sat and racked your brain's for 100 years, you still wouldn't know".

When you have tried every overshoot, undershoot, simile and metaphor known to man and he still *"doesn't know"* and still doesn't provide you with any detail or information, it is reasonable to wonder whether it might be best to try something else.

Lucy

Lucy was completely different to Max. She was lively vocal and sociable. Whereas Max's use of drugs seemed to have a depressing solitude about it, for Lucy her use of ecstasy and alcohol was inexorably linked to a lifestyle that even at the age of 14 involved late nights, partying, fighting and being expelled from school.

Over the months that I worked with her I experienced a comprehensive range of Lucy's moods, behaviours and thoughts about her life. I was made vividly aware of how much she loved drugs, how they made her feel, how they enabled her to easily fit into a social group and how they helped her feel more confident, stronger and more alive. I was also made aware of how much they had cost her already and the fear she had experienced, her lost schooling, the damage to her family life and how she often felt out of her depth in the frightening adult world she inhabited.

Whereas Max gave little away, only providing details if they were eked out of him, Lucy provided a torrent of words and gestures and emotions. The task with Lucy was to keep her focused – and the full range of MI strategies enabled me to do this – for I had plenty of material to work with. She was bright, sharp with a vivid imagination and responded well to hypothetical questions and the use of simile and metaphor. En passant, while working with Lucy, I learned that I should not use the Beatles as an analogy when working with a 14-year-olds - it left me feeling very old!

The target when working with Lucy was not to get her to articulate reasons for change but to try to ensure that they, the reasons, retained a meaning and impact beyond the session itself. She reminded me of somebody who had gone to the cinema to watch a particularly engrossing film. For the time they are in there they are absorbed by everything that they see, hear and experience. The film ends, they leave the cinema and the experience dissipates before the credits have finished rolling. Working with Lucy felt just like this and I always had the feeling that however passionately and expressively she spoke about her unhappiness with drugs it was forgotten by the time her feet hit the pavement outside my office.

What became evident over time was that the hour or so that she spent with me most weeks came to represent the one time when she was allowed to admit that her life wasn't what she wanted. My task was to try to ensure that the 'change talk' that flowed from her in torrents was sufficiently impactful.

When I first encountered MI, change talk, or self-motivational statements as they were then termed, was seen as the predictor of change. The more change talk a client uttered the more likely change became. Subsequently American psychologist Paul Amhrein developed this further. Following a study with drug abusers in 2003 he discovered that not all change talk necessarily predicts change. He differentiated change talk into statements of *desire, ability, reasons, need* and *commitment to change"*.

For example

Desire	- I want to do something about my using
Ability	- I could stop if I wanted to
Reasons	- my using is destroying my life
Need	- I have to do something before it's too late
Commitment	- I'm going to stop this.

Amhrein (2003) concluded that

i)   only client commitment statements ("I will...") predicted abstinence from drugs"

and

ii) verbalising the other four types of change talk- desire ("I want to..."), ability ("I could..."), reasons (" I should because..."),and need (" I have to.....") led to increasing strength of commitment, which in tur presaged behaviour change"

Lucy was an example of a client who freely, spontaneously and regularly spoke of desire, ability, reasons and need, but never made a commitment. As a practitioner I became dogged and persistent in ensuring we returned to *"what do you want to do about it ?"* in a quest for commitment talk.

I articulated many 'grand summaries' highlighting the varied reasons, her belief in her own ability and her desire for a different life and the put that final fatal question, asking directly for commitment *"So what do you want to do about it Lucy?"*

For a long time putting this question was met with blankness, suddenly the flow of conversation was interrupted. Sadly I was no longer a grown-up who understood, but a grown-up who had expectations and was just like the rest --but less obvious about it. I lost count of the number of times Lucy and I aborted this quest for commitment and returned to an articulation of desire ability reasons and need again.

In the end, there was no magical break-through in an MI session. It was another change, one largely initiated by Lucy herself, that began to bring about changes in her drug use patterns. Lucy made a significant change in her relationship with her family. For the first time, following a particularly difficult using experience, she opened up to her parents. From that point onwards they became far more friend than foe. For the first time the work done in our sessions began to reap rewards outside the allotted hour.

So what did MI do for Lucy? The actual breakthrough came independently of our meetings -- and I believe this is often the case. For me the situation is clear. The process of change, particularly change as major as that facing many of my clients, has many different strands to it. Some of these strands, in my case specifically related to the substance use, I may have the chance to change quite dramatically. Others I don't have the chance, but I need to be aware of the bigger picture. Lucy's improved home life enabled her and her family to work together, to learn together and the family to support her through the process of an initial reduction and modification of her using -- replacing it with meaningful experiences and engaging in substantial alternatives to that lifestyle.

Lucy provided for me a prime example of the different qualities of change talk. Many workers have expressed their frustration with an approach which has enabled them to work with a client to a point where change talk flows freely and often unprompted, only to discover that nothing actually changes. With Lucy it was crucial to realise that change talk alone was not the key, commitment talk was.

Concluding Observations

Any professional who works with people 'in need' is likely to dream of the one failsafe, foolproof intervention strategy which in all cases and in all situations will make a difference. The one which will unblock blocked communication, access previously inaccessible places in people's lives and so on. The more complex and unfathomable the individual the more desperate we might wish for the magic answer. It is probably the case that few if any 'straightforward' clients are referred to the helping professions. The mere fact that they have accrued sufficient problems to need the assistance of professionals usually suggests a complexity of issues, often accompanied by a convoluted and intractable lifestyle. However, some clients are clearly less straightforward than others. The term 'special populations' has long been used to describe those clients who by reason of gender, age, culture, disability, complexity of need and so on do not fit into the 'norm'. In my opinion what is undoubtedly the case is that the more complex the client the more work needs to be done in order to 'reach' them and establish a meaningful rapport

One of the most appealing features of MI is the idea of it being 'a way of being with someone'. Shorn of all therapeutic trickery or cleverness it is simply a way of recognizing that the way in which any one of us might like to be treated applies across the board. To this end I have increasingly viewed the clients I see as being no different to myself. Just like them, I'm not keen on being badgered, coerced or pushed into a course of action, even if the particular course of action is one that may well be "better for me".

Max and Lucy were prime targets for a good lecture given by an older, more knowledgeable person just like myself. but there was no point to this.

If one had gone down this route, then it might have had short term benefits for me, the professional. It might assuage the feelings of frustration and helplessness engendered when the client failed to keep an appointment, when only a week ago so many signs were promising and so many promises were made.

When you feel helpless to turn the tide of inevitability sometimes it may be comforting to go home knowing that you had given them a good talking to -- but then one remembers that they have heard it over and over again and that they could probably do it for you and save you the effort.

It is more comforting to go home after a day's work knowing that you have provided for the client an environment based on cooperation, respect for them and for their ability to know what is bad for them. knowing that you have afforded them the courtesy of giving them the chance to find their own way out rather than you being an obstacle to this

...it is the client who knows what hurts, what directions to go, what problems are crucial, what experiences have been deeply buried. It began to occur to me that unless I had a need to demonstrate my own cleverness and learning, I would do better to rely on the client for the direction of movement in the process". Carl Rogers (1961)

I fear and suspect that many of the people I saw are now older people doing much the same thing -- but I know that some aren't.

References

Amrhein, P. C., Miller, W. R., Yahne, C. E., Palmer, M., & Fulcher, L. (2003). Client commitment language during motivational interviewing predicts drug use outcomes. Journal of Consulting and Clinical Psychology, 71, 862-878

Lawendowski L (1997). Motivational interviewing with adolescents presenting for outpatient substance abuse treatment. Doctoral Dissertation, University of New Mexico. (DAI-B59/03, p. 1357, Sep 1998).

McCambridge J, Strang J (2004). The efficacy of single-session motivational interviewing in reducing drug consumption and perceptions of drug-related risk and harm among young people: results from a multi-site cluster randomized trial. Addiction, Volume 99, Number 1, pp. 39-52

The United Nations Convention on the Rights of the Child (CRC or UNCR) (1989),

Slesnick N, Meyers R J, Meade M, & Segelken D H (2000). Bleak and hopeless no more: Treatment engagement of substance abusing runaway youth and their families.

Journal of Substance Abuse Treatment, 19, 215-222.

Rogers C (1961) A therapist's view of psychotherapy: On becoming a person. Boston (Houghton Mifflin)

Learning Applying and Extending Motivational Interviewing Arkowitz H, Miller W R, (chap 1)Motivational Interviewing in the treatment of psychological problems. Arkowitz H, Miller W R, Westra H A, Rollnick S (Ed) (2007) (Guilford Press)

Chapter 5

Using MI with 'Hard to Reach' Parents

Vanessa Wood and Abbey Rice

Nationally, the behaviour of children and young people has been of particular concern to educationalists, government, the media and the public at large. There is considerable interest in working with parents with a view to increasing their ability to nurture children's development. Government policy has reflected this most recently with the Home Office declaring that supporting parents is one of the key elements of their policy to 'promote positive behaviour and tackle antisocial behaviour' (Home Office 2008).

Implicit in government policy is the concept that parent's behaviour and attitudes impact the conduct of their children. The protective nature of good parent-child relationships has been explored in a number of studies (Jenkins & Smith, 1990; Hawley and De Haan, 1996; Sutton, Utting and Farrington 2006). It has been found that a strong relationship between a parent and child or young person is likely to facilitate good behaviour on the part of the child. If parents are to create a positive relationship in which their children can grow, a pre-requisite is the recognition of their part in influencing their child's behaviour.

Miller and Sambell (2003) found that many parents seeking help from support agencies expect to engage with a "dispensing model". They see the child as 'a problem' and the professional as the 'expert', able to dispense the necessary information, advice and knowledge. Furthermore, Miller and Sambell found that parents become highly reliant on the knowledge and skills of the expert and often do not develop confidence and belief in their own skills.

The West Sussex Youth Offending Team Parenting Support Project works with parents who have been referred by any agency or who self refer. The aims of the Project include prevention - and the referred child may or may not be involved with the Youth Offending Service when the family are referred. Parents are offered a maximum of 12 home based sessions to focus on parenting issues. Over the course of the sessions, parents meet regularly with an assigned parenting worker to discuss their issues. The parenting workers receive fortnightly case supervision from an educational psychologist.

Our work focuses on helping parents develop as reflective practitioners who are able to understand their own parenting situation and develop appropriate strategies to bring about positive outcomes. They become the expert on finding solutions within their own lives.

Motivational Interviewing is an approach which has much to offer professionals as they seek to facilitate parent's reflections on their crucial role and the relationship between their own and their child's behaviour. Motivational Interviewing can also engage the parent's motivation to utilise their understanding of the links between their own behaviour and that of their child to make positive changes in their own behaviour with a view to supporting the child.

In this chapter we consider the application of Motivational Interviewing in the context of working with parents to help them explore the impact of their parenting style on their child's behaviour. Within this we look at how we integrate a Solution Focused approach with Motivational Interviewing. We also describe case studies illustrating the effectiveness of working with parents using this approach.

Rationale for using Motivational Interviewing with Parents

In our work with parents we have sought to draw on work which has been shown to be effective in moving people towards successful behaviour change. For example, Hutchings and Lane (2006) have identified a number of factors common to successful interventions with parents, particularly those experiencing difficulties in parenting effectively (see figure 5.1). Such parents may have been called 'unreachable' and labelled as unmotivated, disengaged and resistant to interventions.

- **Build a collaborative alliance with parents**

- **Mobilise parent's resources and work in a way that is compatible with their beliefs and values**

- **Empower families to solve their own problems building on existing strengths**

- **Accept parents' goals at face value, tailoring tasks and suggestions to them and collaborating in exploring material that is relevant to them**

- **Convey an attitude of hope and possibility without minimising the problem or the pain that accompanies it**

- **Encourage parents to focus on the present and future possibilities instead of past problems**

(Hutchings and Lane 2006)

Figure 5.1 Factors common to successful interventions with parents

The factors identified by Hutchings and Lane have much in common with the philosophy of Motivational Interviewing. Miller and Rollnick (2002) point out that positive behaviour change is more likely to occur within an accepting and empowering relationship. The facilitated exploration of relevant experiences enables people to move from a position of ambivalence with respect to behaviour change towards one of positive commitment to behaviour change.

Parents develop confidence through identifying their strengths and exploring how they can utilise these strengths in moving forward.

Not all of the parents we work with could be described as being resistant to change. Many are ready to engage in looking to the future and attempting to make changes. We use a Solution Focused approach (De Shazer et al 1986) with these parents. There are parallels between Solution Focused approach and Motivational Interviewing. Burke et al (2001) identified three similarities.

1. *Responding to resistance* is fundamental to both approaches. In a Solution Focused approach this involves using the client's values and concerns to elicit motivation. At the beginning of the professional-parent collaboration the

parent(s) are invited to share their 'best hopes' for their relationship with their child. In the process of describing a different future, change appears to become more feasible and achievable. For example Ann described her best hopes for her relationship with her son Joe as wanting more co-operation and less conflict. She spoke of how nice it would be to have to only ask him once or twice to do something rather than the hundreds of times she feels that she has to ask him now. The parenting worker asked Ann to reflect upon a single time when Joe had co-operated with her; she described the occasion when she asked him to bring in the shopping from the car as she had a bad back. As Ann described the event the parenting worker listening attentively and was then able to reflect back to Ann the skills that she had used to bring about more co-operation, such as, providing a clear instruction, outlining the behaviour that she wanted to see and how helpful it would be. Ann also mentioned that she said she would make a cup of tea for them both and open a new packet of chocolate biscuits whilst Joe was unloading the shopping, as a reward for his helpfulness. Highlighting to Ann that she has been able to elicit more co-operation from Joe, helped her to feel confident that she could encourage Joe to be co-operative more of the time. In Motivational Interviewing the parent's perception of the issue is 'listened to' and respected without overt challenge. The response to the parent's views might be to reframe the parent's material, perhaps introducing a new angle on which they could reflect.

A pre-contemplative parent might find it very difficult to think of exceptions to their child's behaviour and would therefore benefit from a Motivational Interviewing approach to their resistance to invitations to explore positive aspects of their relationship with their child. Mike was such a parent and by using his own values and concerns motivation to change was built.

Mike was experiencing similar issues to Ann but was unable to identify an exception to Mathew's uncooperative behaviour and is adamant that things are never going to change. The parenting worker listens without judgement to his story, checking out that this behaviour happens all the time, saying, "This sounds really frustrating and you are saying that Mathew is like this all the time, 24/7?" Mike replies, "Oh he will do it quickly enough if it's something he wants to do." The parenting worker then reframes the material saying, "When Mathew is uncooperative you feel really frustrated. However, there are times when he can be co-operative and it may be useful to look at those in more detail."

2. *Supporting and encouraging self-statements indicative of feelings of self-efficacy* is common to both approaches. In the use of both approaches we facilitate the process of identifying times when the presenting issue/problem behaviours do not occur. This enables the parent to identify the contributing factors linked to the occurrence of the exceptions. This insight can in turn lead to successful changes in parenting behaviours. Self-efficacy is also enhanced through the identification of successes in other areas of the parent's lives. By focusing on personal strengths that underpin perceived successes, parents can begin to draw on these in their parenting.

Through actively participating in this process parents appear to develop a greater awareness of their ability to bring about change.

3. An emphasis on eliciting 'change talk' is central to both Solution Focused and Motivational Interviewing. In Solution Focused we notice and celebrate positive change.

When Ann was able to identify times when Joe was more co-operative the parenting worker encouraged her to look at what she had done differently to bring about this change in Joe's behaviour. The parenting worker would begin a follow-up session asking, "What changes have you noticed this week in Joe's behaviour or perhaps in something that you have done differently." Ann replied, "I notice that I am calmer, I am not nagging him to do so much, only the things that are important. I ask him nicely, I don't shout so much." The parenting worker responds "You are asking him nicely and only to do things that are important. It sounds as if that's really working well for you both."

In using Motivational Interviewing we notice and utilise change talk around disadvantage of the status quo, optimism in relation to change and intention to change. Mike spoke about his increasing irritation with Mathew's behaviour; he was worried that he would hit Mathew if the situation continued. The parenting worker replied, "It sounds as if you are saying that things really cannot stay as they are, for everyone's benefit something has got to change." Mike responded, "Yeah, I know that I have to do something about it, and now we are talking about it I feel more positive."

When do we use Motivational Interviewing with parents?

Motivational Interviewing is used with parents who are identified as being at a pre-contemplative stage as described by Prochaska and DiClemente (1983). Their notion of 'pre-contemplaters' or those who appear to be at a 'pre-change' stage is part of an incremental change model. Within this model, pre-contemplation is followed by contemplation of behaviour change and then deciding to change.

Procheska and Diclemente's stages of change are useful because they describe how parents may present during our initial meeting with them. Some parents appear to have a high level of motivation for change and may already be action planning. Others may struggle to identify their preferred future or acknowledge their contribution to the presenting problems. They could demonstrate that they feel unable to identify their strengths and resources which they could helpfully bring to the problem solving process. We identify these parents as being in the pre-contemplative state.

Diclemente and Velasquez (2002) suggest that in contrast to feeling discouraged when encountering parents who are resistant to change, the stages of change model helps us to think about parents in the context of them being at an early stage of the change model and to see this as a position that can be influenced. Furthermore, they make the point that it is helpful to learn more about the parent's reasons for being in that state in order to enable the practitioner in developing and conveying empathy to the parent, the 'empathic alliance'. It also informs strategic interventions underpinned by Procheska and Diclemente's four categories of pre-contemplators.

The thinking patterns of pre-contemplators' resistance to change have been categorised into four categories: reluctance, rebellion, resignation, and rationalisation. Some individuals may present a mixture of some or even all of these patterns at different times.

The *reluctant* parent would either be unaware that their own behaviour was negatively affecting their child or have some awareness but not understand the extent of the problem. For example they might smack their child and not make the link between their aggression and their child's own tendency to hit people. When they become aware of the link, they may decide to find other ways of gaining cooperation from their child.

The *rebellious* parent would be very aware that their behaviour had an impact on their child. They may have tried and failed to make changes in the past and now do not want to engage in the process again. They may be very confrontational towards professionals who attempt to broach the issue of change with them. They seem to have little confidence in their ability to make changes in their situation. For example, they may hit their child – having in the past made some unsuccessful effort to find alternatives to punishment. Their way of avoiding the ongoing possibility of failure is to ensure that the issue is not raised again. Their defensive behaviour, such as rudeness and refusal to engage, is a strategy to deter professionals from exploring the issue.

Similarly, *resigned* parents also have little confidence in their ability to make changes but they may be less likely to be confrontational in their presentation. They may appear depressed and overwhelmed by the apparent obstacles. For example, a parent who is struggling to manage their child and feel that there is no way they could ever find effective behaviour management strategies. They have little belief that they can change their situation. They may report that they have no hope for the future and believe it is futile to try and find any solution.

The *rationalising* parent often has a really clear understanding of the impact of their behaviour on their child and either justify their behaviour or blame other people for their own actions. For example, the parent who hits their teenage child may believe that this is the most effective way of eliciting co-operation. They may produce a very eloquent argument to support their actions. Alternatively they might say that they are only reacting to their teenager's behaviour and therefore it is actually their son or daughter's fault that they, the parents, behave this way. The rationalising parent may seek to persuade the practitioner that their own perspective, ie the parents, is accurate. This is often used by the rationalising parent as a way of avoiding the task of exploring change. The identification of pre-contemplative 'types' enables us to 'tailor' the interventions.

- The resigned parent would benefit from exploring, examples of success, albeit small, or exceptions to the reported failures.

- The reluctant parent could usefully reflect on the effects of their behaviour on their child and the rationalising parent would benefit from being listened to without debate or argument and then being invited to explore possible alternative ways of viewing the issue.

- The rebellious parent requires very sensitive building of an empathic relationship between themselves and the practitioner with a view to exploring within a trusting relationship their perceived inability to change or 'low self efficacy'.

Following the initial meeting with the parents, those parents identified as 'pre-contemplative' are engaged in Motivational Interviewing. When they appear to decide that they want to change, Solution Focused techniques are utilised. We believe that Solution Focused techniques are useful in facilitating the parents' action planning.

Using Motivational Interviewing with pre-contemplative parents

Miller and Rollnick (2002) outline four broad and guiding principles that underlie motivational interviewing, namely; express empathy; develop discrepancy; roll with resistance; and support self-efficacy. Each is valuable in working with pre-contemplative parents and will be considered in turn.

Firstly, the establishment of an empathetic relationship is intrinsic to working effectively with parents. The adoption of a non-judgemental position of acceptance helps the parent to feel heard and understood. This provides the bedrock of trust and respect that allows for further work to take place. Parents are often highly sensitive to judgments about their parenting style and so they should be avoided. In contrast, parents are far more likely to be open to exploring their parenting within a framework of their own elicited goals.

Secondly, *developing discrepancy.* This is the practice of providing an alternative presentation of an unpleasant reality so that the person can fully explore the implications of it and respond to the self-identified implications. Having become aware of the discrepancy between their existing behaviour and what they believe to be important, parents may begin to feel increasingly uncomfortable. As a consequence they may experience a positive shift in their motivational bias towards that of contemplating change.

Thirdly, *rolling with resistance.* Miller and Rollnick (2002) point out that resistance is associated with drop-out - the more a person resists, the less likely behaviour change will occur. Resistance can indicate to the practitioner that the 'pace' of their intervention is uncomfortable for the parents. Responsibility therefore lies with the practitioner to facilitate the parent's reflection on the pros and cons of their current behaviours. Markland et al (2005) point out that by reviewing their behaviour in relation to their hopes and values, parents would become aware of the gap between the two. The dissatisfaction created by the discrepancy between their behaviour and their goals and values would hopefully generate motivation to change. The development of discrepancy is achieved by using variations of reflective responses and other strategies such as shifting the focus, reframing, agreeing with a twist, emphasising personal choice and control, and 'coming alongside (see chapter 2).

Sharon's son Kyle, aged 13 had been excluded from school for hitting a teacher. On numerous occasions the police had been called to the estate where they lived: neighbours had reported seeing Kyle defacing property. Sharon strongly believed that the teachers were picking on Kyle because i) other members of her extended family have a reputation and ii) he is easily led by his friends. Sharon had been served with a Parenting Order and was required to work with the Youth Offending Service Parenting Project.

The parenting worker found Sharon to be highly resistant to any talk about change. Sharon felt that the problem lay with the school and the neighbours. To lower the resistance the parenting worker engaged in the following strategies:

The parenting worker aimed to *'shift the focus'* away from the contentious issues of school and the estate towards exploring Sharon's own thoughts and experiences by saying, "You have given a clear picture of what is happening at school and outside, it would be interesting to hear how things are when Kyle is in the house with you because it sounds as if a lot is going on for you both." Sharon replied, "Things are OK, although I get pretty fed up when he trashes his room because he's had a bad day."

As Sharon began to share her feelings the parenting worker engaged in the strategy of *'coming alongside and agreeing with a twist'*. "Gosh that's tough, he's had a bad day and you get the fall-out." Sharon says "He's always been the same, just like his dad can't control his temper." The parenting worker *'reframed'* the material by responding, "So Kyle hits out at school, on the estate, and at home." Sharon replied, "He's been like it ever since he was a baby, we even had to move because of the trouble he caused in our last street." The parenting worker, emphasising *'personal choice and control',* said "You recognised there was a problem and chose to do something about it."

Fourthly, *supporting statements indicative of feelings of self-efficacy.* By self-efficacy we mean the development of a belief in i) the possibility of change and ii) the ability to make changes. It is the responsibility of the practitioner to convey an abundance of hope. This can be achieved through sharing past casework successes - highlighting the many successful changes that parents have made.

Case Study Involving Pre-contemplative, Rationalising Parent

Gill, was referred at her own request to the Project by the school nurse. Her daughter Sophie, 9 years of age, was presenting major management problems in the home situation. At the initial meeting Gill reported that things were 'worse than ever'. Sophie was being verbally aggressive, defiant and disregarding boundaries. For example, in the supermarket she would demand to be given chosen items. If denied these Sophie would shout and swear to such an extent that the family had to leave the supermarket without their shopping. Gill reported that she did 'a lot' with Sophie and was 'not sure if this is a parenting issue'. However Gill was willing to explore further with the practitioner. During the discussion Gill stated that she had exhausted all possible approaches to the resolution of Sophie's issues. It seemed that Gill could be described as a rationalising pre-contemplator. Gill's best hopes were to have a loving and respectful relationship with Sophie so that they can 'have fun and enjoy being together'.

Gill was cautious about being judged on a number of levels including her parenting within a same sex partnership. The practitioner demonstrated respect for Gill's values by active listening and skilful reflection. The development of trust and the practitioner 'coming alongside' created an empathic relationship, which created a platform for the exploration of family relationships.

The practitioner encouraged Gill to talk about recent incidents and by listening and reflecting them back with a new twist, the impact of Gill's role was highlighted. Discrepancy between Gill's initial position and this new perspective then began to emerge. Gill told the parenting worker, 'Sophie had really 'kicked off' when she came home from school yesterday. She was hungry. I offered her a healthy snack but she wanted biscuits. She persistently asked for biscuits. I tried to go into the other room but she followed me, constantly whining. Eventually I had had enough and gave her the biscuits.' The parenting worker said, 'You were clear that she could not have the biscuits and then changed your mind when she went on at you. I wonder what message she is getting?' Gill then said, 'I'm saying one thing and doing another so I'm not really helping am I?'

Gill's newly adopted position of acknowledging her role opened up the possibility of her achieving change. Gill seemed to move from pre-contemplation to a contemplative stage. Action planning quickly followed with 'ignoring of Sophie's outbursts and speaking to her when things were calmer'.

However, soon Gill's sense of self-efficacy seemed to become an issue. Gill developed resistance when her action plans did not result in successful outcomes. Appearing to revert back to the pre-contemplative stage, Gill phoned the parenting worker following a row with Sophie and said, "Sophie has been worse than ever. I have tried everything I can. Can you talk to her?" The parenting worker suggested that they unpack this at the following session. Later, the practitioner encouraged Gill to report the precipitating events and then reframed the situation highlighting the exceptions. In the exploration of contributing factors to the exceptions Gill was able to identify several successful strategies including engaging in enjoyable activities with Sophie and talking with her about feelings. As a result of this intervention Gill became more hopeful and began to re-engage with the original action plan. At the following session Gill reported that they had noticed positive outcomes.

At the end of the intervention (6 sessions) Gill reported that she was spending time with Sophie and enjoying the experience. Sophie was more respectful and co-operative. Gill was able to set clear boundaries and consistently apply them. Gill and Sophie were able to talk more openly about how certain behaviours made them feel. Gill reported that she and Sophie shared lots of 'cuddles'.

Four months after the intervention Gill reported that the relationship between herself and Sophie was still positive. This could be attributed to the development of the parent's ability to adopt a Solution Focussed approach in response to any new issue that arose.

Case Study Involving Pre-contemplative, Resigned Parenting

Jane, was referred to the Project by the Family Link Worker because she reported feeling 'at the end of her tether' with the behaviour of her youngest child, Chloe aged 8. On numerous occasions Chloe hit her mother and siblings and displayed tantrums which were affecting the well-being of the whole household. Jane also reported concerns about the difficulty Chloe experienced in making successful peer relationships. Jane felt that she had tried a number of strategies including 'time out chair', charts and praising, all with limited degrees of success. In the past she has had considerable contact with other agencies but failed to find any long-term solutions. Jane was therefore sceptical about engaging with yet another agency.

Jane's feelings of being overwhelmed seemed to indicate that she was a resigned pre-contemplator. These problems had existed for a long time. She had little confidence in her own ability to bring about change; although she was able to identify two 'exceptions' to Chloe's bad behaviour. These were 'when Chloe got what she wanted' and 'when Chloe had individual time with mum'. Jane said that her best hopes were for Chloe to 'listen and be reasonable' and for the household not to 'revolve around Chloe'. It was significant that these hopes were related to changes in Chloe's behaviour.

Skilful summarisation and reflecting back of Jane's experience demonstrated that the parenting worker understood the level of difficulty. In response to hearing Jane's story the parenting worker replied, "It sounds exhausting as these problems have been around for a long time. You've tried really hard to make things better and you have had some success, e.g. when she has time alone with you, which you want to build on".

This allowed the practitioner to 'come alongside' Jane thus establishing an empathic relationship. During the exploration of personal strengths and resources the focus was shifted away from past parenting experiences to past successes in Jane's wider life story. This enabled Jane to develop a greater understanding of personal strengths and resources which fed in to her sense of self- efficacy.

The practitioner used 'reframing' as a strategy to redress the balance of Jane's recollection of weekly events from negative to positive. This was achieved by listening for the small nuggets of constructive experiences and reflecting them back in a new light.

Jane reported that nothing had really changed from the last session. Chloe was still swearing and taking forever to go to bed, "If she went up and down those stairs once, she went a thousand times. I know patience is virtue but it's enough to drive a saint mad! This morning wasn't so bad though." The parenting worker replied, "You have had a good morning with Chloe, I wonder if we look more closely at what happened whether we might learn something that would help to improve the bedtimes." Jane responded, "Well I do prepare her for the morning the night before, getting everything ready and making sure that she knows the routine." The parenting worker said, "I'm curious, I'm wondering what would happen if you did that in the evening." Jane responded, "Usually I just say 'time for bed now Chloe', which I know she doesn't like because everyone else is still up. I don't mind reading her a story though and perhaps that would help. I could also give her more notice for bedtime. I think I'll have a chat with her about it and see what she thinks will help."

The process allowed Jane to view her interaction with Chloe more optimistically. She then began to creatively approach her 'parenting action planning' by exploring how she would achieve her own best hopes in this area.

The initial change that Jane made was significant. This involved 'actively listening' to Chloe, 'reflecting back' what she had heard and 'empathising'. This is the strategy which had been modelled by the parenting worker throughout the intervention. Jane reported consistently throughout the ensuing sessions that this active empathic listening strategy was successful in developing her relationship with Chloe and leading to positive behavioural outcomes. Jane now viewed Chloe more positively and she was able to consolidate change very thoroughly and steadily. Jane seemed to be able to approach apparent set backs by problem-solving as opposed to viewing them as failure.

At the end of the intervention (a total of 7 sessions) Jane reported that Chloe now had a co-operative and responsive attitude towards everyone in the family. Jane spoke of the potency of positivism, adding that she now enjoyed spending time with Chloe and that this had significantly improved the quality of their relationship. Chloe was also reported to have developed her skills to form relationships with her peers. Chloe herself had begun to develop the active listening and empathic approach within her own social networks.

Four months after the intervention had finished Jane reported that the changes had been maintained.

Case Study involving Pre-contemplative Reluctant Parenting

Simon, a father, was referred to the parenting project by the school. His daughter Zoe, aged 11, had been displaying aggressive behaviour at school. She was becoming unpopular and isolating herself from her peer group. Furthermore his ex-wife reported that Zoe was temperamental at home and often lashed out at her younger brothers. In Simon's opinion his relationship with Zoe was pretty good, they talked and did fun things together, although he did notice that Zoe would 'get into a strop' if she didn't get her own way, "But isn't that the same as a lot of kids?" Simon asked.

Simon said that it was his ex-wife who felt that he should have parenting support, whilst he saw the service as an example of 'professional meddling.' Simon was reluctant to consider the possibility of working together. The parenting worker responded empathically, sensitively reflecting back what Simon had told her. "It sounds as if you are pretty frustrated at being told you need parenting support, particularly as you feel that your relationship with Zoe is good, you chat and have fun." Simon responded "It's not personal like, but I get fed up at my ex always pointing the finger at me, and you coming here makes me feel like I've failed. I am doing the best I can and I want to help Zoe." By acknowledging Simon's viewpoint and allowing him to feel listened to, and not judged, the parenting worker was able to create an empathic alliance, within an atmosphere of trust and respect.

To encourage Simon to reflect upon the impact of his parenting on Zoe's behaviour the parenting worker utilised the strategies of *'reframing'* and *'agreeing with a twist'*, saying "You have done your best and you are wondering what you could do differently to help change Zoe's behaviour." This reframe also highlighted Simon's ability to exercise *'personal choice and control'*.

Through the process of reflecting upon examples of when Zoe's behaviour was good, Simon was enabled to identify more specifically the role that he played. The parenting worker asked, "Can you give me an example of something good that has happened this week?" Simon replied, "The other night Zoe was playing up, I physically intervened so that she didn't hurt her sister. Zoe went to her room, after a few minutes I followed her. I sat on the bed and asked her if she was OK. She then told me what had happened and why she was upset. We had a hug and she said she felt better. This turned out a lot better than the other night when I ended up shouting and losing my rag with them."

Allowing Simon to verbalise his reluctance and for that to be taken seriously and listened to, broke down the barriers and allowed for the establishment of an empathic alliance. Maintaining the optimistic outlook Simon was able to reflect upon the impact of his parenting role without undermining the quality of the relationship that he felt he already had with Zoe.

At the end of the intervention (4 sessions) Simon reported that Zoe was doing a lot better at school and that Zoe had developed ways to help her calm down when she felt a strop coming on. Simon felt that he listened more effectively and tried to see situations from Zoe's point of view as well as his own. Furthermore he said that he was also doing this in his relationship with his ex-wife and things were a bit calmer between them. Simon said he still had a way to go but he had developed the confidence and strategies to be able to take things forward.

Case study involving Pre-contemplative Rebellious Parenting

Jack, a single parent, was referred to the parenting service by the family Social Worker. Jack was a full time carer for his severely disabled daughter aged 7 and son Max, aged 14. Jack experienced Max's behaviour at home as rude, occasionally violent and often confrontational. Jack said, "It's always been like this and I worry that Max might hit his sister when he's copped a strop, usually when I've told him I've no money to buy a new computer game."

Initially Jack presented as being in favour of receiving parenting support and said he was in agreement with the philosophy that individuals cannot be forced to change; they have to make that decision themselves. The parenting worker listened empathically to Jack's story summarising his experience "It sounds really difficult when you are doing so much and receiving little support or co-operation from Max." Jack replied, "Well Max is a teenager you can't expect him to do too much and anyway it's easier to give in for a quiet life. He does love his sister." Trying again to build an empathic alliance the parenting worker replied, "It sounds like you are saying that you have been successful in gaining co-operation from Max, which involves you giving him what he wants." Jack, becoming increasingly hostile responded, "No, I don't have the money to buy him all the games that he wants but I do try". He ended the conversation by saying, "I don't think this (the parenting sessions) is going to help. Things have been like this for ages, not great, but we rub along and get through it. I've tried stuff like this before and Max never changes."

The observation of Jack's hostile behaviour and hearing that he may not wish to continue working with the service indicated to the parenting worker that he was a rebellious pre-contemplator. This informed the parenting worker's thinking about appropriate strategies to utilise in further meetings with Jack. The Columbo technique (see chapter 1) was used to great effect. The parenting worker, acknowledging that she is not an expert on Jack's life, allowed Jack to feel less threatened and elicited a helping response from him. The parenting worker said, "I know that you have tried lots of this stuff before and I'm wondering what might be of use to you in helping to bring about change". Jack replied, "When Max and I watch our TV programmes together its great we have a laugh every now and again. It makes it all feel better somehow. The other night he even got up and made us a cup of tea and biscuits." The parenting worker came alongside Jack agreeing with a twist, "When you and Max spend time together you get along well, things are calmer and he is more co-operative."

Skilful summarisation highlighted to Jack the possibility and optimism for change by reflecting upon examples of where things had gone well and identifying what Jack was doing that helped to bring about Max's positive behaviour. Focussing upon Jack's skills enabled him to feel more confident and less threatened. His self-efficacy began to grow, alongside his willingness to contemplate an action plan for further changes in his parenting style.

At the end of the intervention (10 sessions) Jack and Max both reported positive outcomes. Jack couldn't believe how different he felt, "I really enjoy spending time with Max and I've mastered the art of saying no and meaning it. OK, so Max isn't always happy about it, but when he's calmed down we often have a quick chat and smooth things out. His famous strops are now saved for the football pitch!" Max had also told his dad that home was a far happier place to be these days, it felt like they were a real family helping each other not arguing and fighting.

Motivational Interviewing and a parent centred philosophy

The philosophy of our work is to build a collaborative alliance, share the parent's agenda and to accept parental goals without challenging them. In our work context, Motivational Interviewing aims to encourage parents to change their perspectives on an aspect of their relationship with their child: this may sometimes appear to clash with a parent's agenda. For example, a parent may report that their agenda is to pursue removal of their child from the family home by Social Services as they believe that they cannot manage their child any more. The practitioner seeks to explore the parent's interactions with the child in order to identify possible factors vis a vis parent behaviour which negatively influence the child's behaviour. The Practitioner seeks to find exceptions to the perceived negative picture of the relationship between the parent and child. In turn this may build the parent's confidence in their management of the child. While this is contrary to the parent's initial declared agenda, the philosophy of the project is not compromised through the use of Motivational Interviewing because the agenda for the child's behaviour change is a shared desired outcome. However, the parent and practitioner might take a different view about how this outcome can be achieved. The parent may, for example, believe that the child requires medical or social services intervention, whereas the practitioner may take the view that by changing their own behaviour the parents can effect change in their child's behaviour. Through Motivational Interviewing the practitioner seeks to facilitate the parent in looking afresh at the impact of their own behaviour on their child's. It is hoped that the parent will begin to reflect on the importance of their role in their child's behaviour with a view to contemplating the possibility of change.

Conclusion

We have explored the rationale for using Motivational Interviewing with pre-contemplative parents. The timing and use of the approach has been considered with reference to Prochaska and Diclemente's cycle of change. The way that Motivational Interviewing compliments Solution Focused approaches has also been addressed with the view to proposing a model by which, following the use of Motivational Interviewing at the pre- contemplative and contemplative stages, the solution focused approach is introduced at the action planning stage of the change cycle. Case studies demonstrating approaches to working with resigned, rebellious, reluctant and rationalising parents have been presented, demonstrating the application of the four general principles of Motivational Interviewing. Finally, some possible ethical issues have been identified and considered.

We have presented a creative way of using Motivational Interviewing with pre-contemplative parents, integrating with Solution Focused techniques at the action planning stage.

It is intended that the chapter has captured the effectiveness of the approach in supporting parents in developing nurturing relationships with their children, which in turn result in positive behaviour outcomes for the children, and for the parents themselves.

References

Burke, B., Arkowitz, H., & Menchola, M. (2001). The efficacy of motivational interviewing: A meta analysis of controlled clinical trials. *Journal of Consulting and Clinical Psychology 71* (5), 843-861.

De Shazer, S., Berg., I.K., Lipchik, E,. Nunnally, E., Molnar, A., Gingerich, W., & Weiner-Davis, M. (1986). Brief Therapy: Focused solution development. *Family Process, 25, 207-222.*

DiClemente, C. C. & Velasquez, S. K. (2002). *Motivational Interviewing and the stages of change in Motivational Interviewing: preparing people for change* (2nd Edition), Eds Miller, W. R. & Rollnick, S. NY Guilford Press.

Jenkins, J. & Smith, M. (1990). Factors protecting children living in disharmonious homes: maternal reports. *Journal of Academy of Child and Adolescent Psychiatry 29, 1: 60 – 69.*

Hawley, D. & De Haan, L. (1996). Towards a definition of family resilience: integrating life span and family perspectives, *Family Process 35 (3) 283-298.*

Home Office. Tackling antisocial behaviour and its causes: Parenting (2008). Available from the worldwide web (http://www.respect.gov.uk).

Hutchings, J. & Lane, E. (2006). *Reaching those who need it most.* The Psychologist, 19; 8, 480- 483.

Markland, D. Ryan, R. M., Tobin V J. and Rollnick S. (2005). Motivational interviewing and Self Determination Theory. *Journal of Social and Clinical Psychology, 24 (6) 811-831.*

Miller, W. R., Rollnick, S. (2002). *Motivational interviewing: preparing People for Change (2nd Edition).* NY: Guilford Press.

Miller, S. & Sambell, K. (2003). What do parents feel they need? Implications of parent's perspective for the facilitating of parenting programmes, *Children and Society, 17, 32-44. Wiley Interscience www.interscience:wiley.com DOI:10. 1002/CHI.726*

Prochaska, J. O., & Diclemente C. C. (1983) Stages and Processes of self and change of smoking:Towards an Integrative Model of Change. *Journal of Consulting and Clinical Psychology, 51, 390 -395.*

Sutton, C., Utting, D., & Farrington, D. (2006). Nipping criminality in the bud. *The Psychologist, 19, 8, 470-475*

Chapter 6

Combining Solution Focussed Approaches with Motivational Interviewing

Mawuli Amesu

Introduction

Motivational Interviewing (MI) is a counselling approach which originated within the field of addictive behaviours (Miller and Rollnick, 1991) and is becoming increasing widely used in clinical settings (Miller and Rollnick, 2002) and in social work practice (Corden and Somerton, 2004). MI is based on the premise that people are not always at a stage of readiness to change behaviours, such as smoking, drinking or drug use, which are perceived by others to be problematic.

Miller and Rollnick (1991) linked MI to the Transtheoretical Model of Change proposed by Prochaska and DiClemente (1982) who looked at over 300 psychotherapeutic interventions and identified a series of stages that people pass through when changing their behaviour. McNamara (1992; 1998) later adapted this model for evaluating pupil readiness to change within academic settings.

In adult counselling interactions and working with families to resolve difficulties in their relationships, often an individual or the family will seek help and sometimes be referred with their consent, to a professional at the point where they recognise that a particular behaviour, such as drinking, smoking or being unable to resolve challenging issues, has got the potential to break up the family relationship without a mediator. Whether the family has recognised the need for intervention or not, the joint approach of MI and Solution Focussed Approaches (SFA) is valuable to use with the family, meeting them where they are and hopefully nudging them through the process of change.

Recently Lewis and Osborn (2004) identified similarities between both the theory and practice of MI and Solution Focused Counselling (SFC) and called for them to be used together in therapeutic practice. SFC examines the individual's ability to make positive changes to their life by accessing and using their inner resources, strengths and skills. Solution Focused Brief Therapy (SFBT) was pioneered by de Shazer (1985) and has become a popular approach in therapeutic and educational settings.

Amesu (2004) proposed that solution focused language and questioning might be used to help children, young people and their families to explore and problem solve behavioural/family relationship issues and could also help to facilitate movement through the stages of change. In the sections below are described more fully issues that may be present at each of the stages of change and the use of solution focused language that may be useful at each of these stages, is considered.

Stage 1 – Precontemplation (not yet thinking about change)

Prochaska, Norcross and DiClemente (1994) observe that precontemplators usually have no intention of changing their behaviour and will typically deny there is a problem. Furthermore, there may be strong factors influencing a young person's choice to maintain behaviour that is seen by others to be problematic, such as an aggressive display of anger which seem to engage some attention, albeit negative attention.

At this stage asking the young person to recognise how their behaviour is impacting on the rest of the family does not normally work. Phrases such as, *"Think about how your parents feel!"* or, *"Can't you see how this makes your parents/siblings angry?"* may actually increase resistance from the young person and mean that it is difficult for the adult facilitator to develop a supportive relationship with them.

Useful strategies at this stage might include:

Asking for a third party perspective

This involves getting the young person to explore how others that have concerns might see the situation. This line of questioning addresses the issue and makes the point without making an enemy. It also helps to avoid direct confrontation and challenge about a particular behaviour. Asking the following questions might provide useful information about how the young person feels about the situation and about the views of others. The following approach can also be used to engage any member of the family, whose behaviour/decisions are affecting the rest of the family in a negative way.

- *Someone looking at your situation might say you find it difficult to control your temper. What would you say to someone who thought that way about you?*

- *Someone looking at your decisions might say you don't seem to be aware of how it is affecting the rest of your family? What would you say to someone who thought that way about you?*

- *How could you show them that they were wrong about you?*

If the young person or the family member is able to identify concerns expressed by others, further solution-focused questions can be used to establish what they might be able to do to make a difference. In this situation possible questions might include:

- *What small things could you do differently that would convince them?*

- *Who would notice first?*

- *What would they notice?*

- *What difference would that make? What could you be doing differently that would prove them wrong?*

Scaling

Another solution-focused approach that is useful at the Precontemplative stage of change is to ask young people or the family member to be explicit about their motivation to change by using scaling questions. One example might be:

> *On a scale of 1-10, 1 is that you don't need to do anything different and 10 is that you are willing to look at how things could be better, where would you put yourself on the scale?*

If the response indicated that they did not wish to change their behaviour, the following scale could be used.

> *On a scale of 1-10, how confident are you that your parent/other family members would share your view that there is no problem?*

A low response to this question might represent some acknowledgement that there is a problem. The facilitator might want to explore this further with the young person/family member, for example:

> *So how come you're a 3, not a 2 or a 1.*

The facilitator (the person supporting the young person/family) can also ask follow up questions to identify what might be different if they are able to go up one point on the scale the following week, for example;

> *If we come back next week, and you put yourself on a 4 instead of a 3, what would have to happen between now and next week?*
>
> *What would it take for that to happen?*
>
> *Can you remember a time you did that in the past?*

Stage 2 - Contemplation (Weighing up the pros and cons)

At this stage, people acknowledge that they have a problem but may not be prepared to do anything about it. Prochaska et al (1994) note that although contemplators may think seriously about solving a problem they may be a long way from actually making a commitment to action. Prochaska and DiClemente (1983) suggest that contemplators should be given the opportunity to explore their beliefs about the future while McNamara (1998) suggests that at this stage they are evaluating the pros and cons of changing.

Some useful strategies for a family or a young person who may be at this stage are listed below.

Exceptions

This is a helpful way of looking at times when the problem does not exist or when the problem still exists but the family coped or managed the difficulty better. It can be used once the family has identified that a behaviour or a situation might be problematic. It is also a helpful way to engage them in looking at past solutions rather than only concentrating on the problem. The facilitator might help the family to look for:

- Times when the problem does not happen

- Times when the problem happens less often or when the problem bothers or restricts them less.

- Times when the problem is more manageable or when they are able to cope better (for example, *"Tell me about the times when you felt like losing your temper but didn't"*.

Using this approach can also help to identify times they find things difficult as a family and when they might need further support or strategies. It can also reveal situations in which they feel confident about managing family difficulties which will highlight their strengths and past successes, however small.

Looking for a preferred future

This set of questions focuses on how life might be different in the future. If the family is able to think that life might be preferable without the problem behaviour, the likelihood of change is increased. Example questions include:

- *How was your life before this problem?*

- *Lets imagine that tomorrow turns out to be a good day, how would you know that it is going well?*

- *When the current difficulty/alcohol/drugs are no longer an issue in your life, how will life be different for you?*

- *When you resist the temptation to go back to the behaviour/smoke/ steal what will you be doing instead?*

The Miracle Question

Linking to the idea of thinking about a preferred future, asking the Miracle Question is a popular solution focused approach. It helps the whole family to begin to envisage how life might be without the problem. A suggested script is:

> *Suppose tonight while you are asleep a miracle happens and the problem no longer exists. You don't know immediately that it has happened because you were asleep. When you wake up what is the first thing you will notice that will let you know that there has been a miracle?* (DfES, 2003, page 30).

Practitioners wishing to avoid possible cultural connotations associated with using the term 'miracle' may adapt such a script and consider words like "something amazing" or "magical" for younger children. The Miracle Question is non-threatening, it sets the stage for imagination of their own solution and encourages them to consider a potential preferred future.

Deciding not to change

Having weighed up the pros and cons of changing their behaviour, it is possible that a young person/family might appear to be making an informed choice to do nothing and carry on as before. In such instances a third party perspective may again be useful, for example:

> *Someone looking at your situation may say you want to keep this problem. What would you say to them?*

Stage 3 – Preparation (getting ready for change)

This stage was previously referred to as 'Determinism' (Prochaska and DiClemente, 1982; McNamara, 1992; 1998) and represents a time at which people choose to change their behaviour, or carry on as before. However, after further research into the processes of behavioural change (Prochaska, et al, 1994; Prochaska and DiClemente, 1998) an alternative stage of 'Preparation' was proposed, in which people get ready for making behavioural changes. For example, an overwhelmed parent wishing to resolve pressing family issues, such as relationship difficulties, housing or debt issues, may find out about ways they can access support.

At this stage the facilitator can help the family to identify practical ways in which they can achieve and maintain future change.

In getting the family ready for change, some useful questions to explore include:

- *What has worked for you in the past?*

- *Who has helped you?*

- *How will you know that things are changing in your family?*

- *Who would notice that things are changing and what might they say?*

Scaling questions (as previously described) may also be useful to assess the thoughts and feelings of every family member about the impending change and how confident they are that their goals will be achieved, for example:

> *How confident are you that the skills/strengths you have as a family will enable you to make changes?*

It is important at this stage to help them develop their personal resources, on the assumption that they are the expert of their own situation, and to allow them to implement desired change.

Stage 4 – Active Change (putting the decision into practice)

The action stage is the one at which people most overtly modify their behaviour. It is a busy period and one which requires commitment in terms of time and energy from both the young person, their family and the facilitator (Prochaska et al, 1994). Once a decision has been made to change behaviour, shared contracts and targets can be negotiated with the young person/family and jointly monitored, allowing them to take increased responsibility for their own situation/behaviour management. Solution focused approach can help establish what is helpful to the young person/family at this stage.

The facilitator can help the young person/family evaluate the process of change by asking questions that help them to explain and evaluate what impact it is having on their life.

- *What is better since we last met? (Who has noticed? What did they say?)*
- *Who is doing what?*
- *What are you doing instead of [fighting]?*
- *What difference has it made to you and your family as a result of the changes you have made?*

5. Maintenance (actively maintaining change)

Prochaska et al (1994) note that, just as at every other stage, there are great challenges associated with the maintenance of behavioural change. The young person/family may be keeping the change going, but this should be an active process. Supporting the young person/family by recognising their progress and achievements can reduce the likelihood of relapse.

Questions useful at this stage include:

- *What is better?*
- *What helped you as a family to achieve it?*
- *How did you manage it?*
- *How did you get through that time?*
- *So what did it take to do that?*
- *How confident are you about keeping this up?* You can use confidence scaling to help the young person/each family member to assess this.
- *What does this tell you about yourself/family that you did not know before?*
- *What would be the first sign that will tell you things are beginning to slip back?*

6. Relapse (returning to previous behaviour)

Most people, when trying to change their behaviour/resolve their conflict, will relapse at some point. However, providing that this is anticipated and support and encouragement is provided, this can be temporary and the individuals can return to maintaining previous behaviour/resolution.

Preparing for relapse

Preparing an individual or a family for relapse and helping them to understand that change can be a "two steps forward, one back" process. If a plan for relapse is addressed before difficulties arise, the family is likely to find it easier to get back on track, taking comfort in the fact that two steps forward, one step back, still equals one step forward.

Sometimes factors beyond the family's control can contribute to difficulties in maintaining positive behaviour, such as illness or difficult unforeseen events. If this is the case, maintenance of change may be difficult. The facilitator can provide emotional support and stability for the family and enable other agencies to be supportive, until they feel more settled.

Here are some examples:

- *What are you doing to stop things from getting worse?*
- *What is it about your family that keeps you going no matter what?*
- *What is keeping it from getting worse?*
- *What helps you to stay on track*
- *Who can help?*

One potential limitation of MI and SFBT approaches is that they are language-based and rely to a large extent on the ability of individuals to express their feelings about a particular set of circumstances.

Dalton (1994) notes that young people can have difficulties controlling or expressing their emotions, particularly when they have language or communication difficulties. It is also important to note that for many families sitting down together as a family to resolve family conflict through dialogue may be unfamiliar ground for them, and they therefore need more support through the process.

Facilitators using MI and SF approaches may also have to take into account additional considerations when using them with children under 11 years old or with children and young people with learning difficulties. In such circumstances, using additional visual prompts, pictures or activities may be one way of facilitating the young person's involvement.

Summary

The examples above describe ways in which techniques from MI and SFBT approach can be combined to help children, young people and their families work through the process of change. All of the approaches described here can be used flexibly. The overall aim is to create an ethos based on the principles of MI and solution focused thinking where the responsibility for change is left with the individuals as they are treated as the expert of their own situation. The facilitator works in a non judgemental way, demonstrating understanding and empathy with the young person and their family. Thinking about where they are on the Model of Stages of Change will help the facilitator select the right strategies for supporting the young person and their family, thus enabling them to explore and challenge their own patterns of behaviour.

Acknowledgements

Thank you to Dr Cathy Atkinson for her encouragement, support and contributions. Eddie McNamara, for his continuous enthusiasm in the subject and encouragement.

References

Amesu, M. (2004) *'Solution Focused Approaches and Motivational Interviewing'*. Paper presented at the Association of Educational Psychologists Conference, Stratford-Upon-Avon, November 25.

Atkinson, C. and Woods, K. (2003) 'Motivational Interviewing Strategies for Disaffected Secondary School Students: a case example', *Educational Psychology in Practice* 19 (1), pp 49-64.

Corden, J. and Somerton, J (2004) 'The Trans-Theoretical Model of Change: A Reliable Blueprint for Assessment in Work with Children and Families?' *British Journal of Social Work,* 34, pp 1025-1044.

Dalton, P. (1994) *Counselling People with Communication Problems.* London: Sage Publications Inc.

De Shazer, S. (1985) *Keys to solutions in brief therapy.* New York : W.W. Norton

DfES (2003) 'Focusing on solutions: a positive approach to managing behaviour,' in *Behaviour and Attendance: developing skills.* London: HMSO

Lewis, T. F. and Osborn, C. J. (2004) 'Solution-Focused Counseling and Motivational Interviewing: A Consideration of Confluence', *Journal of Counselling and Development,* 82 (1), pp 38-49.

McNamara, E. (1998) *The Theory and Practice of Eliciting Pupil Motivation: Motivational Interviewing – A Form Teacher's Manual and Guide for Students, Parents, Psychologists, Health Visitors and Counsellors.* Ainsdale, Merseyside: Positive Behaviour Management.

Miller, W. R. and Rollnick, S. (1991) Motivational Interviewing: *Preparing People to Change Addictive Behaviour.* New York: Guildford Press.

Miller, W. R. and Rollnick, S. (2002) Motivational Interviewing: *Preparing People for Change.* New York: Guildford Press

Prochaska, J. O. and DiClemente, C. C. (1982) 'Transtheoretical Therapy: Toward a More Integrative Model of Change', *Psychotherapy: Theory Research and Practice,* 19 (3) pp 276-288.

Prochaska, J. O. and DiClemente, C.C. (1983) 'Stages and Processes of Self-Change of Smoking: Toward and Integrative Model of Change,' *Journal of Consulting and Clinical Psychology,* 51, pp 390-395

McNamara, E. (1992) Motivational Interviewing: The Gateway to Pupil Self-Management. Pastoral Care in Education, 10(2), 92-98.

Prochaska, J. O. and DiClemente, C. C. (1998) Comments, criteria and creating better models: In response to Davidson, in Miller, W. and Heather, N. (Eds) *Treating Addictive Behaviours,* 2nd edition. New York: Plenum Press.

Prochaska, J. O., Norcross, J. C. and DiClemente, C. C. (1994) *Changing for Good: A Revolutionary Six-Stage Program for Overcoming Bad Habits and Moving Your Life Positively Forward.* New York: Quill.

Chapter 7

Assessment of Motivation to Change

Section 1
Assessing Pupil Motivation for Change: a Questionnaire Approach

Vanessa Wood

Section 2
Assessing Pupil Motivation for Change: Using Card Sorting Methodology

Martin Hughes and Vicky Booth

Section 1

Assessing Pupil Motivation for Change: a Questionnaire Approach

It can be a common experience for school staff to be met with silence or one-word answers to questions when attempting to discuss a serious behaviour incident or even general behaviour with a student.

Within the school context students may be unwilling or unable to verbally explore their attitude towards their 'problematic' behaviour and to indicate their attitude towards changing their behaviour. However, they may be willing, albeit sometimes reluctantly, to respond to a questionnaire which largely requires them to tick boxes indicating the extent to which they agree or disagree with given statements.

The 'Have Your Say' questionnaire was devised to access student views about their behaviour and their attitude to behaviour change. This tool can be used as a springboard for Motivational Interviewing, either at the time of questionnaire completion or at a later date. Reading the student's responses back to them can be a powerful strategy to engage the student in active listening dialogues.

If the student is extremely reticent to talk, the information gathered through the questionnaire can be used by staff when considering further actions/interventions.

The Questionnaire

The questionnaire is completed either independently by the student or with the help of an adult. It is useful for an adult to support the student during the completion of the questionnaire as the adult can encouraged the student to expand and develop the answers to the questions. The 'Have Your Say' Questionnaire consists of 3 sections.

The first section consists of 46 statements that sample the student's views on their experience of school, behaviour in school and motivation for change. Students are required to tick one of four boxes to indicate the degree to which they agree with the statement - See Figure 7.1.

In the second section students are asked to give examples of lessons in which they behave and lessons in which they misbehave. They are invited to describe their behaviour by writing what an observer would see if they, the observer, recorded the scene with a video camera. The students also rate their behaviour in the lessons on a scale from 1 to 7 (1= really badly behaved through to 7 = really well behaved). Students are asked to give reasons for their compliance and misbehaviour as appropriate. The invitation to give examples of 'good' behaviour in lessons enables the student to provide examples of 'exceptions' to their misbehaviour.

HAVE YOUR SAY!

	Agree A lot	Agree A bit	Agree Not at all
* I argue with teachers			
* I argue with other students			
* I think the teachers are responsible for the way I behave			
I enjoy making friends			
* I don't like getting the work wrong in class			
* Things that are going on outside school are affecting me			
* I do things without thinking			
* I say things without thinking			
* Other students affect my behaviour			

Figure 7.1 Sample questions from the 'Have Your Say' questionnaire

In the third section of the questionnaire the student is asked to explore possible solutions to the issues that were identified by questionnaire completion. The section consists of 14 possible ways in which their, i.e. the student's, situation could be improved. The student is required to tick solutions that could make a difference- see Figure 7.2.

Things that could make a difference

(tick as many as you need to)

If I could manage my anger   ....
If I could understand some subjects better   ....
If adults in this school treated me fairly   ....
If I was better at getting on with my work   ....
If my parents helped me   ....
If I was better at managing my relationship with teachers   ....
If I had more friends   ....
If I knew how to sort it out when my friends and I fell out   ....
If adults help me with my work   ....

Figure 7.2 Sample items from "Things that Could Make a Difference" Protocol

The student then indicates which option they believe would be most effective in 'making a difference' to their experience of school. Finally they are given the opportunity to suggest further actions that they or school staff might take to resolve presenting issues.

The *'Have Your Say'* questionnaire explores five different aspects of the student's perception and evaluation of his or her situation. These are:

1. The student's views on the behaviours of concern to others

2. The student's 'explanation' of the behaviour

3. The student's views about the need or otherwise to change his or her behaviour – and ability to engage in such change

4. The student's judgement about the situation – ie is/isn't a problem

5. The nature of the support/intervention that the student judges would be helpful (If the student is motivated to change).

The contents of Figure 7.3 illustrate the relationship between the areas of enquiry covered in the Questionnaire and the Stages of Change model – which in turn facilitate the identification of the appropriate MI techniques to emphasise.

Emphasis of enquiry	Example statement	Link to Stages of Change model and MI
Identify the presenting behaviour	'I argue a lot with others'	Indicates whether the student is aware of and concerned about the behaviour of concern to others
Gather information about why the behaviour is occurring	'Things outside school are worrying me'	Explores the student's interpretation of the 'causes' of the behaviour – and the extent to which it is contributing to resistance
Ascertain how the student feels about change	'I think I can change my behaviour'	Shows whether the student is ready, willing, and believes able, to change
Explore reasons for the attitude towards change. May indicate what type of pre-contemplator the student is	'I don't think my behaviour is a problem'	Identifies which type of pre-contemplator the student is
Indicate which type of intervention the student believes might be effective	'It would help if I had another student to talk to'	Indicates whether the student is ready for action planning

Figure 7.3 The Relationship between the 'Have Your Say' Questionnaire
Areas of Enquiry and the Stages of Change Model

Areas of Enquiry

Identifying the present behaviour

An assessment of whether the student believes himself to be misbehaving is achieved by asking the student to i) rate questionnaire statements and ii) describe their behaviour in specific lessons. This information is also used to compare the student's perspective with that of school staff. Discrepancies between staff and student reports can act as a conversation starter with students who have a different view to that of their teacher about their behaviour. Raising the student's awareness about the extent of the concern that others have about their, i.e. the student's, behaviour can be effective in developing dissonance in a student who might not previously have been aware that their behaviour was seen as 'a problem'.

Examples of student responses to the statement 'If you had a video camera in lessons you would see me doing these things':

> *'Swinging on my chair and shouting out'*
>
> *'Mucking about, talking and doing no work'*
>
> *'Shouting, not doing my work, ignoring the teacher'*
>
> *'I would be swearing and shouting at the teacher'*
>
> *'Being horrible and mouthy to Mr Smith for reasons'*
>
> *'Just minding my own business'*
>
> *'Getting on with my work'*
>
> *'Trying to listen'*

Exceptions to the behaviour described above are also explored through the questionnaire. Students are asked to describe their behaviour in lessons where they believe their behaviour to be appropriate.

Examples of such exceptions in response to the statement 'In these lesson i.e. lessons that 'work for them'

> *'Enjoy them and get on with most people in these lessons so I don't mess around and I like the teachers'*
>
> *'Work'*
>
> *'Sometimes ignore what other people say to me when they try to wind me up'*
>
> *'Sometimes concentrate'*
>
> *'Have fun and learn new skills'*

Gathering information about possible reasons for the inappropriate behaviour – by exploring the student's 'explanation' of the behaviour

The questionnaire informs thinking about factors that may contribute to the behaviour of concern. This information can help to indicate why the student may not want to change his or her behaviour. The student may have a lot invested in their behaviour. For example, the student might be disruptive in class because it makes other students laugh, thus leading to that student feeling that he is liked and accepted by his peers. The student may believe that the problem lies with someone else and their own behaviour does not need to change. For example, the student may feel that the teachers talk to them in a way that is unacceptable to them ie the student. Further, the student may feel that he or she is completely justified in responding to this inappropriate teacher behaviour by leaving the lesson or shouting at the teacher. Some students may believe that their behaviour is less of an issue than staff suggest. Alternatively, the student may feel that he or she have so many problems in their life that they are overwhelmed and powerless to influence such issues. Information of this nature can give school staff an insight into the student's perspective on the issues and inform further interventions or conversations.

Examples of student responses to the statement 'My reasons for behaving like this' are given below:

> *'I was annoyed, stressed and angry'*

> *'Because Mr Smith is patronising'*

> *'Because I hate Mr Brown and he hates me'*

> *'Pupils find it funny watching the teacher getting mad with me'*

> *'I get no help in Geography and I'm no good at it. He doesn't explain it well either'*

> *'I can't get on with the teachers and some of the pupils and the work is too hard'*

> *'I was bored and the work was too hard'*

> *'The teachers don't treat me like other people in the class'*

Students' perceptions of the reasons for behaving well in certain lessons are also elicited through responses to the statement 'These lessons work for me because…:

> *'The lessons are fun and easy to understand. Teachers help you when you need it'*

> *'These lessons are really exciting and in Drama and French we are left to work on our own'*

> *'The teachers are really nice'*

> *'The teachers treat me with respect'*

> *'I can learn stuff in the lessons because I get some help'*

Explore reasons for the student's attitude towards change

For a person to achieve change Miller and Rollnick (2002) believe that they have to feel *ready, willing* and *able* to change. The questionnaire responses allow judgements to be made about where the student sees themselves with regard to each of these facets of readiness to change.

Furthermore, the questionnaire responses provide an evidence base from which to formulate hypothesises with regard to the reasons for the student's seeming unwillingness to change – if such is the case. For example, the student may indicate that his/her behaviour is serving a purpose, that he/she has tried many times to change but failed or that he/she believes that his/her behaviour is not a problem at all.

Prochaska and Diclemente's (1984) pre-contemplative categories (reluctant; rebellious; resigned; and rationalising) can be used to identify the nature of the student's pre-contemplative state – which in turn can inform the counsellor as to the bias to be put on responses to the student's utterances.

Statements in section 1 of the questionnaire explore why the student feels they cannot, don't want to or don't feel ready for change. An example of such a statements is *'I have not been able to change my behaviour when I have tried in the past'*.

The student responses to these statements are important as each category of pre-contemplator needs to be approached in a specific, slightly different way. For example, those who indicate they have no hope of changing will respond to different approaches from those who believe the problem lies with the teachers and not with them at all.

Examples of some responses to the questionnaire by a student who could be described as *resigned* are reproduced in Figure 7.4.

This student who volunteered the information in Figure 7.4 appears to be overwhelmed by her issues and cannot report any exceptions to her negative classroom experiences. She has no confidence in her ability to change, although she would really like things to be different. She does not seem to be able to identify why she behaves in this way but her responses to the statements given in Section 1 of the questionnaire indicate what some of the issues might be. This information would point to the student as being a resigned pre-contemplator.

The student ticked the box **'A lot'** in response to these statements	The student ticked the box **'Not at all'** in response to these statements	Behavioural Descriptors and reasons for the behaviour
'I am worried about a lot of things' 'I have difficulty with some subjects at school' 'Things that are going on outside school are affecting me' 'I do things without thinking' 'Anything other students do in class distracts me' 'It's hard for me to finish work in lessons' 'I think I'm different from other students' 'Other students treat me as different' 'I think the teachers treat me as different from other students' 'I would like to change the way I behave'	'I can cope with working with lots of teachers in this school' 'I usually follow the rules in this school' 'Teachers at this school help me when I need it' 'I am able to do the work in this school' 'I feel I belong in this school' 'I think I can change the way I behave' 'I am responsible for the way I behave'	'If you had a video camera in lessons you would see me shouting, not doing my work, ignoring the teacher' 'I don't have good lessons' 'I behave badly in all my lessons' 'I don't know why I do it. I've always been the same' 'I feel oppressed'

Figure 7.4 Examples of a "Resigned" Student's Responses

Indicate possible interventions

The questionnaire also gives the student an opportunity to indicate whether he/she feels that there is a strategy which will help him/her solve the problem(s). It may be that the student says that he/she does not believe that any intervention would be helpful. This, along with other information gathered from the questionnaire, may indicate that the student does not feel that change is possible. On the other hand, if the student is able to indicate that he/she has clear ideas about possible ways of moving forward then the student could be at the action planning stage of the change cycle. If this is the case then the student would be supported in devising an action plan.

Examples of these student generated ideas are:

'If I tell people to leave me alone'

'I would want the teachers to listen to me when I tell them I'm being bullied and do something about it'

'If the teacher helped me a bit more in maths when I needed it'

'If I got on with the teachers more in the classroom'

'If the teachers listened to me instead of telling me to shut up all of the time in the classroom'

'If I could have more patience when teachers don't come and help me'

Summary

The *'Have Your Say'* Questionnaire provides the teacher with a tool for accessing the views of students, particularly students who are reluctant to respond verbally to teacher initiated interactions.

- It enables the teacher to explore student attitudes towards their problematic behaviour.

- It samples student views on their experience of school; identifies current behaviours across a variety of lessons and indicates factors that may contribute to the student's inappropriate behaviour.

- It gives information on the student's attitude towards change which can then point to strategies for building motivation.

- It provides the student with the opportunity to indicate possible interventions which would help them solve their problems.

- It can give staff an insight into the student's perspective on the issues and inform further interventions or conversations, particularly Motivational Interviewing.

A person must be motivated for behaviour change to occur and a student's motivation can be influenced by any number of factors. With the student's voice at the centre of exploration of such factors, a targeted and coherent approach can be taken to effectively increase their motivation for real change.

References

Miller, W. R. and Rollnick, S. (2002) Motivational Interviewing: Preparing People for Change. New York. The Guilford Press .

Prochaska, J.O. and DiClemente, C.C. (1984) The Transtheoretical Approach: Crossing Traditional Boundaries of Therapy. Homewood.Il., Dowe Jones/Irwin

Section 2 - Assessing Pupil motivation for Change: Using Card Sorting Methodology

Introduction

An important part of the role of Educational Psychologists (EPs) is to facilitate hope and change within situations involving young people which have become 'stuck'. It is not uncommon for an EP to hear a young person described as *'the most difficult young person I have had in thirty years of teaching'.* Once challenging and demanding situations concerning young people are 'presented' as crises, an EP may find that it is more necessary than ever to work creatively to foster hope and to achieve positive change for the young person and the school. It can be hard and time consuming for an external support worker to make a positive input, especially when staff might see the solution in terms of a change in provision i.e. the removal of the young person from the school, and expect the EP to facilitate this change.

Even when there is time and opportunity for early intervention, some practitioners find it hard to work effectively with these young people, run out of ideas, and experience the young people and families as 'hard to reach'.

As practitioners charged with supporting staff in schools and the children and young people in them who are of concern, our focus as EPs in responding to challenge is on developing approaches which encourage youngsters to engage and which are respectful and effective. Our positions both as researchers and practitioners overlap where we attempt to explore methodologies which

i) are ethically sound ii) are effective with regard to engaging young people and iii) enable young people's voices to be heard and responded to.

We explored the theory of change model described as the Trans-Theoretical Model (TTM) and Motivational Interviewing (MI) practices in order to consider how they could be employed to engage young people in a respectful and effective manner.

Beyond this, we explored how MI and the TTM can be integrated with a card sort activity derived from Q methodology -see Stenner et al, 2008 for further description. The card sorting activity was developed as a way of eliciting what young people think about their behaviour. It was particularly effective with pupils who experienced difficulty putting their thoughts into words and/or were uncomfortable talking to an adult about their views on their life situation.

Motivational Interviewing and the Trans-Theoretical Model

The main appeal of using MI with young people stems from the fact that it provides a way of addressing a 'problem' situation in which a young person may not feel there is a problem or want to change his or her behaviour. However, another feature is important when considering a model of change.

From an *interactionist perspective,* we wanted in some cases to facilitate a change within adults' views of the youngster. We wanted the adult to move away from a problem-saturated 'story' of the young person to a more optimistic solution-oriented narrative. The TTM provides a 'map' which can chart progression through different stages of change. This contrasts with an 'all or nothing' approach to behavioural change. Consideration of the TTM 'map' by adults can facilitate a move away from a solely within-young person analysis of the problem towards an interactive analysis. For example, during a consultation around a young person, the EP linked the TTM model to everyday experiences within the teacher's life e.g. being motivated to go to the gym, give up smoking and so on, so that a joint understanding emerged between the EP and teacher of the significance for the young person of moving from being at the 'pre-contemplative' stage to being at the 'contemplative' stage of change. MI therefore seemed to provide both i) a 'way in' to working with young people who may be at different stages of change (from not wanting to change to actively implementing plans to change) and ii) offer adults an alternative way of viewing the 'problem' situation. Two reasonable questions to ask at this point are i) where did the model of change which MI uses originate from? and ii) does it, ie the model, uphold evidence-based practice? Observations about the first question follow. Observations about the second question are made in the concluding chapter of this publication.

A search for the evidence base for the Trans-Theoretical Model

Prochaska and DiClemente's Transtheoretical Model (TTM) of Change emerged from a meta-analysis of 18 major theories of psychotherapy and behavioural change from Freudian to Rogerian schools of thought (Brown 2005). Prochaska, DiClemente and Norcross (1992) analysed a range of research into addiction, including the process of giving up smoking, and then combined Prochaska's early TTM into the Stages of Change Model.

This model proposes the intuitively plausible idea that when considering an aspect of their behaviour which could potentially be changed, people move between different stages of change. For example, at one stage the person may feel that they don't need or want to change, *'It's not me, it's the teacher's fault'*, then later an ambivalence towards the change *'I don't know – I suppose I do want to go to the gym more often, but it's hard work fitting it in'*, and finally signing up to the change. *'I've not smoked for 2 months – so far, so good!'*

How can 'stage of change' be assessed?

Some approaches to assessing the stage of change (in relation to the TTM) involve the use of questionnaires - see Miller and Tonigan, (1996). Shortcomings of the methodology of questionnaires can be found described in the literature. For example, Stainton Rogers (1991), is critical of methods such as questionnaires with a limited range of questions where concepts are predetermined. The response analysis, he believes, is more likely to tell us something about the researcher who constructed the questionnaire, rather than the social world being investigated. Brown makes a similar point when he considers social science scales and how an observer (or researcher) imposes their will on reality, 'by defining ahead of time, what a response is to mean' (Brown, 1980, p3). Stainton Rogers is also critical of some interview strategies – because of the difficulties they pose with regard to mutual understanding. In our work, we are keen to go beyond the notion of using method to transfer information from a research participant's head into our own, as if we were emptying a vessel. If we are serious about the voice of the child, then we need to explore and understand approaches which facilitate co-construction between researcher and researched.

Card sorts represent one way in which youngsters can be more involved in a 'hands-on' approach which relies less on the conventional interview. Also, such an approach can encourage conversation to be opened up more easily.

With the above considerations in mind, we developed the card sort activity as a way to determine which stage on the six stage model (Prochaska et al, 1994) a youngster might be at. We aimed to develop a tool which could also be used after a youngster had been excluded from school – a tool which would provide us with a better understanding of the excluded pupil's view of their own behaviour. We saw this as a first step towards the identification of appropriate interventions aimed at re-engaging a youngster and preventing further exclusions. The tool can, however, be used with any young person to explore their views about their behaviour in more detail.

During the development of this assessment tool various versions of this activity have been designed. The first was a 48 statement card sort, the second a version with 12 cards with statements. We have also been developing two different versions of the Motivational Interviewing assessment tool, including a picture card sort version, and an electronic version which enables a young person to show their responses on a computer, with the responses being automatically scored at the end.

Literature on the practical use of MI contains descriptions of the therapeutic process and of practical resources for use when working with young people e.g. Atkinson (2005). The approach is increasingly being used within the field of Educational Psychology e.g. Boyle (2007), as a means of working collaboratively with young people to increase feelings of self-efficacy through active listening – which is developed to include the central MI principles of:

- Expressing empathy

- Developing discrepancies

- Avoiding argumentation

- Rolling with resistance

Atkinson and Woods (2003) provide a useful case study to illustrate their use of MI strategies - strategies based on the work of Rollnick, Heather and Bell (1992) and McNamara (1998). To develop the approach further, they suggested that it would be useful to explore i) a means by which the young person could be involved in assessing which stage of change he or she feels they are at and ii) a means by which MI could be used in contexts where there is limited time for working in depth with a young person. In response to these suggestions, we developed the Sheffield MI 12 card sort assessment activity.

The 12 Card Sort Assessment

Statements which a young person may say at each stage of change were developed from McNamara's (1998) examples. After consulting young people and reflecting with colleagues, a number of statements representative of each of the stages of change was decided upon. For the purpose of using these statements when working with children, each statement was printed on a card. The 12 statements which constitute the Sheffield MI 12 card sort assessment tool are reproduced in Figure 7.5

P1
There's nothing wrong with my behaviour – I'm OK as I am

P2
It's the teachers – they are always getting at me

C1
I could behave better

C2
Sometimes I mess about and disrupt the lesson

D1
I want to keep out of trouble

D2
I'd like some ideas on other ways of keeping out of trouble

A1
Some of the things I do keep me out of trouble

A2
I know some ways to change and they are helping

M1
When I feel like something is about to go wrong I can figure out what to do

M2
It's hard work, but I feel like my behaviour's getting better

R1
Things have been going well until recently

R2
I do try to behave better but I can't keep it up

Figure 7.5 Cards for 12 card sort

The letters on the cards relate to each stage of change. There are 2 statements from each stage of change: P = Pre-contemplative, C = Contemplative, D = Deciding, A = Action, M = Maintaining, R= Relapse. The numbers are simply for ease of recording.

Card Sort Method

1. The cards are handed to the young person.

2. The young person is told that he/she is to place each card on one of three piles, namely *agree* (with the statement on the card), *disagree* (with the statement on the card and *neither* (agree or disagree with the statement on the card).

3. The first card is read with or to the young person.

4. The young person is asked whether he/she felt that this was the sort of thing she may say, and to place the card on the appropriate pile.

After a few cards are sorted, the card sorting process is individualised. Some young people choose to read the statements themselves, and quickly understand the card sorting process. For other young people, the cards are all read for them and they are helped throughout the sorting process.

After completion of the first level sorting task, the young people are introduced to a 9 point *strongly disagree* to *strongly agree* continuum scale. This continuum scale ranges from -4 (strongly disagree) through 0 (neither agree nor disagree) to +4 (strongly agree).

5. Cards from the strongly agree and strongly disagree piles are taken in turn.

6. Based on how strongly the young person agrees with the statement, she places the card underneath the scale at points ranging from +4 through +3 and +2 to +1.

7. Based on how strongly the young person disagrees with the statement, she places the card underneath the scale at points ranging from -4 through -3 and -2 to -1.

8. Cards from the 'neither' pile are placed at position 0 on the continuum

For some young people, including younger pupils, we simplified the process by just asking the young person to put the cards into the initial three piles, namely 'agree', 'disagree' and 'not sure'.

Using this method, the young person could talk as much or as little as he/she felt comfortable doing – for the only requirement was for the young person to decide how far she agreed with the statements on the cards; an activity which doesn't require any verbal communication at all if the young person feels comfortable communicating her views by 'doing' (placing cards in different places) rather than by talking. In our experience, it was often the case that verbal interactions increased as the card sort progressed.

Figure 7.6 A typical arrangement for 12 Card sort

A further understanding of the young person's views was possible by asking questions about where the cards were placed once they had been sorted e.g. "I noticed you strongly agreed with the card that said *"Some of the things I do keep me out of trouble' – what sorts of things help you?"* and *"Would it be OK for me to share your ideas with other people who are more stuck for ideas than you are?"*

However, the use of questions is only indicated if the judgment is made that questions will not inhibit the young person's engagement in the sorting task.

Card Sorts – the Young Person's Perspective

The reactions of young people completing a questionnaire compared with responding to the same items presented as a card sort activity, was explored. One boy, reported that in contrast to the card sort, the questionnaire completion made him feel that he was *'not welcome...like you've done something wrong'.*

An articulate 15 year old student was asked to complete the 12 card sort and was then asked for written feedback. She reported as follows:

'The card sort would be good for people who don't like to talk about themselves or find it difficult (to talk about themselves). Also it's easier than writing down information about how you're feeling because the thoughts are there. And because they are thoughts that relate to the person but aren't actually volunteered by that person, that makes it easier for the person to describe how they are feeling but not feel as if they are giving too much away or finding it difficult'.

We believe that this might be the case for other young people who undertake such an activity, but who do not have the reflective or communication skills to report back in this manner.

By using this 'hands-on' card sorting approach youngsters can be engaged with by a process which relies less on the conventional talk orientated interview. In addition, such an approach can sometimes encourage conversation to be opened up more easily than would otherwise be the case.

Assessment and intervention over time

Educational Psychologists often use models of assessment which take place over time – models that are closely linked with interventions. We have found that by using the 12 card sort with a young person at intervals, we can explore the young person's attitudinal change over time. For example, we have used the card sort before and after an intervention using MI to determine how far the young person has moved round the cycle of change. We have also used the card sort to assess a young person's views about his behaviour across different settings, for example when the young person has changed school.

When engaging with 'hard to reach' young people, particularly young people who are at risk of permanent exclusion, the card sorting and subsequent MI activities are driven by a number of general research questions, namely:

What do young people say about, or what accounts do they give for, their behaviour?

What reasons do young people who are close to permanent exclusion give for their behaviour?

How might these accounts help a practitioner to understand how to best engage with and talk to a young person so as to support them effectively?

What do young people think about the help that is offered to them?

How could the help that is offered be improved?

What are young people's views of help and how might there be an effective match between helper and helped?

How does change happen - what and who helps change?

How do young people account for change?

Case study 1: Liam - Using the MI 12 card sort over time

Liam was a Year 8 boy who had recently moved schools within the Local Authority. The 12 card sort was used at the beginning of the placement in the new school, and again after two months, to explore changes in attitudes, if any, towards behavioural change. In the first session, Liam seemed to be within the *Pre-contemplative* stage. For example, he agreed most with *"It's the teachers, they are always getting at me"*. He least agreed with statements including *"I want to keep out of trouble"*, and *"I know some ways to change and they are helping"*. On the second card sort, two months later, Liam agreed strongly with the Action statements *"When I feel like something is about to go wrong I can figure out what to do"*, *"I know some ways to change and they are helping"* and the Decision statement *"I want to keep out of trouble"*.

On the second sort, he agreed least with: *"It's the teachers – they are always getting at me"*. By jointly reflecting on these sorting responses with Liam, and after the session with his teacher, it could be concluded that Liam had moved through the *Pre-contemplative* stage and, by the later session, he was within the *Deciding* stage and beginning to make definite plans for *how* he was going to make the change. By sharing these assessment outcomes with teaching staff, they could be 'witnesses' to, and therefore support Liam's plans for making changes at school.

With the 12-card sort approach, we also developed a method for *visually quantifying* the results of the card sort in graph form to present to the young person in the next session. This constituted an effective prompt for discussion and eliciting change talk. An example of such a graph is included in the following case study;

Case study 2: Gita -Using a graphical representation of the card sort outcome to elicit change talk

Gita was a Year 9 girl who had been permanently excluded from school and was attending a Pupil Referral Unit. The 12 card sort was used to explore how best we could work together to support her reintegration to mainstream school. Gita preferred visual, "hands on" activities, and the 12 card sort therefore seemed well suited to her learning style.

Gita's card sort can be seen in Figure 7.7.

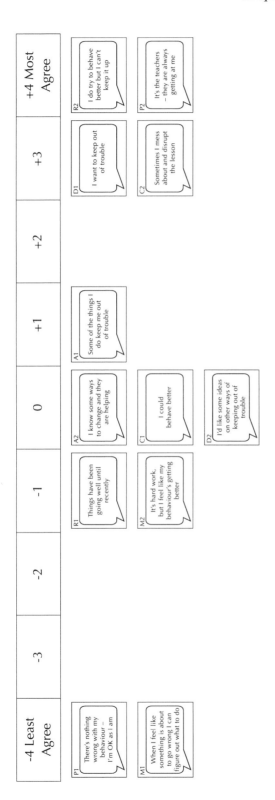

Figure 7.7 Gita's Motivational Interviewing 12 card sort

By sorting the cards as shown in figure 7.7, each statement was given a value (-4 to +4) depending on how far Gita agreed with the statement. The values were then totalled for each stage of change. For example, for the Pre-contemplative stage of change (those cards marked with a P), the total value for the stage was 0 (-4 plus +4) as shown in figure 7.8 below

	Precontemplating	Contemplating	Deciding	Action	Maintaining	Relapse
	-4	0	0	0	-4	-1
	4	3	3	1	-1	4
Totals:	0	3	3	1	-5	3

Figure 7.8 Gita's Motivational Interviewing 12 card sort scores.

The totals for each stage of change were then converted into a bar chart

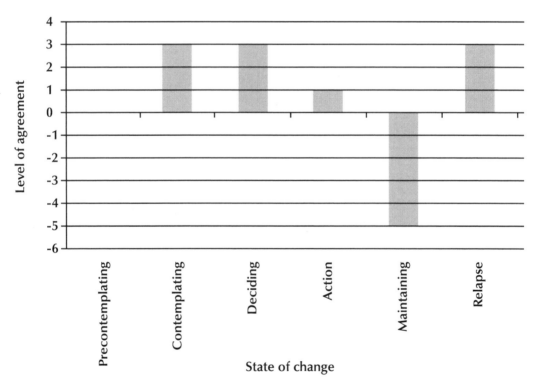

Figure 7.9 An example of a graph based on Gita's card sort

There is much to explore with the young person when using such an approach. It is always emphasised that this is a 'snap-shot' of what the young person felt on one occasion, rather than 'the truth'. The key to 'using' such a graph with the young person is that a curious 'not knowing' stance is adopted, so that the practitioner and the young person can *jointly* work as detectives, analysing what the graph seems to be saying, and exploring ideas to take a position in relation to the data.

The chart in figure 7.9 suggests that Gita is starting to want to change her behaviour as indicated by positive values for Contemplating, Deciding and Action. However, she is not yet able to maintain the change, and has already been through the Relapse stage of change – perhaps this is not Gita's first time round the cycle of change. A common feature of behavioural change is that the individual may relapse, perhaps on more than one occasion, before sustained change is achieved. Sharing this observation with the young person often helps the young person stay motivated to change when relapse has occurred.

In this example, it was helpful to explore Gita's ambivalence about change - ambivalence evident by Gita agreeing strongly with *"It's the teachers, they are always getting at me"* and disagreeing strongly with *"There's nothing wrong with my behaviour"*, both are Pre-contemplative statements, but ambivalence can be hypothesised as Gita is claiming that there is a problem but that it, the problem, is precipitated by teacher behaviour.

There are a range of other conversations which this graph can open up, especially when discussed with the young person alongside a copy of the cycle of change. It may be that the contents of this discussion are a better indication of how the young person feels than the 12 card sort alone, as an understanding of the reasons why the young person made his or her choices can be explored.

We have found that a range of solution-oriented approaches can be used throughout the Motivational Interview. For example, exception finding questions such as *"When things were going well, what were you doing?"* and *"What things might I see you doing when you are trying to behave better"*.

Using this solution-oriented approach, the 12 card sort was used again with Gita. Gita was asked to sort the cards in response to the question 'where do you want to be next year, in Year 10?' This again provided plenty to discuss. Gita placed the two Action stage statements in the 'most agree' column, and the two Contemplative stage statements in the -3 'disagree' column. It is hypothesised that by Gita rehearsing this positive story of what will happen in future (with her more fully within the Action stage of change), and by strengthening this story through sharing it with key people in the school who can support her with her plans for change, her preferred narrative about herself will strengthen further and may become self-fulfilling - see Morgan (2000) and White and Epston (1990) for a description of working therapeutically using narrative approaches.

In order to plan for maintenance and eventual exit from the cycle it is important to explore how to strengthen some of the young person's own self change strategies - perhaps slightly adapting these through discussion with the young person. Such practice both reduces the possibility of relapse and increases the probability that the young person will re-enter the cycle of change at the planning and active stage phase. Activities to achieve this include working through role-play scenarios, discussing comic strip drawings in which a scene involving a possible relapse situation is depicted e.g. a close friend is trying to encourage the young person to truant from school. In this activity the young person is encouraged to problem solve and use rehearsed strategies to overcome the potential difficult situation.

The identification of adults who can support the pupil's plans for change and maintenance is also important. The Facilitating Change DVD resource (Atkinson 2005) has been found to be useful to achieve this end. The clearly structured session plans in this resource describe activities which aim to support the young person in working towards the 5 goals of MI as described by McNamara (1998):

- To increase knowledge

- To increase concern

- To promote self-efficacy

- To promote internal attribution

- To promote self-esteem

Case study 3: Sam - Using MI and Positive Psychology

One of the authors (VB) has drawn upon ideas from Positive Psychology e.g. Seligman (2002), Robinson (2006),in order to emphasise the therapeutic aspect of the spirit of MI within an intervention with Sam, a young person at risk of permanent exclusion.

Sam was a Year 8 boy at High School, who for some of his time accessed Valleydale, an alternative curriculum centre. The 12 card sort was used alongside some of the ideas from the Positive Psychology conversation plan (see chapter appendix) and the Strengths profile to explore ways of helping Sam in acquiring a more positive self-perception as a learner and thus facilitate change.

Throughout the conversation with Sam notes were made of Sam's identified skills and competences and these were written on the 'Strengths profile' leaflet. Then we began to explore how these skills could be generalised. For example, Sam enjoyed motocross racing, so we drew out the skill 'determination to succeed'. From this we explored ways in which this competency could be used in school.

Intervention as a collaborative endeavour

As part of the therapeutic work, a letter was written to Sam to ensure that he was fully included within the process and felt some ownership of it. The letter also acted as a record for Sam of some aspects of our conversations, with an emphasis being given to i) positive messages affirming strengths and ii) prompts for generalising aspects of our conversation. The written content of the letter was kept simple and focussed and was made more interesting to Sam by including coloured pictures which complemented the written content – see Figure 7.10 below.

Figure 7.10: Letter to Sam

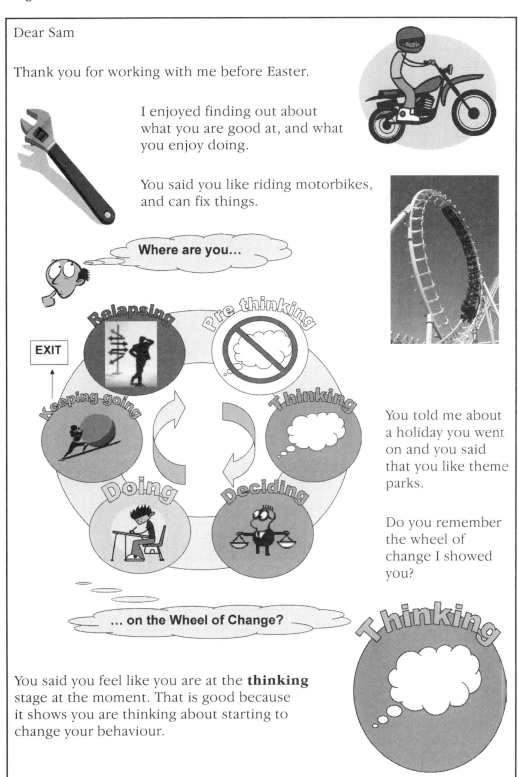

Dear Sam

Thank you for working with me before Easter.

I enjoyed finding out about what you are good at, and what you enjoy doing.

You said you like riding motorbikes, and can fix things.

Where are you...

EXIT

... on the Wheel of Change?

You told me about a holiday you went on and you said that you like theme parks.

Do you remember the wheel of change I showed you?

You said you feel like you are at the **thinking** stage at the moment. That is good because it shows you are thinking about starting to change your behaviour.

You agreed that when you feel like something's about to go wrong you can work out what to do. That's an important skill. What sort of things do you do?

I hope that you work out ways of getting to the next stage of change – the next stage is the **deciding** stage. From what you said to me before the holidays, it sounds like you are

nearly there!

I enjoyed finding out about how well you are getting on at Valleydale. Your teachers said that you are good at woodwork and canoeing.

It sounds like you are learning a lot by doing the activities.

I have finished working in Valleydale now, but my friend Karla visits your school, and so you will see her after Easter.

Good luck in the future, and thanks again for being such an interesting person to get to know!

Yours sincerely,

Vicky Booth

Distribution

I have sent this letter to you at home, and one to school.

Observations

Ashton (2007) has described useful strategies to use when writing letters to young people. For example, it is useful to prepare the family for the arrival of the letter, so that the young person is more likely to receive the letter personally. Ashton found that the letters were valued by the young people: for example, they are often shown to teachers and family members.

As part of the intervention, Motivational Interviewing and Positive Psychology approaches were shared with Sam's Learning Mentor at the school. Atkinson's (2005) *Facilitating Change* Motivational Interviewing resources recommended to in-school support staff, so that the work with Sam could be continued by his teachers.

Outcome

Positive outcomes of the intervention for Sam included Sam being able to talk about his strengths, through competence profiling. Discussions with Sam based around the 12-card sort suggested that Sam felt that he was at the Thinking (Contemplation) stage of change. Collaboratively with Sam, we developed an Individual Behaviour Plan Target based on the Motivational Interviewing intervention. The success criteria for this target involved Sam moving towards the Deciding (Determination) stage of change – the success to be evaluated by Sam's choices when using the 12 card sort.

Concluding Observations

Our continued exploration of the use of card sorts has encouraged us to consider using pictures and simple phrases or single words as the content of the sorting exercise e.g. those found on the 'Strength Cards for Kids' (St Luke's Innovative Resources).

In the future, we believe that digital photographs perhaps taken by the youngsters themselves, could also serve as items for them to sort. We have also considered ways of trying to engage youngsters more effectively, right from the start of an EP's involvement, by looking at the issue of informed consent. Sheffield and Wigan are two of many Educational Psychology Services who have developed leaflets and booklets which explain carefully what EPs do and why adults might be asking for the young person in question to become involved with one. Sheffield and Wigan are also two of a number of services actively exploring ways of involving youngsters in evaluating the service that they have received.

Perhaps one of the most significant limitations of using MI when working with young people relates to one of the fundamental differences between using MI with adults, who are perhaps thinking about changing their behaviour specifically relating to a substance addiction, and using MI with young people who are thinking about changing their behaviour at school. In the former case, there is *usually one clear behaviour change target* e.g smoking, and although there may be many reasons as to why the client maintains the behaviour, the surface level behaviour itself is clearly manifest and understood. In contrast, a young person's behaviour relating to their disaffection in school may result in a range of 'unacceptable' behaviours influenced by context factors such as i) differences in the approaches of various adults ii) the type of activity the young person is being asked to engage in and iii) social relationship changes with peers. The young person's stage of change may therefore be different for different behaviours. For example, he or she may be maintaining regular attendance in lessons (Maintenance stage): however, within lessons she or he may be perceived as being disruptive, blaming the teacher for targeting him or her unfairly (Pre-contemplative stage).

By using MI, even though we are facilitating the autonomy of the individual and moving at his or her pace, we are nonetheless at least to a degree implying a within-young person causation of the 'unwanted' behaviour. Acceptance of this could be at the expense of exploring contextual and systemic factors which may be contributing to the 'problem' situation. Indeed, it could be that the young person does not feel that he or she needs to change because the behaviour is a protective mechanism and the result of contextual factors beyond his or her control. While MI may encourage the individual to explore his or her context in more detail, it is the individual who is being facilitated to change rather than elements of the context. Therefore MI can be part of 'the story', but is not the whole story.

Conclusion

In spite of these limitations and reservations, we remain optimistic that this work offers young people an alternative to the kind of encounter with an adult which can all too often involve a question-answer routine and a downward spiral which descends into monosyllabic responses from a youngster. The hands-on approach described in this chapter can help to develop trust and rapport with youngsters who may feel more at ease by doing something rather than talking - particularly when the subject is their behaviour. Our work continues to identify statements which are a good representation of what is said by young people about their behaviour so that we can offer them the opportunity to sort statements in ways which maximises their choices. We continue to explore methods to hear and act uponyoung people's voices which are ethical, respectful and effective.

Appendix Figure 7.11 A plan for a Positive Psychology conversation adapted from Turner (2007)

References

Ashton, R. (2007) Learning from writing to students. Debate journal: Division of Educational and Child Psychology. No.122.

Atkinson, C. (2005). Facilitating Change. Stockport, Facilitating Change Ltd.

Atkinson, C. and K. Woods (2003). Motivational Interviewing Strategies for Disaffected Secondary Students: a case example. Educational Psychology in Practice 19(1): 49 - 63.

Boyle, C. (2007) The challenge of interviewing adolescents: Which psychotherapeutic approaches are useful in educational psychology? Educational & Child Psychology, 24:1, pp.36-45.

Brown, K. M. (2005). Transtheoretical Model/Stages of Change. Retrieved 05.08.05, Accessed online at: http://hsc.usf.edu/~kmbrown/Stages_of_Change_Overview.htm.

Brown, S. (1980) Political Subjectivity. Applications of Q Methodology in political science. Yale University Press, New Haven.

McNamara, E. (1998). The Theory and Practice of Eliciting Pupil Motivation: Motivational Interviewing - A Form Teacher's Manual and Guide for Students, Parents, Psychologists, Health Visitors and Counsellors. Positive Behaviour Management.7 Quinton Close, Ainsdale, Merseyside PR8 2TS UK

Miller, W. R., and Tonigan, J. S. (1996). Assessing Drinkers' Motivation for Change: The Stages of Change Readiness and Treatment Eagerness Scale (SOCRATES). Psychology of Addictive Behaviors : Journal of the Society of Psychologists in Addictive Behaviors. 10 (2), 81.

Morgan, A (2000) What is Narrative Therapy? An easy-to-read introduction. Adelaide: Dulwich Centre Publishing.

Prochaska, J. O., DiClemente, C. C. and Norcross, J.C. (1992). "In search of how people change." American Psychologist 47(9): 1102 - 1114.

Prochaska, J. O., Norcross, J. C. and DiClemente, C. C. (1994) Changing for Good: The revolutionary program that explains the six stages of change and teaches you how to free yourself from bad habits. W. Morrow, New York.

Robinson, K. (2006). What can be learned from Positive Psychology to help Educational Psychologists in their practice? The University of Sheffield, Unpublished EdD (Educational Psychology) assignment.

Rollnick, S., Heather, N., & Bell, A. (1992). Negotiating behaviour change in medical settings: The development of brief motivational interviewing. Journal of Mental Health, 1, 25-37.

Seligman, M. (2002). Authentic Happiness. London, Nicholas Brealey Publishing.

St Luke's Innovative Resources (1996), Strength Cards for Kids. Bendigo Victoria, Australia. (see www.innovativeresources.org)

Stainton Rogers, W. (1991) Explaining health and illness : an exploration of diversity. Harvester Wheatsheaf, London.

Stenner, P., Watts, S. and Worrell, M. (2008) Q Methodology, Ch13 in The SAGE Handbook of Qualitative Research in Psychology. SAGE, London.

Turner, K. (2007). Positive Psychology conversation prompt sheet. Unpublished resource, Blackburn with Darwen Educational Psychology Service.

Whie, N and Epston, D (1990) Narrative Means to Therapeutic Ends, London: Norton

Part 3

MI and Systems Level Intervention

Chapter 8

Section 1

A Short Term Qualitative Evaluation of MI Inset in an EBD School Setting

How we can encourage disaffected students with EBD to become self change agents, rather than 'problems to be sorted'?

Jonathan Middleton and Tricia Lunt

Section 2

Using the Stages of Change Model to Facilitate Change at a whole School Level

Stuart Duckworth

Section 1 - A Short Term Qualitative Evaluation of MI Inset in an EBD School Setting

In the first part of this chapter Dr Jonathan Middleton describes how MI was used as a framework to support students with emotional and behavioural difficulties (SEBD) who were seen as, 'difficult to engage.' In the second part Tricia Lunt describes how the intervention framework was evaluated for impact, focusing at child level, staff level and school level.

Part 1

Background

For many years I have worked as an E:P (Educational Psychologist) with young people labelled as experiencing social, emotional and behavioural difficulties. Such labels are subjective and socially constructed. Indeed I'm not sure what professional descriptions would have been given during my formative years on a Sheffield council estate! However, in recent years I have become increasingly uncomfortable about my own role when working with similar young people and their families. Am I actually changing anything profoundly or merely tinkering at the margins? What impact have I really made? What long term transformations have there been?

In order to help me address these questions at a theoretical and clinical level, I began to research the area, culminating in a Doctoral Thesis exploring the perceptions of young people placed in special SEBD provision (Middleton,,2004). Throughout the research one major fundamental postulate emerged relating to the need for engagement with young people, sharing of perceptions, and utilizing a 'bottom up' framework of engagement.

Legislation such as the U.N Convention on the Rights of the Child (1989), the Special Educational Needs and Disability Act (2001) and the Children Act (2004) had made reference to this process, although my experience told me that this was not necessarily happening effectively on a day to day basis.

At the same time as making this philosophical shift, I also began to re-address my clinical practice particularly in schools and particularly with a special school in St. Helens catering for students evidencing social, emotional and behavioural difficulties (SEBD).

I gained credibility with the establishment based upon the traditional EP route of 1:1 assessment work, feedback and training. This credibility was helpful with regard to both myself feeling confident to engage in systemic change activity with the school and with regard to the school personnel being open minded and receptive to the possibility of such change.

The Head Teacher and Senior Leadership Team (SLT) within the school were open to new ideas, challenge and the idea of progressive change. In a sense we shared a vision for 'future travel'.

The vision, which did emerge was based upon two major themes. Firstly, the school wanted to develop the notion of pupil participation and wanted to hear the pupils' voice. Secondly, they saw the need for a therapeutic aspect to intervention. In other words, there existed a willingness to engage in a philosophical change - a philosophical transition from highly structured behaviourist principles determined by staff to a more therapeutic approach, particularly for the most difficult to reach pupils.

It was agreed that such a process should have a timeframe of 12 to 18 months and should be formally reflected within the school development plan. It was further agreed that the EP would be the primary driver in the process.

In the first year I was heavily involved in whole school training. Some of these sessions were traditional in content e.g. Dyslexia, ADHD and so on, although they had an underpinning commonality based around the student voice. However, other sessions were, more focused upon staff participation and therapeutic intervention. Such themes included Personal Construct Psychology, Person Centred Counselling and Solution Focused Techniques.

Out of these training sessions, staff developed a series of pupil based activities which included; an empowered school council; creative writing tasks such as "'What's it like to be me!'? 'My life' and the creation of a DVD on pupil perceptions.

It was clear at this point that the school as a body was changing both its thinking and practice, and that staff were engaging more effectively with pupils. This view was reflected in an Ofsted report at the time. At this point I was keen to move the agenda on further towards an overarching theoretical model of delivery based upon the framework of Motivational Interviewing (Miller and Rollnick, 1991). Such an approach was in my opinion capable of unifying many of the principle themes we had been working on in school for over a year.

I worked, with SLT in order to formulate a delivery model. At this stage it was decided that I would work alongside four members of staff, both teaching and non-teaching staff, on a fortnightly basis in order to help them acquire the skills and knowledge necessary to engage with young pupils using an M.I approach.

Staff were initially asked to volunteer and then an internal selection process identified four staff members. Staff were selected and the delivery model agreed within two months of the whole school training on M.I.

A number of young people were chosen to work with the staff members - using the concept of informed consent. They were carefully matched with the staff member on the basis of who it was felt they would relate to best. Consent forms were signed by parent/guardian and the young persons.

The meetings I held with the sub-group of staff in school had a specific agenda in order to 'take them through' in the sense of 'describe and discuss' the trans-theoretical model. However, the meetings were also beneficial in respect of mutual support and problem solving. When we met to discuss how the sessions were going and plan our next session, individuals were able to share their good practice and when experiencing difficulty look for support/ideas from colleagues.

Whilst the EP maintained the central role in the meetings, it was as a facilitator and not as an expert practitioner dictating a top-down process.

The agenda for delivery focused upon:-

a.)

- Theory and history of M.I. (values and principles).
- Aims and Objectives of the intervention process.
- Facilitating change and the trans-theoretical model of change.
- Recording mind mapping techniques.
- Fostering secure and positive relationships.
- Rating scales/miracle questions/good times and not so good times/good lessons and not so good lessons.

b.)

- Contemplative/Pre-contemplative. Where is the pupil at?
- State of readiness.
- Information giving.
- Active listening skills.
- Zone of actual development and zone of proximal development i.e. exploring with the pupil the pupil's perception of their potential and comparing this with how close they are to reaching it.

c.)

- Re-capping/rating scales.
- Solutions.
- Target setting.
- Self efficacy and esteem.
- Notion of relapse.
- Letter writing-using letters to communicate self-generated targets to significant others, i.e. parents/teachers.

d.)

- Monitoring and reviewing.
- Concluding.
- Letter of thanks.
- Notion of long term support.

It was envisaged that the agenda would not be prescriptive. The ideas and concepts were communicated within the sessions and staff were given freedom and autonomy to share and use these concepts with their clients. Each staff member then reported back on their activities at the next meeting. In this way the four staff were supported on a fortnightly basis: during this time they were developing their own theoretical understanding whilst in parallel working with pupils. This relatively high frequency of meetings was necessary – as there was a need to combine both an overview of previous sessions and identify and develop new skills required to deliver the next stage of the model.

The next part of this chapter focuses on the evaluation of the MI intervention.

Part 2

Background to the evaluation study

Whilst I was training as an Educational Psychologist and on placement at an Educational Psychology Service (EPS) I was asked to evaluate the MI intervention aspect of the work carried out by Jonathan Middleton. This project resulted in a dissertation entitled: 'Evaluating the effectiveness of training school staff in Motivational Interviewing (MI) to support disaffected secondary students with EBD'. (Lunt, P 2006).

I first became aware of MI being applied within an educational setting several years ago when I was a research assistant in a MI project. Since then I have applied MI within many classroom settings.

My intention throughout this study was to understand the practitioner's perceptions and views about the MI intervention to engage disaffected students. I also explored how the students theorised their thinking about actions and decisions they made during the MI process. I was aware that I needed to be as objective as possible and to take into account the 'politics' and 'stresses' that school life can bring. I believe that the participants' stories have been interpreted so that an accurate account of what actually happened has been recorded. I found on many occasions that I had to clarify meanings of words and intent of sentences with the practitioners and students – illustrating how easy it is to attribute different meanings to the same words.

Listening to children and young people

Before I started to evaluate the MI framework I first read the students' files in order to gain background information. However, while sifting through the many reports I realised that most were just a paper chain of events retold by the authors and not the pupils themselves. This gave rise to the question, 'What are we actually doing as practitioners' and 'What can we do to help the hard to reach children and young people who are at the margins?'

From a government policy-making perspective, student disaffection, both in and out of school, is seen as a widespread problem. In order to address issues around disengagement and social inclusion, there have emerged a number of publications and guidance documents since the publication of the document, 'Excellence for all children' (DfEE, 1997). Children and young people often attract a great deal of media attention, particularly following news releases about poor discipline in schools, growth in disaffection, juvenile crime and parental accountability for children's behaviour. Unfortunately such attention tends to lead to reactive management responses rather than focusing on: i) the key issues which underpin a child's difficulties and ii) preventive, proactive work with young people.

Practitioners are often aware of the social pressures children and young people face outside school. Disaffected students can present a major challenge to the calmest of practitioners. Some practitioners working with disaffected students, especially violent or challenging ones, may judge their behaviour from "outside in," ie see it arising from "within child" deficits. The pupil on the other hand may analyse the situation as 'the teacher picks on me' ie 'inside out'. This polarisation of belief systems may impede collaborative working to address difficulties or difficult situations.

All school practitioners are constantly involved in listening to the views of children and young people. I often ask myself, 'Why does this young person feel the need to express themselves in this negative way?' and 'How can we, as practitioners, encourage disaffected students to become their own change agents?' One of the greatest achievements for many school practitioners is to enable disaffected students to access learning and become involved in school and in the wider community when they previously experienced difficultly in doing so.

As I begin to reflect upon the journey of accounts of the MI intervention and the findings, it is my intention to write in a journalistic style informed by the diary of weekly events I maintained throughout the project.

What actually happened?

The MI intervention had already been undertaken before I joined the EPS and, therefore, I was unable to plan and collect pre-intervention baseline measures for the students involved. I carried out a qualitative retrospective evaluation. Ideally I would have collected pre intervention data in the areas of attitude towards school, motivation, self-efficacy, self-image and the students' views concerning their behaviour and school attendance. However, the only pre and post intervention data collected was the students' school attendance figures.

The work was carried out in a Special Needs Resourced School designated for boys and girls aged between 9 and 16 years who had been identified as having social, emotional and behavioural difficulties (SEBD). Jonathan Middleton, the school EP, trained four members of the teaching staff, one allocated to each of the four student volunteers. However, due to personal circumstances, one of the students left the school shortly after the intervention, resulting in three students taking part in the MI intervention evaluation. Their parents'/carers' consent was requested by school via a letter and the parents'/carers' were asked if they would like to participate in the study. Offers were all declined.

The evaluation of the MI intervention took place over a ten week period.

Participants

Four members of the teaching staff received the MI training, three of whom conducted the MI sessions with the three students. The fourth member of the teaching staff, Headteacher and school EP were all interviewed after the MI intervention. Other members of the teaching staff, including the pupils' form teachers, were also interviewed.

There were twelve participants in this study, as shown in figure 8.1 below:

Kevin	**Larry**	**Martin**
A Year 9 boy, aged 14 years.	A Year 10 boy, aged 15 years.	A Year 11 boy, aged 16 years.
Practitioner A: (teaching staff who conducted MI intervention with Kevin).	Practitioner B: (teaching staff who conducted MI intervention with Larry).	Practitioner C: (teaching staff who conducted MI intervention with Martin).
Form teacher A.	Form teacher B.	Form teacher C.
School EP.		
Headteacher.		
Practitioner D, teaching staff who received MI training.		

Figure 8.1 List of participants

Students

Three students, one each from Year groups 9, 10 and 11, were involved in the study. All the students were boys and of white ethnic origin. The selection criteria for the students involved the MI intervention were:

- They were experiencing disaffection from school and school staff saw this as a significant cause for concern.
- They displayed aggressive behaviours and temper outbursts.
- Poor attendance.

Brief pen portraits of the three students, based on information from teaching staff, reports from various agencies and individual work, are reproduced below.

Kevin

Kevin was a Year 9 student, aged 14 years. He lived at home with his mum, dad and younger brother. He moved from a mainstream school to the EBD School in 2001 as a result of experiencing learning difficulties (making slow academic progress) and displaying aggression and temper outbursts at home and in school. He evidenced receptive language difficulties, was very literal and found it hard to follow oral conversations and instructions. Kevin's strengths were swimming, football and I.C.T.

Larry

Larry was a Year 10 student, aged 15 years. He lived at home with his mum, grandfather and younger sister and brother. From an early age Larry had witnessed incidents of domestic violence towards his mum. Larry volunteered the information that he did not have a good relationship with his sister, brother or grandfather. In a letter from school it was reported that Larry displayed a great deal of control at home. School staff observed that Larry presented as a solitary boy who was reluctant to develop meaningful relationships or seek the company of other students or adults. He displayed physical and verbal aggression towards other pupils and school staff. He had refused to accept rules/boundaries and was known to vandalise property after engaging in verbal aggression. Larry's strengths were maths, art and P.E, especially football.

Martin

Martin was a Year 11 student, aged 16 years. In Martin's previous mainstream school his behaviour was described as 'volatile, confrontational and aggressive towards other pupils.' It was reported by the class teacher that Martin seemed unstable as he was erratic, eccentric and bizarre at times, looking for 'victims' to pick on. It was noted that he had no friends, as most pupils felt threatened by him. Martin's strengths were football and art work.

Research methods

Consideration was given to the use of interviews, observations, questionnaires and what these methods could offer. Finally, it was jointly decided by the practitioners that I would carry out classroom observations and conduct interviews.

Interviews

Before each interview I discussed a list of pre-requisites with each participant, such as appropriate venue, the need for privacy and time scale.

All of the interviews took place in school and most of the questions were open-ended. This allowed for further probing and clarification of key issues. I interviewed the teaching staff, head teacher and Jonathan Middleton before the students in order to gain background information. The importance of confidentiality and anonymity was acknowledged and demonstrated at all times. Each member of the teaching staff was asked if they would be willing to participate in a 45-50 minute semi-structured interview that would be taped for ease of recording. Permission was obtained to record the sessions with the guarantee that, once the data had been analysed, the tapes would be erased. It was judged unethical to audio-tape the students' responses. It was made clear to the students that they could "pass" on any of the questions and that they were free to terminate the interview at any time. Notes were taken during the interviews and responses to questions were hand written and recorded verbatim. I offered to read back the notes to the students. I was aware that the students may have wanted to show themselves as being helpful and co-operative and tell me what they thought I wanted to hear.

However, the students appeared to show great respect for the school practitioners when they gave their account of the MI intervention.

Data analysis

The tape recordings were analysed by making a partial transcript of the interviews from the recordings. I first coded the data either by words, line of text or by direct quotes or paraphrasing common ideas. The first pattern of experience listed was the practitioners' concerns about the students' emotional and behavioural difficulties before the start of the MI intervention. The participant's aspirations, hopes and initial views of MI were also explored.

The three cases will be discussed separately and common themes will be discussed in relation to the Goals of MI as described by McNamara (1998).

Analysis of interviews

As themes emerged from the practitioner interviews I began to relate some of these to the elements of MI as described by Miller and Rollnick, (1991).

Whilst clustering the themes together I discovered even more pertinent links to the Five Goals of MI described by McNamara (1998) namely:

- Increased knowledge.
- Increased concern.
- Self-efficacy.
- Internal attribution.
- Self-esteem.

Therefore, the findings were reviewed under these Five MI goals.

Goal of MI 1: To increase Knowledge

Practitioners reported that, at the beginning of the MI intervention, all the students were at the "pre-contemplative stage" of the Model of Stages of Change. The practitioners all thought that it was a significant achievement for the students to actually attend the MI sessions. One of the first major themes to emerge was that all the practitioners expressed their surprise at the students' willingness to discuss personal issues around change.

Practitioner C reported that his previous experience was that getting students to think about personal issues was a big challenge and had proved to be a difficult hurdle to overcome. Practitioners reported that their ie the practitioners, knowledge and, awareness of the Model of Stages of Change enable them to behave differently towards the students and consequently the students to 'opened up' to them.

Practitioner A reported; *"It made Kevin think about things he hadn't talked about or things he didn't want to think about. It gave him time to consider the relationships he had within his family."* Practitioners B and C reported that Larry and Martin both perceived that they didn't have any behavioural problems – indicating that they were at the pre-contemplative as they externalised onto others the 'causes' of problematic situations. Larry blamed his behaviour on both his mum and teachers and said that they 'nag': Martin externalised the causes of his behaviour on rejection issues - blaming society in general. Both practitioners stressed that it was a breakthrough when Larry and Martin discussed personal family issues. They both emphasised that the stage was useful to elicit *".what Larry thought of himself and how he thought others perceived him."*

Practitioners B and C reported that, as the students' knowledge and concerns increased, they noticed how the students started to think about how other people perceived their behaviours. During the pre-contemplative stage Practitioner C helped Martin draw a path of consequences for keeping his behaviour the same and a path of consequences for changing it. The practitioner reported that this visual aid helped the student increase his knowledge and concern which, in turn, helped him to move on to the contemplative stage.

Goal of MI 2: To Increase Concern

During the contemplative stage the school practitioners used other strategies and techniques such as Solution Focused Brief Therapy (SFBT) - including goal setting and scaling questions. The practitioners stressed they were aware that they needed to be sensitive and to express empathy when implementing the active listening strategies. The practitioners reported that, at the contemplative stage, the students started to think about their behaviours and attitudes towards school.

Practitioner C noted that Martin expressed some concern regarding his attitude towards his teachers. Martin had also reported that one of his future goals was to be able to trust people. Practitioner C reported that *"During the intervention, Martin said he felt for the first time in his life, he could trust someone."*

A common theme that emerged from the student interviews and from the MI evaluation forms was that the MI strategies had succeeded in helping the students think about their attitude towards their families, teachers and school.

Practitioners reported that at the school most of the students with SEBD liked to feel a sense of control. It was when the students felt out-of-control that they would 'kick off.' Practitioners reported that they believed the students liked MI because the students felt a sense of control around making their own decisions about change. Both Martin and Larry during an interview with me said they liked MI as they felt in control and the teachers didn't tell them what to do.

The headteacher also reported that he had noticed a change in Martin's behaviour and reported an incident to me. Practitioner C confirmed the incident. *"Oh, yes! There was another time when Martin and another pupil got caught doing something and they both got sent to the headteacher's office. Both of them were about to get sent home and the other boy was really kicking off... he was shouting," I'm not f****** staying here." Now Martin would normally be kicking off, defending himself, denying all knowledge of the incident and blaming the teaching staff for picking on him. But this time the headteacher said that Martin just sat in his office and asked him "How can I resolve it, Sir?" The head said you basically need to do this.......Which he would not have done before as Martin would have kicked off and said it's not my f****** fault. Later on in the day the headteacher said to me that Martin had really made an effort to control his behaviour. He said, 'that's you, that's all your hard work during*

*the MI sessions paying off. MI made me (Practitioner C) feel re-invigorated!
There have been many positive situations that other members of staff have
reported to me. I think MI involvement was a positive experience for him."*

In summary, all three students reflected not only on their own personal views
about their behaviours but also on how others may perceive their behaviour. It was
reported that some of the students were able to contemplate and investigate the
reasons behind some of their aggressive behaviours towards others. Practitioner
C noted that, throughout the MI process, Martin became aware of his behaviour;
*"....he used to like it when he wound teachers up and they would shout at him,
as he said this gave him a chance to shout back without feeling guilty."*

Goal of MI 3: To promote self-efficacy

Analysis of the data suggested that both Larry and Martin showed some belief
that change was achievable for them. They also showed some short-term
improvements in their attitude towards their teachers and school. It was
reported by the headteacher and other members of the teaching staff that
these two students generalised some of the behaviour strategies identified and
discussed in the MI sessions and used them to turn negative situations into
positive ones.

For Kevin, the data suggested that there appeared to be no directly observable
changes in his behaviour. Practitioner A reported that even though the MI
intervention made a positive contribution, by moving Kevin on from pre-
contemplative to making a verbalised commitment to change, *"Kevin seemed
to come up against a brick wall when it came to actually implementing the
changes that we had actually talked about."*

Goal of MI 4: To promote Internal attribution

MI aims to promote internal attribution which, in turn, may help some students
to believe that their commitment to change can be realised. An important
assumption of attribution theory is that people will interpret their environment
in such a way as to protect their positive self-image. This was not the case with
Kevin, Martin and Larry. It was reported that before the MI intervention they all
had negative self-concepts. Practitioner C recalled that, before MI, Martin would
reject any form of praise and compare his successes to those of his peers by
saying their work was better than his. Practitioner C also reported that, when
Martin contemplated change, Martin said that his behaviour was part of him and
that he couldn't change.

During the MI sessions the students were encouraged to focus on their positive
achievements. Both Larry and Martin were able to discuss situations about which
they felt proud because they had succeeded in something due to effort and hard
work. Martin discussed his GCSE Art course-work file, whilst Larry spoke about
how he had spent a long time fixing a bike. However, during an interview with
Larry I noted that he attributed any 'failures' he had experienced to external
factors, such as blaming his peers for him getting him into trouble.

Goal of MI 5: To promote self-esteem

After analysing the common themes, all three practitioners suggested that the MI process had helped them to promote and 'boost' the students' self-esteem. It would appear that school practitioners are in a powerful position to be able to do this.

Practitioner C reported that, during the MI process, Martin's self-concept seemed to change for the better as improvements in his feelings of self-worth became evident. It was also reported that Larry felt 'good' about himself when Practitioner B focused on his positive achievements. Both Larry and Martin reported that the MI sessions made them feel good about themselves. Kevin, on the other hand, reported that he felt no different after the sessions – but did report that he liked talking to his teacher.

Practitioner A noted that Kevin's self-esteem seemed to improve during the MI intervention, reflected in him being more sociable and outgoing: but afterwards he reverted to being quiet, moody and withdrawn.

Maintenance

Would the student outcomes have been different had the intervention gone on longer? The practitioners spent the greater part of their time working in the pre-contemplative to action stages and did not progress to Stage 5, Maintenance - maintaining the changes. This may have been because of the half-term holidays. McNamara (1998) suggested the Maintenance Stage is the 'test' of the effectiveness of the intervention programme. Even though MI is supposed to be a short intervention programme, all of the participants reported that it should be an ongoing process, especially within an SEBD school. Practitioner C put forward the view that students with SEBD evidence multiple and complex behaviours of concern - and as one problematic behaviour ceased it was replaced by another. However, MI and a functional analysis approach did give the practitioner an insight about the functions of different behaviours.

Summary of Outcomes

Kevin

The data seemed to suggest that Kevin achieved the first two goals of MI, as both his knowledge of and concern about his situation increased. This indicated that he moved from the pre-contemplative to the contemplative stage. Although, Kevin verbalised his commitment to change he never put his words into actions and became static at the deterministic stage – illustrating that there is a difference between knowing what to do and actually putting it into practice. On a scaling question, Kevin indicated that he thought his behaviour had improved slightly, moving from 3 to 5. Both Practitioner A and Kevin indicated that they had wished that the MI activities had continued longer. Practitioners reported that Kevin seemed to be a student who needed continuous support due to the complexity of his behaviours. In this case short term intervention was not successful. The MI intervention required more time to be spent with the student than the practitioners could give.

Larry

For Larry, the data suggested a short-term, moderate improvement in behaviour. He seemed to achieve the first three goals as his knowledge, concern and feelings of self-efficacy appeared to increase. Teaching staff reported that there had been a reduction in Larry's extreme problematic behaviours and that his general day-to-day behaviours had shown a slight improvement - or that at least had become no worse. On a scaling question Larry indicated that he thought that over the past term, he had moved from 4 to 6 on behaviour within the classroom, indicating improvement, and that "he couldn't be bothered to get into trouble anymore". He told me that he did not want to be "perfect" but would like to move to 8 and thought that he could do this by changing his attitude and behaving better. He thought that this would be difficult as others got him into trouble and the teachers always thought it was his fault when things went wrong. This would suggest that while Larry was actively seeking to change his behaviour he was still externalising 'the cause'.

Martin

The results seemed to indicate that Martin showed improved positive adjustment to school after the MI intervention. Martin seemed to achieve all the MI goals, as he actively made a public commitment to change. A number of the teaching staff reported that Martin's general attitude had improved and that they had observed him engaging in much more positive behaviour. On a scaling question Martin put a cross on number 10. This which indicated that he thought the MI had helped him. The most successful outcome that Martin reported was that, for the first time in his life, he trusted someone to help him.

It was reported that Martin appeared to have developed some resilience factors and positive values about his future. During an interview with him he appeared to realise that it was up to him to make the right choices.

Overall, the outcome appears to be that the MI intervention had a positive short-term effect on Martin's adjustment more so than with Larry. It seemed that during the MI intervention Kevin showed some initial improvements but regressed when the MI stopped. It appears that MI holds a great deal of promise within an educational context cf the case of Martin. It appeared to be effective - with a relatively small amount of input (7 sessions) achieving comparatively large effects.

All participants believed that the students had acquired some strategies from the MI process and closer pupil-adult relationships had developed.

Practitioners Perceived Outcomes

During an interview with the headteacher he reported that positive feedback had been received from all the members of staff who had been involved in the MI intervention. The headteacher stated that the teaching staff had indicated that; *'they had not only learnt more about the students but also about themselves.'* This was reiterated during the semi-structured interview, with Practitioner A reporting; *"MI gave me a feel good factor for myself."* Practitioner C reflected; *"It made me feel reinvigorated."*

Before the MI intervention some of the practitioners made the judgement that the students selected were not ready for change, as they were angry and exhibited other negative attributes. The Practitioners considered these characteristics to be indicators of a poor prognosis. This judgement proved inaccurate. For example,, Practitioner C acknowledged that she 'was proven wrong' - as MI seemed to be effective with Martin, who had seemed less ready and motivated for change, than with Kevin or Larry.

Building stronger relationships with the students.

A major finding from this study was that the MI intetvention appeared to help build a stronger relationship between the practitioner and the student. At the end of the study Practitioner C reported that that the MI sessions with the students had been enjoyable.

The Practitioners also reported that they had started to view the students differently and to empathise with them more as they began to appreciate a sensitive side to their natures. The Practitioners also reported that the MI process helped to facilitate secure, trusting and lasting relationships between the students and themselves. The students commented that they valued having teachers who knew them well while the practitioners reported that they enjoyed getting to know the students. Both the students and practitioners said they saw each other in a positive light. This would support the views of Miller and Rollnick (1991), McNamara (1998), Lambert (1992) and Geldard and Geldard (2004) who all stressed that the client-counsellor relationship is a critical part of the change process.

There seem to be many gains associated with practitioners being given the opportunity to view the students in a different way. All the practitioners at the school showed empathy and warmth towards the students. Both Practitioners B and C reported that they had learnt a lot from the MI process and had started to view the students in a 'new light.' Practitioner B established an empathy with Larry which evolved as Larry began to show a sensitive side to his nature, a side which was not evident before the MI intervention. Larry was perceived as a child who did not get along with his mum and was violent towards her. However, while this may have been the case on some occasions, during the evaluation process Larry told both Practitioner B and me that all he wanted was for his mum to feel proud of him. This aspiration was considered with Larry and means of achieving it explored.

Promoting the voice of the student

Practitioners reported that the MI process helped the students to express their views from their own perspective. It helped students to bring into consciousness their thoughts about their positive self-attributes.

The students discussed family issues as well as school issues. Practitioner C reported that she could now see how Martin's domestic social difficulties spilled over into his school life.

Individual Behaviour Plans (IBP's)

The MI process provided a structure to plan and discuss goals/targets for IBP's. Practitioner C reported that Martin was more involved in setting his own targets and agreed to type them up on the computer.

Counselling techniques

A further common theme that emerged from the interview data was that the Practitioners felt empowered, for they had learnt new counselling techniques to help the students. Practitioners B and C reported that they integrated many of the MI strategies acquired into classroom practice. Practitioner C reported that she particularly valued acquiring questioning techniques, for they helped the students explore their own solutions to a problem.

Motivational strategies

The MI process yielded information for Practitioner C about the external rewards Martin liked in order help him feel 'good'.

Practitioner C reported that, in the past, Martin had focused on the material things around him. However, since the MI intervention Martin had started to internalise and positively value the kind of things people had actually said or done for him. He really valued the pictorial mind map and the personal letter he received from Practitioner C during the MI sessions.

During the study the Practitioners stressed that they thought it was useful to identify personal motivational strategies for the students. They recognised that different things motivate different students and that a reward which was important to one student may not be important to others. For instance, Larry did not like it when the teaching staff praised him in front of his peers.

The Practitioners also reported that MI process had the following personal benefits:

- A valuable form of continued professional development for teaching staff to enhance their counselling skills.

- Stronger student/practitioner relationships were built up as both practitioners and students began to view each other differently, ie more positively.

- Facilitated the student voice.

- Supported the setting of goals/targets for IBP's.

General benefits

- It was cost effective.

- Student consultation was viewed as a valuable tool for promoting whole school changes.

- School adapted MI to suit their needs and, as a result, developed ownership.

- Staff sharing resources and ideas promoted collaborative teamwork.

- MI could be employed for issues other than behaviour. (See Atkinson 2005).

Implications/limitations of MI within an educational context

After analysing the interview data and after further discussion with the participants around their own personal views of the strengths and limitations of MI, the following common themes emerged:

- *Time constraints:* Practitioners reported timetable implications for both the student and themselves. Not having enough time to plan for the next MI session was an issue.

- *Organisational issues:* Finding a quiet room sometimes was a problem. One practitioner stressed that a sign on the door, 'do not disturb', would have been useful to eliminate interruptions. The establishment of an agreed finish time at the start of the session was identified to be helpful.

- *Teacher/student pairing* needs careful planning, as some students may have better relationships with certain members of staff.

- Practitioners reported that, as they got familiar with MI, they became more flexible and they integrated some of the strategies and techniques into their everyday practices.

Practitioner C reported that, recently, she used the Model of Stages of Change when contemplating a career change. A desire for more training to develop counselling skills in order to help students was also expressed by Practitioner C. She stressed: *"...the nature of teaching staff, especially here at an SEBD school, is to want to help the students solve situations and prescribe answers and solutions."*

The use of other techniques and strategies to support the MI process

As in Atkinson and Woods (2003) study, MI was viewed as a process and the Model of Stages of Change integral to the process. Techniques and strategies from other paradigms were applied at different stages, such as SFBT, scaling questions, realistic goal-setting and PCP, as proposed by the Cheshire Model (Cheshire 2000).

Conclusion

As demonstrated in this study, the outstanding common theme that emerged was the need for positive, supportive relationships.

Working with vulnerable students with turbulent lives who are operating on the margins of their social environments can be a challenging task for anyone. The change process can be both messy and complicated and the day-to-day pressures of school life cannot be underestimated.

This being so, an important question to ask is, 'how can an MI intervention encourage practitioners to promote social inclusion and support disaffected students to become agents of their own change process?' More research involving children and young people to evaluate the MI process may provide new insights into how practitioners can support young people during the change process.

It seems that the use of MI within educational settings has been slow to gain acceptance and be widely implemented. This may be because knowledge of the theory and practice of MI has not been widely disseminated to educationalists. It is my belief that MI can help motivate the students and transform negative views of school into positive ones, and consequently be a very valuable tool for working with individual pupils and classroom practice.

References

Atkinson, C. (2005). Motivational Interviewing and boy's views and perceptions of reading at Key Stage 3. *Doctorate thesis, Manchester University.*

Atkinson. C. and Woods, K. (2003). Motivational Interviewing strategies for disaffected secondary school students: a case example. *Educational Psychology in Practice,* 19 (1), 49-64.

Cheshire County Council (2005) Multiple Intelligence Theory. Retrieved [7/7/06], *http://www.salt.cheshire.gov.uk/mfl/THEORY/MULTIPLE.HTM.*

DfES. (1997). Excellence for all children. London DfEE.

Geldard, K. & Geldard, D. (2004). Counselling Adolescents. 2nd Edition. Sage: London.

Lambert, M. (1992). *Outcome Research in Counselling.* Hillside, NJ: Lawrence Erlbaum Associates.

Lunt, P. (2006) *Evaluating the Effectiveness of Training School Staff in Motivational Interviewing to Support Disaffected Secondary Students with EBD* . Centre for Educational Support and inclusion, Research and Teaching Group. University of Manchester.

Middleton, J (2004) Exploring the perceptions of young people placed in special SEBD provision. *Doctorate thesis, Manchester University.*

McNamara, E. (1998). *The Theory and Practice of Eliciting Pupil Motivation: Motivational Interviewing – A Form Teacher's Manual and Guide for Students, Parents, Psychologists, Health Visitors and Counsellors.* Ainsdale, Merseyside: Positive Behaviour Management.

Miller, W. R. and Rollnick, S. R. (1991). *Motivational Interviewing: Preparing People to Change Addictive Behaviour.* New York: The Guildford Press.

U.N Convention on the Rights of the Child (1989),

the Special Educational Needs and Disability Act (2001)

and the Children Act (2004)

Section 2 - Using the Stages of Change Model to Facilitate Change at a Whole School Level

This section of the chapter describes how the Model of the Stages of Change (the Model) (Prochaska and DiClemente,1982) was used to facilitate the implementation of Continuing Professional Development (CPD) for school staff after the merger of two Primary schools. The process was designed to share with staff the rationale underlying the Model and utilise this to motivate staff towards change. Focus groups were used as a 'tool' for providing staff with an opportunity to share their views. The Model was used to facilitate action planning for development in areas that were identified as priority areas by staff for school development. The process is ongoing and this chapter describes aspects of the work undertaken.

The work with the school staff was aimed at helping the staff from the two previously separate schools to 'come together' as a team and tackle issues of concern that required change at the whole school level.

The author of this chapter engaged in the work in the context of an action-research paradigm and identified two questions of relevance to the project, namely:

- Does the process of using The Model in action planning at the whole school level develop teachers' motivation to change?

- Do the developed action plans lead to sustained change?

Background

The structure of service delivery for Educational Psychologists (EPs) in the Authority in which I work involves termly 'planning meetings' with senior school staff. Two schools that were 'covered' by the author had recently been merged into one school due to falling numbers of children on their rolls. The two schools that merged were not yet on the same site. Through working in each of the schools, I had gained the impression that both sets of staff and respective Senior Management Teams (SMTs) were viewing the other with a degree of suspicion and apprehension. At the first planning meeting under the banner of the new school, the Headteacher requested INSET on the topic of 'Restorative Justice' for the whole staff i.e. staff from both merged schools.

Negotiating the work done in schools through the planning meeting affords EPs the opportunity to negotiate the nature of any work undertaken. I felt that the effectiveness of delivering 'Restorative Justice' training would be limited due to the fact that staff did not know each other and may not view the content of the planned training as reflecting their needs as a group in the existing stressful circumstances they were in, ie the very recent school amalgamation. I voiced my concerns to the HT and asked the question, 'Why would the staff be motivated to take Restorative Justice training on board at this time?' The HT agreed that this was not necessarily the right content for the first post amalgamation staff development meeting. I agreed to explore the possibility of some other whole staff development work that would address staff current concerns and priorities.

This conversation with the HT triggered me to consider the school's situation in the context of the work of Deci and Ryan (2000) in the areas of self-determination theory of motivation. The theory emphasises the need for people to have a sense of:

- 'competence i.e. that they have skills and can achieve
- 'relatedness' i.e. that they have bonds with those around them and feel valued
- 'autonomy' i.e. that they can make choices with regard to their behaviour and make their role consistent with their view of themselves

The process that I developed was designed to meet these three needs.

Overview

Firstly, discussions were held with the HT regarding the underlying issues that she felt would be addressed through the 'Restorative Justice' training. These issues were reflected in questions that were put to a focus group of staff members. The use of a focus group was designed to meet the need for staff to feel listened to and make their own choices.

'Themes' were then derived from the compiled focus group data and fed back to the whole staff, e.g. the theme of the school having a consistently applied behaviour policy. Staff were then asked to choose a theme that they were particularly interested in or had skills to develop. Using the Model as a visual 'tool' for understanding the process of change, the staff then reflected on the process of change in relation to their chosen theme. The action plans that were eventually formulated were reviewed 3 months later.

Setting

The setting of the study was a school that was newly built as part of a bigger Children's Centre in a northern industrial city. Both staff had recently moved on site. The area has a high degree of social deprivation and numbers at local schools had been falling for some time. As a result of the falling numbers in schools, the Local Authority had merged two of the local primary schools and relocated to the new site. This was a new school with a new name and a high profile within the Authority - due to the expense of the new-build and also its' 'Children's Centre' status.

Staff

Staffing at the school was made up of staff from two Primary schools that had been merged. It was necessary for some teachers to re-apply for certain key posts, including Headteacher (HT), Deputy Headteacher (DHT) and Special Educational Needs Co-ordinator (Senco). As some staff failed to be given the same post in the new school context they had held previously, there was a certain degree of tension between key figures.

Staff in the amalgamated school appeared to be divided along the lines of the previous schools in which they had taught. Their differences and difficulties were contributed to by a number of factors. Firstly, the composition of the new SMT resulted in teachers feeling 'disloyal' if they followed one member of the SMT's direction over another. Additionally, neither of the amalgamated schools had high reputations within the Authority and had been in the shadow of neighbouring schools with similar pupil intakes that were high achieving. This situation appeared to lead to a culture of blame, e.g. *'We get all the difficult children, because they (the high achieving schools) turn away children and say that they have no places'.* Some of the project schools' staff also viewed each other with suspicion. There was a tendency for the view to be held that before the schools merged the 'other school' did not do things as well as 'our school' and that standards would suffer. Most members of staff seemed to be very wary and defensive regarding the merger.

My Role

In my Local Authority work in schools is agreed and allocated through planning meetings which are held on a termly basis. This is a structured meeting that discusses areas of EP work in schools under a number of headings. One of these headings is 'Intervention from EPS at a whole school level'. During the planning meeting a request was made for the specific topic of 'Restorative Justice' to be delivered to staff via an INSET (In-Service Education of Teachers) session. This request was then discussed in the context of the school's current newly amalgamated situation. It was agreed that before specific initiatives such as 'Restorative Justice' were undertaken, more immediate staff concerns should be addresses, namely -

- Team building and motivation
- Sharing of skills between the newly amalgamated members of staff

Method

Discussions were held with the HT regarding the underlying issues that she felt would be addressed through 'Restorative Justice' training. These issues were incorporated into questions that were put to a focus group of staff members.

The use of a focus group was designed to meet the need for staff to feel listened to and involved in decision making. The questions put to the focus group reflected areas of concern for the Headteacher, particularly around the need for the staff to become a cohesive 'team'. The areas, team building and the sharing of skills, were agreed with the Headteacher before the focus group questions were formulated.

The focus group participants were chosen from a range of school staff, mainly teachers, but also included administrative officers, learning mentors and a school governor.

The focus group questions were written in an open ended way and began with phrases such as, "How do you feel about", "What is your opinion of" and "Please describe". When drawing up the questions we were aware that:

- questions beginning with "how" are particularly effective
- there is a need to be wary of asking questions beginning with the word "why", particularly at the beginning of focus group work - because they may lead participants to justify their actions or opinions rather than reflect on them and question them
- there is a need to arrange the questions into topics and avoid bias in the wording of the questions.

The areas explored and the relevant related questions are reproduced below:

Empowerment

What do you understand by the phrase 'empowerment'?

What is an empowering environment?

How can you empower others?

Behaviour Policy

What is the role of the behaviour policy in the school?

Do you feel your daily practice reflects the behaviour policy?

Is it possible to standardize teacher practice in the area of pupil management?

Would this, ie attempting to standardise practice, be a worthwhile exercise?

Is there a need for teachers to model appropriate behaviour for children?

What is the role of punishment/negative consequences?

Is there a role for 'telling children off'? If so, how should this be done?

Happiness

What makes someone happy in their work?

How can a school promote happiness for staff?

Restorative Justice (RJ)

What is your understanding of RJ?

What, if any, is the role of RJ in schools?

Do you have confidence in using an RJ approach?

What approaches, other than RJ, have been useful to you in the past?

What was useful about these approaches?

Making a contribution

Do all staff contribute to the school?

How can this be promoted?

Are their any barriers to this?

Value

What do you value in a colleague?

What do you need to make you feel valued?

Relationships/ Cohesive Team

What is a cohesive team?

What makes a cohesive team?

How would you know if you were working in a cohesive team?

Themes' were then derived from the compiled focus group data and fed back to the whole staff. The themes were:

- Teambuilding
- Behaviour Policy
- Modelling appropriate teacher behaviour for observer colleagues
- Having a shared vision

Staff were then asked to:

- Choose the theme that they were particularly interested in or had the skills to develop
- Reflected on the process of change model in relation to their chosen theme of interest
- Make a judgement in terms of what stage they were at vis a vis the model of the stages of change
- What actions they had taken that had placed them at the above stage
- Decide the stage they would like to get to in the model
- Identify the skills and resources they might use to help them get there.

Staff used the Model as a visual 'tool' for understanding the process of change. Action plans in each of the theme areas were developed by interested groups of staff during a twilight session. The action plans were then reviewed 3 months later.

Summary of the Process

The process comprised of seven phases. These were:

Phase One: The planning meeting at which the initial request for staff development was made and the type of work discussed, negotiated and agreed.

Phase Two: The meeting with the HT to discuss and formulate focus group questions that would address her ideas for continuing staff development (CPD).

Phase Three: The focus group session with staff volunteers.

Phase Four: The analysis of data and formulation of feedback. For details of how the themes were produced see Goldenkoff (2004).

Phase Five: The content of the proposed feedback to whole staff was discussed and agreed with the HT. Sensitive issues that were deemed inappropriate for whole staff discussion at an initial stage were identified and alternative means of addressing these concerns were agreed e.g. through SMT meetings .

Phase Six: Feedback was given to staff at a twilight INSET. Action planning was undertaken using the Model of Stages of Change as a structure for discussing where the school i) was at and ii) wanted to be with regard to the five identified themes.

Phase Seven: The evaluation of the process described in phases one to six above using a semi-structured interview - undertaken with a member of staff from each of the action planning groups.

The Use of the Model of Stages of Change

The rationale underlying the use the Model was that:

- It was a visual way of representing the cycle of change that the staff were already engaged in.

- Groupwork would help the staff agree on where on the Model they were as a collective group in relation to key themes that had been identified as a concern to themselves.

- Once staff had collectively established where they were on the Model with regard to the identified themes, It was anticipated that then they could plan, using their own skills and resources, how they might move onto the next stage.

The work that involved using the Model was undertaken during a two-hour twilight session with all staff. Prior to this session, the focus group work had established the themes that staff saw as most relevant to them at that time, namely – i) Teambuilding ii) Stress Prevention and Management iii) Behaviour Policy iv) Modelling appropriate teacher behaviour for observer colleagues and v) Having a shared vision.

At the twilight session, the staff were engaged in a structured sequential process. This unfolded as follows:

- The nature of the focus group was explained

- The principles of using the Model to engage them, the staff, to utilise their own resources and skills to move forward together were explained.

- Each theme was presented to the staff with quotes from the focus group to support why it had been identified as a theme.

- Staff were then asked if they felt that the theme was reflective of their views about the theme topic. It was agreed that adaptations would be made to the language used if this was thought to be helpful.

All staff agreed with the themes as initially identified.

In order to clarify thinking in terms of the changes that staff might like to make in relation to the theme topic, a 'preferred future' was identified and outlined for each theme ie staff were required to describe how they would like things to be. The preferred future was initially formulated by myself, based on information volunteered by members of the focus group. This enabled a 'starting point' to be established to stimulate staff in their thinking. The opportunity for staff to amend or change the vision of the future was built into the process. However, all staff without exception expressed the view that the preferred future as initially described and presented to them, was consistent with their own view.

The 'preferred future' for each of the identified themes is outlined in table 8.2 below:

Theme	Preferred Future
Teambuilding	"We are a coherent team which has developed honest, helpful and trusting relationships"
Stress Management	"We have the time to reflect on planning and supporting each other to make things run smoothly"
Behaviour Policy	"We have a consistent, positive behaviour management policy that allows for individualisation and flexibility"
Modelling Behaviour	"Staff believe that modelling expected behaviour for children is essential for developing appropraite behaviour in children"
Vision / Role of Our School	"We have a mission statement that is reflected in practice throughout the school"

Figure 8.2 Identified 'Preferred Future' for the School

Developing an Action Plan

The model was again explained to and discussed with staff. The language for the model was adapted in order to make it more meaningful and accessible for the staff see Figure 8.3

Figure 8.3 The Stages Model of Change: 'The Wheel': A visual way of understanding 'where we are and where we want to go'

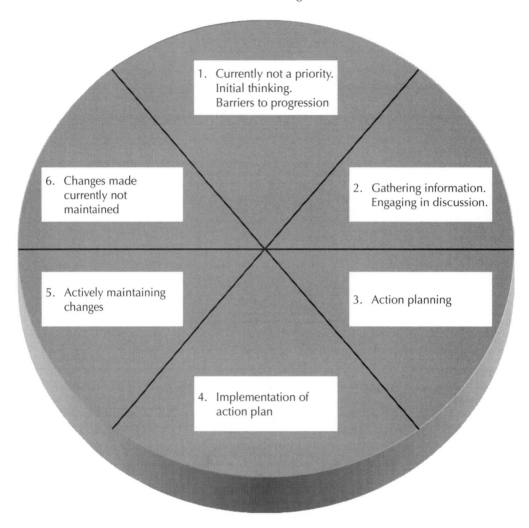

1. Currently not a priority.
   Initial thinking.
   Barriers to progression

6. Changes made
   currently not
   maintained

2. Gathering information.
   Engaging in discussion.

5. Actively maintaining
   changes

3. Action planning

4. Implementation of
   action plan

1. Before starting	2. Consider change	3. Decision Making
4. Making Changes	5. Maintenance	6. Relapse

An example of how the model had been used to facilitate school development at a different school was then presented – see Figure 8.4. The reasons for this presentation were fourfold (McNamara, 1998, p.19), namely, it –

- Illustrates what has to be done

- Shows that it can be done

- Creates the expectation it will be done

- Creates the expectation of a positive outcome

I started from the premise that it was essential for the school staff to understand how the use of 'the Model' could be helpful: for this was a pre-requisite for the school staff to engage in the process of self assessment of their own and 'whole staff' position with regard to where they are in terms of the model of the Stages of Change vis a vis the theme or topic being considered. Specifically, I felt that it was necessary for the staff to appreciate that

- 'change' itself is a process that can be broken down into identifiable stages and

- through identifying 'where we are now' a vision of 'where we want to go' can become clearer.

Figure 8.4 Using the Model of Stages of Change for identifying the stage at which a school is engaging with Emotional Health and Social Well Being

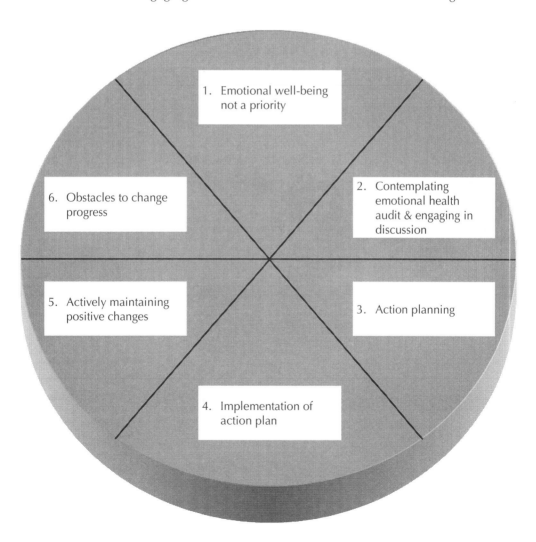

For the purposes of the task set the staff, I felt that it was important for staff to understand the concept of how "it worked", i.e. that the model was a visual representation of the process of change and that they might use it as a means of planning ways forward ie moving from where they where to where they wanted to be – movement achieved by the staff utilising their own skills and resources.

It was important that a practical example be used at this stage so that the link between the theory and the practice was made explicit. The illustration used was of a school implementing ideas around emotional health and well-being. Each stage of the stages of change model was discussed in terms of what it might entail in relation to the theme of how a school might conceptualise it's current engagement with the emotional health and well-being agenda. This provided a meaningful example of how current and relevant issues might be addressed. A copy of the illustration is reproduced in Figure 8.4

The illustration of the Stages of Change model completed by the 'other' school staff in relation to their ie the school's, current situation regarding Emotional Well-Being was discussed. Following on from this, an example of the action plan produced by the staff of that school in order to address the emotional health and well-being agenda was presented and talked through. A copy of this plan is reproduced below. The aims of this were those previously described ie to i) Illustrates what has to be done ii) Shows that it can be done iii) Creates the expectation it will be done and iv) Creates the expectation of a positive outcome.

Action Plan

Current Stage :

- Implementation of Action Plan.

How we can move to the next stage as a school?

- Whole staff course on Emotional Literacy
- Further peer observation of teacher classroom behaviour strategies
- Additional training/support from Lead Behaviour Professional

Support/Resources Needed:

- Await outcome of whole school training

Additional Information:

- Lots of strategies for managing effects of teaching and learning
- All children to be set individual targets
- Teaching and learning strategies in place - but not clearly linked to behaviour
- Helpful to set a review date

Support for those at an earlier stage in the wheel

- Modelling classroom techniques for colleagues (peer observation)
- 'Easy to access' reading material to be provided

Individuals with knowledge/skills/interest

- Mr Green – Circle time trained
- Mrs Sweet - Peer mentoring

Next Action: Peer observation – selection of pairs

By Whom: all staff

Review Date: _ term

When it was apparent that staff of the amalgamated school understood how the Model 'worked' and how it might be helpful in terms of developing their own action plans, the task of action planning was presented to them. Staff were organised into groups on the basis of the theme that they had a particular interest in. Using the illustrative model presented as a guide, they were set the task of planning for positive change around the theme that they had chosen.

Prior to the session, for each theme a large Model had been prepared on flip chart paper. At the top of each of the five pages was i) the name of one of the five themes and ii) a description of the preferred future.

Each sheet of flip chart paper was then placed on its' own table along with resources such as 'post-it' notes, pens and copies of blank action plans.

Staff were then guided with instructions being given and questions asked ie

1. Stand by the wheel that most interests you

2. Do you agree with your preferred future? - If not, re-write it

3. Indicate on your wheel what each part would represent with regard to the issue/theme being addressed, particularly with regard to the first 2 stages.

4. Place an initialled post-it note on the part of the wheel that reflects where you think you are at present

5. Attempt to establish a consensus with others at the same table where on the wheel you are at as a school

6. Complete an action plan pro-forma

7. Select a spokesperson to feedback

Staff were given 30 minutes to complete the task and 5 minutes each to feed back.

It was the author's impression that nearly all staff were very enthusiastic and engaged in the task, which was perhaps 'surprising' when one bears in mind the context of the session - being the final part of a two-hour long twilight CPD activity. The author circulated amongst the groups and supported the teachers while they were engaged in the activity. A summary of the action plans that were developed by the five groups and one example from the five Models of Stages of Change produced by the staff are reproduced in Figure 8.5 below.

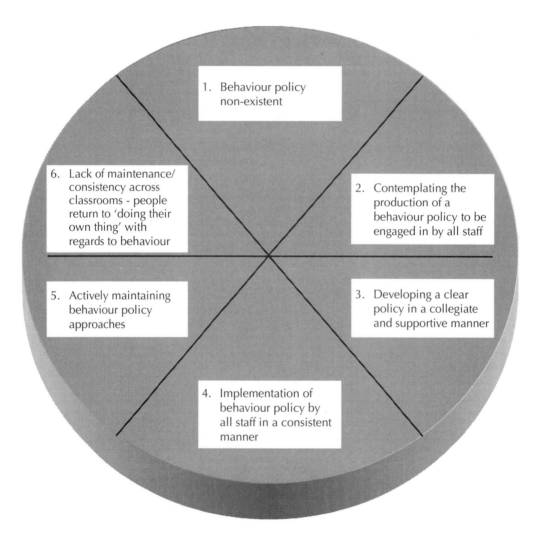

1. Behaviour policy non-existent

6. Lack of maintenance/ consistency across classrooms - people return to 'doing their own thing' with regards to behaviour

2. Contemplating the production of a behaviour policy to be engaged in by all staff

5. Actively maintaining behaviour policy approaches

3. Developing a clear policy in a collegiate and supportive manner

4. Implementation of behaviour policy by all staff in a consistent manner

Figure 8.5 The Model of Stages of Change produced by staff for the preferred future of, *'We have a consistent, positive behaviour management policy that allows for individualisation and flexibility'.*

The staff decided that they were at Stage 6 (relapse) and outlined a plan, focussing on consistency and monitoring.

Theme	Preferred Future	Current Stage	How to get to the next stage	Next Step (Who? What? When?	Support Resources required
Behaviour Policy	We have a consistent positive behaviour management policy that allows individualisation and flexibility	Relapse	• Communication • All groups involved - dinner staff, teachers, TAs, supply • Collaborative INSET - concrete decisions made and agreed • Ongoing monitoring and support from colleagues		• Training for all staff • Mentors required for different groups
Staff Stress	We have the time to reflect on planning and supporting each other in making things run smoothly	Consider Changing	• Audit re: staff stress levels, causes and beliefs • Shared planning (on hard drive • Increased levels of communication		• IT • EP input into stress audit
Teambuilding	We are a coherent team which has developed honest, helpful and trusting relationships	Consider Changing	• Time and opportunities to get to know one another better • Audit of resources • Organise storage of all resources in school • Increased communication across whole school • Staff meeting time to resolve issues		• Teambuilding events?
Modelling Behaviour	Staff believe that modelling expected behaviour is essential for developing appropriate behaviour in children	Decision Making	• Increased staff awareness • Development of Emotional Literacy approaches		• Further Emotional Literacy Training • Access to materials e.g. SEAL

Figure 8.6 Completed Action Plan

Outcomes

Three months after the twilight session at which the Action Plan was formulated, information was gathered through interviews with key staff who had been allocated responsibilities at the action planning stage. The information gathered was aimed at answering the two questions reproduced below.

Question 1. *Did the process of using The Model of Stages of Change in action planning, increase and develop teachers' motivation?*

The process appears to have been highly effective in terms of enabling staff to feel that they have strengths and skills that can be utilised. Each member of staff that was interviewed gave very positive feedback in this area. The HT stated that the process *"allowed us to develop our own ideas based on the individual skills and strengths of staff"*. Staff reported being able to reflect their own strengths in the action plans that were developed, with one member of staff remarking, *"I'm good at I.T. and I managed to get that in there!"* In addition to harnessing the specific skills that staff possessed, the process also seemed to allow people to express their own personal characteristics. For example, one teacher remarked, albeit with humour, that *"I was able to be honest and I'm good at that"*.

In a broader sense than simply reflecting individual skills, the process also appears to have facilitated staff's understanding of each other's strengths. One member of staff stated that, *"We all have individual strengths and weaknesses but we all want the best for the kids"*. The fact that people were given an opportunity to discuss their own and others competencies was viewed as very positive.

With regard to facilitating stronger positive relationships between colleagues, the outcome appears to be generally positive - but there were some concerns expressed that relationships had not improved across the whole staff. One teacher summarised the process as further establishing relationships, *"with the ones that I was already getting close to"*, but that, *"some staff need a bit more to move them closer"*. The theme that already existing bonds were made stronger but new connections were not made was also reflected in another teacher's view that, *"the ones who need to get on the most didn't bother. Some just stay in cliques"*. These existing bonds were further cemented by, *"a good staff night out"* which was written into the action plans.

There were indications that some relationships became stronger, but also indications that other relationships needed more 'intervention' in order to develop and become established. It was also acknowledged that weak relationships would take more time to develop and become stronger. The HT observed that, *"we are in a slow process of moving closer as a team"*. Another teacher observed that, *"we need more time to learn from each other but don't always feel that this is prioritised"*.

The findings were mixed with regard to the process of developing a sense of volition and choice regarding practice amongst staff. Staff appeared to feel able to reflect their own choices in the action plans but then sometimes did not feel that they had the level of autonomy that was necessary in order to carry through the plans. One member of staff summarised the situation as follows, *"Yes, we had a choice about what went down on the paper (action plan)... but some staff are scared to act on them because of inconsistency in the leadership"*.

The above quote suggests that one reason for staff not feeling that they can move forward on the ideas they put forward in action plans was the fact that they were wary of being 'corrected' by the SMT. This suggests that the sense of autonomy felt by staff in the INSET sessions was not one that transferred outside of these process sessions into the real life school situation. The HT did feel a sense of autonomy and remarked that, *"we could develop our own ideas. Things that mattered for us were being addressed"*.

Question 2. *Did the action plans lead to change that was sustained three months later?'*

Teachers felt that there had been some individual changes and were aware of specific actions that had been taken. One teacher commented that there had been some change, *"in some staff and the people who needed to be included were involved"*. Another teacher stated that the change process *"relies on the SMT. The SMT has all the information and it needs to drive it(the change process)"*. These comments appeared to reflect a general theme of more individual changes being achieved than systemic changes. Staff appeared to believe that systemic change was the responsibility of SMT – and that a lack of enthusiasm on the part of the SMT accounted for systemic changes not being wholly achieved.

Some action outcomes were reported with regard to the 'stress audit' recommendations that had been written into one action plan. Teachers appeared to be highly motivated to carry out this aspect of the action plan but felt that the audit was not reflective of the true situation - due to the possible negative implications of being perceived as 'stressed' by the SMT. As one teacher put it, *"We have done a questionnaire and audit of stress but people aren't sure about telling the truth because if they say that they are stressed they think that the management might think that they aren't coping".*

The HT was unequivocal that the process had brought about sustained change: she presented evidence as to what had actually been put in place. At the general level, the HT reported that it was valuable for people *"to reflect and take time to think about how they do things"*. An example of a specific action outcome that was that the focus group themes and action plans had been written into the school's Self-Assessment Framework.

Summary and Future Directions

The use of the Model does seem to have been effective in enabling staff to generate plans with great enthusiasm, incorporating their own skills and interests. Staff also learnt more about each other's strengths and what they and others could bring to 'the team'. Another benefit of the process was that it brought some colleagues closer together and there was a sense of group empathy generated. However, the sense that colleagues became more socially connected with each other was not universal across the staff and those who were furthest apart remained so. The sense of autonomy that the process allowed for was not consistently supported by implementing action plans at the systemic level, and therefore the sustainability of these plans was varied.

The process does appear to have been very effective in terms of identifying the needs that are not currently being met for staff. With regard to the current motivational climate in the school, the process can be viewed as 'assessment through intervention'. The processes engaged in could be 'reframed' as an assessment tool rather than viewed as direct intervention.

Perhaps the major conclusion that can be drawn from this project is that if the climate and leadership do not support staff needs then it is difficult to generate the motivation for whole school change. This conclusion has implications for the delivery of all INSET training to school by EPs or other professionals see Harris and Lambert, (2003) and Joyce and Showers (1995).

A further implication of these findings is the identification of the client group that this type of intervention should be targeted at. Given that we know that leaders have the major influence on school ethos and on creating a 'motivationally friendly climate', it may be more effective to work directly with headteachers in order for them to achieve an understanding of the principles and theory and how this could be put in place in their school. This conclusion has further implications for how EPs work in schools, particularly with regard to how EP's can broaden their focus and apply psychological principles to the subject of leadership.

References

Deci, E.L., & Ryan, R.M. (2000). The 'what' and 'why' of goal pursuits: Human needs and the self-determination of behaviour. *Psychological Inquiry,* 11, 227-268.

Goldenkoff, R. (2004). Using focus groups. In J.S. Wholey, H. P. Hatry, & K. E. Newcomer (Eds.), *Handbook of practical program evaluation* (2nd ed.) (pp. 340-362). San Francisco: Jossey-Bass.

Harris, A., and Lambert, L.(2003) *Building leadership capacity for school improvement.* Buckingham, Open University Press

Joyce, B & Showers, B, (1995), *Student Achievement Through Staff Development* (2nd edn). White Plains, NY, Longman

McNamara, E. (1998). *The Theory and Practice of Anxiety Management*
PBM (Positive Behaviour Management) 7 Quinton Close Ainsdale, Merseyside PR8 2TD: Positive Behaviour Management.

Prochaska, J. O. and DiClemente, C. C. (1982). Transtheoretical theory: Toward a more integrative model of change. *Psychotherapy: Theory, Research and Practice,* 19, 276-288.

Chapter 9

Incorporating Motivational Interviewing Strategies into a Consultation Model for use within School-Based Behaviour Management Teams

Joe Duffy and Patricia Davison

In this chapter we describe the development and implementation of a group process consultation model. The model was designed as a means of supporting mainstream Primary and Secondary schools in their work in the area of pupil behaviour management. A particular feature of this model was the adoption of Motivational Interviewing (MI) within a solution-focused approach as a means of facilitating monthly behaviour management team meetings, involving teachers and trained Education and Library Board (ELB) facilitators.

Historical Context

The five Educational Psychology Services (EPS) within Northern Ireland (NI) have historically offered a direct model of service delivery following the referral of children and young people for assessment by an Educational Psychologist (EP). The direct service delivery model in conjunction with open referral has led to ever increasing referral lists for EPs and Outreach Support Teachers. Schools also tended to see such services as having a "gatekeeper's" role in relation to their ability to access special educational provision. It was also felt that, because of the referral opportunity, not enough attention was being paid by schools to assessment and intervention of pupils with Special Educational Needs (SEN) at Stages 1 & 2 of the Code of Practice – stages at which schools have primary responsibility.

During the 1990s ELBs experienced a dramatic increase in referrals of children and young people with social, emotional & behavioural difficulties (SEBD). Then in 1998 a Discipline Strategy for schools was established by the Department of Education, entitled *Promoting and Sustaining Good Behaviour: A Discipline Strategy for Schools.* (DENI, 1998b) As part of this strategy, it was recommended that multidisciplinary Behaviour Support Teams (BST) should be established in order to provide support for schools at a systemic level in relation to pupil behaviour management. In the two ELBs in which the authors work this was developed as an indirect service delivery model, which was almost exclusively school and teacher-focused.

In 2005 the Special Educational Needs & Disability (Northern Ireland) Order (SENDO) was introduced in NI. This marked a further change of emphasis towards more "inclusive" education with mainstream schools being required to take more responsibility for the management of special educational needs, including SEBD.

This led the present authors to meet to discuss the possibility of developing and implementing a school-based consultation model as a means of supporting schools with regard to pupil behaviour management. Through initial support and facilitation, our aim was that schools would become more empowered to manage pupil behaviour more effectively. We also aspired to develop a consultation model that would reflect i) the systemic work we were already doing in schools as part of the Behaviour Support Team (BST) and ii) our personal interests in collaborative work, MI and solution-focused approaches. We considered that this particular combination of theory and method of delivery would be most suitable as a consultative way of working with teachers in schools.

Rationale

School psychology has had a long history of consultation in schools e.g. Gutkin & Curtis (1982). Over the last 10 years many EPSs have developed consultative approaches to service delivery to schools (Larney, 2003). We were particularly drawn to the well-established, solution-focused framework outlined by Wagner & Gillies (2001) and process consultation e.g. Schein (1988), Farouk (2004).

In our work domain EPs and BST members were already using solution-focused approaches in their work with pupils and individual teachers in schools. Following MI training for EPs in 1999, some EPs, including the authors, began integrating aspects of MI into their work in schools as a means of further promoting behavioural change in children and young people with SEBD.

Although MI was initially established as a brief therapeutic intervention in the treatment of people with alcohol, drug and substance misuse e.g. Miller, (1983); Miller & Rollnick (1991), it has since been applied as an intervention for a range of health-related behaviours e.g. eating disorders, (Treasure & Ward, 1997), chronic illness, (Bundy, 2004).

In the early 1990s McNamara started to apply MI to EP work in UK schools (McNamara, 1992) and further applications have been described elsewhere by others - most notably Atkinson & Woods (2003) and Atkinson & Amesu (2007). They wrote about interventions with children and young people with social, emotional & behavioural difficulties (SEBD). Following their work with young people, Atkinson & Woods (2003) recommended further application of the structure, principles and techniques of MI to school consultation e.g. using the Stages of Change Model (Prochaska & DiClemente, 1982) to assess a teacher's motivation to include or exclude a child with SEBD. Due to the nature of our work in the BST we were keen to integrate aspects of MI and solution-focused approaches into a school-based consultation model as a means of supporting and empowering teachers.

Others have combined aspects of solution-focused questioning and MI in both health and educational settings. For example, case studies are presented by Lewis & Osborn (2004) involving an adult with alcohol–related problems and Atkinson & Amesu (2007) involving a 12 year old evidencing SEBD, in which both approaches were successfully integrated.

There are also some examples of MI being used in school consultation with teachers. For example, in the USA, Reinke (2006) developed a Classroom Check-up (CCU) as a consultation model in order to support individual teachers in US schools. The CCU, a classroom consultation assessment intervention, was used to provide teachers with feedback and support when they were engaged in implementing behaviour change strategies - MI viual performance feedback strategies were used in the feedback and support work with the teachers.

In developing a model of school consultation, we were particularly drawn to applying aspects of Schein's (1988) process consultation model to a school setting. He defined the process of consultation as "... *a set of activities on the part of the consultant which help the client to perceive, understand and act upon process events which occur in the client's environment.*" (p.11) It is very much based on collaboration and partnership between consultant and consultee.

Farouk (2004) combined aspects of Schein's model with Hanko's (1989, 1995) approach to group work with teachers to establish consultation groups in schools, with the EP as consultant, in order to support teachers primarily in relation to their work with pupils with SEBD. Farouk (2004) also used solution-focused questioning in his approach.

There is therefore a strong evidence-base with regard to the use and effectiveness of school-based consultation by EPs both in the USA and GB. Solution-focused thinking has been increasingly incorporated into models of consultation used in a range of Local Authorities in the UK e.g. Wagner & Gillies, (2001). MI is also a well established and well documented intervention with adults and young people with health-related and, more recently, educational problems. The authors recognised its potential as a way of facilitating change in teachers in relation to the management of pupil behaviour. We were keen to both incorporate MI principles and strategies into a consultation model based on that outlined by Farouk (2004) and also to develop a group consultation approach to support schools in their work around pupil behaviour management. The approach we developed is described below.

Farouk's Process Consultation Model

Farouk's (2004) model is a group consultation approach, based upon four phases, namely

Phase 1.   description and clarification.

Phase 2.   reflection.

Phase 3   personal theory generation

Phase 4.   strategy generation.

These phases reflect distinct roles and functions for group members - see Farouk (2004). These roles and functions are described in Figure 9.1.

Figure 9.1: Farouk Model of Consultation (adapted from Farouk 2004)

Description and Clarification Phase **(Phase 1)**	The referring teacher outlines his/her concerns. Group members listen actively, asking only clarification and information-seeking questions.
Reflection Phase **(Phase 2)**	The referring teacher is asked to reflect on his/her concerns. Group members are encouraged to ask questions about the referring teacher's concern and to share similar experiences.
Personal Theory Generating Phase **(Phase 3)**	All group members (including the referring teacher) are encouraged to share their personal theories regarding the nature of the problem situation.
Strategy Generating Phase **(Phase 4)**	Possible strategies are discussed by the group. The referring teacher is given time to reflect on these and may or may not follow them up after the meeting.

Development of the SEBD Consultation Model

Our overarching aim was to enhance and supplement existing ELB services within schools by developing schools' ability to manage and respond to SEBD at the early stages of the Special Educational Needs Code of Practice. We envisaged our initial work to be primarily preventative in approach. It was targeted at supporting teachers of pupils at Stages 1 and 2 of the Code of Practice.

At the beginning of the initiative key personnel from Behaviour Support Services and senior management from the ELB were consulted. Following this, a steering group was set up and agreed that a pilot should proceed, initially targeting 5 schools in each ELB i.e. 2 primary, 2 secondary and 1 Special school. Although 2 special schools were initially involved in the pilot, our focus was primarily on mainstream education.

The steering group drew up an Action Plan and the aims for the pilot were established.

The aims of the pilot

- to complement existing SEBD support for schools;
- to promote a process consultation model of support for schools in relation to management of pupils with SEBD;

- to further empower schools to deal more effectively with pupils with SEBD within the already established Code of Practice framework and to further develop school autonomy;

- to encourage schools to become more solution focused in relation to behaviour management;

- to encourage schools to be more self-evaluative/reflective and independent in relation to pupil behaviour management;

- to promote inclusive practice;

- to further develop a working partnership between the BST and behaviour outreach services;

- Following the evaluation, to extend the model to other ELBs.

The approach the authors developed and implemented is based on Farouk's (2004) model (see Figure 9.1). We also decided to use group process consultation (after Schein, 1988), integrating key elements of MI and solution-focused thinking in order to establish behaviour management teams in the pilot schools. The process involved in the development of our approach to consultation was also influenced by Senge's (1990) concept of the learning organisation.

The procedure for the initiation, staff awareness raising and setting up of the consultation group, the Behaviour Management Team (BMT), was also similar to that outlined in Farouk, 2004. As we work within a BST framework there were a number of key differences in our process.

1. We involved as facilitators in the process all BST members, including those from an exclusively teaching background as well as EPs and all the teachers from both ELBs' Behaviour Outreach Support Service;

2. All facilitators received intensive 3-day, skills-based training focusing on facilitation skills and questioning techniques, with particular reference to MI and SFBT;

3. Two facilitators were selected to work together in schools involved in our initial pilot. In order to encourage collaboration and joint working at this level, we attempted to ensure that the two were from different disciplines;

4. Two teachers from each of the schools involved in the pilot received a day's training on facilitation so that they could take over the facilitation role from the two Board facilitator's at a mutually agreed time;

5. Facilitator "scripts" were developed and used at each of the consultation meetings in order to provide structure and consistency of approach. This was important as the process was to be evaluated;

6. The co-facilitator recorded structured notes on a Summary Record Form which was used for ongoing and final summary. A copy was presented to the referring teacher (RT) at the end of the meeting;

7. Supervision was provided for the facilitators;

8. The pilot was evaluated by initially exploring teacher self-confidence and self-efficacy with regard to behaviour management, pre and post intervention. A reflective evaluation was also held at the end of each consultation. This involved asking group members and the referring teacher to reflect and comment upon 4 questions. These were:

- On a scale of 1-10, how to you feel the consultation went, with 1 being "not well" and 10 being "very well"?

- What went well?

- What didn't go well?

- How could we improve the consultation if we were to do it again?

The 3-day training for the facilitators took place in September 2006 and November 2006. Following selection of pilot schools, a whole staff briefing session was held in each of the schools in January 2007. A BMT was then set up, during term 2 of the 2006-2007academic year, and started to meet on a monthly basis to consult on one referral per session. A follow-up meeting was held the following month along with a consultation on a new referral.

Rollnick et al (1992) outline how a brief intervention, using a "menu of strategies", can be carried out in a 40 minute session. We therefore aimed to limit our group sessions to 40-45 minutes, with the follow-up, with its emphasis on feedback, being much shorter e.g. 15 minutes.

As with Farouk (2004), after support over a period of time – in our case, one academic year, external facilitator support was faded and eventually withdrawn. Following a one day training course for nominated staff, the school then took over responsibility for the process. The ELB facilitators continued to support the BMT in a more advisory capacity rather than through direct involvement cf Bozic & Carter (2002) who emphasised the importance of *"extensive training and on-going support"* (p.199) for school-based consultation groups.

Motivational Interviewing - Overview

The most frequently quoted definition of MI is that of Miller & Rollnick (2002) where it is described as *"a client-centred, directive, method for enhancing intrinsic motivation to change by exploring and resolving ambivalence"* (p.25)

Ambivalence is a central concept in MI. It is a feature of any decision-making in which there is a degree of doubt or hesitation about the maintenance of the status quo or commitment to change. EPs and outreach support teachers will recognise such ambivalence in relation to teachers who are experiencing pupil behaviour management difficulties – especially ambivalence towards a possible intervention or indeed whether to make a referral in the first place. It is easy to be judgemental in such situations and label the teacher as unmotivated, inflexible or uninterested. However there may be a range of reasons as to why the teacher concerned did not initiate or follow through with a suggested intervention, including lack of confidence in their ability to do so, not seeing themselves as having ownership of the intervention once the "outside expert" becomes involved or not yet ready to change but perhaps pushed into an initial referral by a concerned Head Teacher.

Another possible reason for ambivalence, highlighted by McLean (2003), is the possible fear of losing the little control or authority the teacher may currently have. McLean sees this as being a result of low self-efficacy, something we will return to later.

Teachers inevitably come to meetings with a certain degree of ambivalence about change. A focus of MI is that of exploring the costs and benefits of change for the client or referring teacher (RT) in our case. It is then up to the RT to make a more-informed decision about change at the end of the process.

The concept of *ownership and responsibility* are dealt with at an early stage in our consultation process. In line with Schein's (1988) view on process consultation, it is made clear to staff at the initial briefing session that responsibility for any tasks resulting from the consultation lies with the RT and then collectively with the school. The facilitators are only responsible for the process. Similarly, Rollnick et al (2008) highlight the importance of the responsibility for the decision to change being placed with the "client" and that it important for the client to make choices for him/herself.

Staff are also told that that referrals to the BMT are voluntary and that the culture of the team is supportive, empathic, reassuring and non-judgemental.

Collaboration

Collaboration has been an essential element in the development of school-based consultation in the USA (e.g. Gutkin & Curtis, 1982; Gutkin, 1999). Similarly in the UK, Wagner (2000) refers to EP consultation as a "collaborative and recursive process." (p.11) Process consultation is also seen by Schein (1988) as a collaborative, problem solving process.

It is also a key premise in MI e.g. Rollnick et al, 2008; Rollnick & Miller, 1995. Rollnick et al (2008) define the "spirit of MI" as a therapeutic partnership involving ongoing cooperation and collaboration between "client" and therapist". Consultation within an MI framework is seen as "an active collaborative conversation and joint-decision making process" (Rollnick et al, 2008 p.6). In our pilot we hoped to develop collaborative consultation not just at the individual but also at a systemic level within the schools involved i.e.

1. Collaboration between the RT and BMT;
2. Collaboration between the two facilitators who were coming from distinct educational backgrounds;
3. Collaboration within the BMT;
4. Whole school collaboration following the consultation meeting.

This was in line with Wagner's (1995) view that consultation can operate at an individual, group and/or organisational level.

General Principles of MI

Miller & Rollnick (2002) outline the four principles of MI as follows:

1. Express Empathy

2. Develop Discrepancy

3. Roll with Resistance

4. Support Self-efficacy

In our approach to consultation we try to ensure that all 4 principles are adhered to.

Express empathy

The process of establishing rapport, setting the agenda and assessing the readiness to change are the first three of eight steps that allow the therapeutic process to work (Miller & Rollnick, 1991). These three steps form the basis of Phase 1 of our approach. One of the facilitators' key roles is to ensure that the BMT creates an environment in which the RT can feel safe and secure and explore the problem situation in a non-blaming way.

During training, facilitators were introduced to a range of strategies to enhance interpersonal, communicative and group dynamic skills, based on the "task and maintenance functions" of group management e.g. after Schein, 1988 and also implemented by Farouk (2004). These help to express empathy as defined by Miller & Rollnick and also to keep the group together as a cohesive, supportive unit.

According to Miller & Rollnick (1991) behaviour change is only possible when the "client" feels accepted and valued and is not judged in any way. They see this as the key to the principle of expressing empathy. In order to achieve this, in the facilitator's script for the introduction to the meeting, he/she in welcoming the RT to the group and thanking him/her for making the referral, highlights the empathic nature of the meeting and then gives the RT a chance to "tell their story" (problem talk).

We tried to ensure in this initial phase of the consultation that the client is heard and understood by other group members, without interruption other than clarification or information seeking questioning. Such questioning was done in a reflective manner, an essential aspect of MI – this is considered in more detail further on in this chapter.

Develop Discrepancy

The principle of developing discrepancy is similar to that of creating "cognitive dissonance" (Festinger, 1957) i.e. a difference between the current state, "where we are" and the desired or target state, "where we want to be". The role of the BMT, aided by the facilitators, is to explore the RT's current behaviours in relation to the problem situation with the aim of generating awareness of the discrepancy between the RT's current state and the target state.

In the consultation meeting this is done in a solution focused way. For example

Scaling questions are asked prior to (in the referral form) and during the meeting:

> *"On a scale of 0-10, where 0 means no concern and 10 means most concerned, where are you now regarding the problem situation?*

This establishes 'Where the person is'.

This is counter-acted by goal-setting questions during Phase 1 and at the start of Phase 2

> *"What needs to happen during this meeting for it to have been useful to you in dealing with the problem situation?* or

> *"What do you hope to get from this meeting?*

This establishes 'Where the person wants to be'.

The use of decisional balance questioning is also used at this stage e.g. weighting up the pros and cons of things remaining the same and the pros and cons of change.

Roll with Resistance

When engaged in MI, arguments, debates and confrontations are avoided. In any situation where a person's modus operandi is being challenged, resistance may occur. However, as RTs in our model are 'voluntary referers', they tend to arrive at the meeting as "customers" (DeShazer, 1985), i.e. they are prepared to engage because they recognise the potential benefits of consultation.

But on occasions we have encountered a degree of resistance from RTs. When such is the case it tends to be evident from the very beginning of the meeting, at the point when the RT is asked to "tell their story". Facilitators are trained to listen carefully to what the RT says about the problem situation, looking out for statements that may be challenged later during Phase 2 e.g.

> *"He never does what he is told to do"*

> *"She's always interrupting me when I give the class instructions"*

> *"I taught his brother and he was exactly the same"*

> *"There's nothing more I can do. I've tried everything. It's now over to the experts"*

We find that when other group members are being empathic eg by sharing similar, difficult experiences, some RTs can manifest "passive resistance" e.g.

> *"I know what you are saying but I can't say I've ever seen that side of him"*

It is at this stage that the facilitators must ensure that group members don't become argumentative and oppose such resistance.

We have found that resistance to change is not a significant issue at the meetings. During training facilitators are introduced to techniques to help in situations when a RT, or indeed another member of the group, is particularly resistant. For example, we introduce adaptations of the "Menu of Strategies" outlined by Rollnick et al (1992), "task and maintenance functions" (Schein, 1988), solution focused (De Jong & Berg, 1998; Harker, 2001) and "rich" questioning (Frederickson, 1990). We also adapt the use of the Miracle question to make it more relevant to the school setting:

"Imagine we have moved on ……….. it's the end of term/end of the school year ……….. and everything has gone really well ……….. it's all much better that it has previously been ……….. the concerns you outlined at the beginning of the meeting have all gone ……….. it's been a very successful term/year

Looking back from this perspective…..where everything has gone well…..

What has happened?………………………………………………. (after De Shazer,1985)

Support Self-Efficacy

Bandura (1997) defined self-efficacy as *"belief in one's capabilities to organise and execute the courses of action required to manage prospective situations."* (p.2). Applied to behaviour management within an educational setting, teacher self-efficacy would therefore be linked to whether or not teachers felt they have the resources or capabilities to manage pupil behaviour effectively. We felt from the outset that a major aim of the consultation pilot was to enhance the RT's confidence in their ability to manage behaviour in the classroom.

McLean (2003) indicates that teachers with low self-efficacy in relation to their management of pupil behaviour tend to teach in an authoritarian way, relying on strict rules, sanctions and punishment. They also tend to attribute blame for the problem behaviour to "within-child" factors e.g. low IQ, personality traits.

For change to occur, the RT must believe that change is possible and that he/she has the ability to make it happen. Arkowitz & Miller (2007) highlight this i.e. that a key goal of MI is to increase a person's intrinsic motivation in relation to behaviour change. In order to enhance both motivation to change and self-confidence i.e. self-efficacy, the facilitator helps the RT to explore past successes and encourages group members, through their sharing of similar experiences, to act as successful role models that the RT can identify with. This is achieved by helping the RT reflect on exceptions to the problem situation and by encouraging him/her to consider effective past and current coping strategies. The use of "exceptions" and coping questions is also an important element of Phase 2 of the original Farouk model.

 The group's belief in the RT's ability to change is paramount, but it is the RT, not the facilitators or other BMT members, who is responsible for deciding on and carrying out change.

The RT is helped to recognise that there are times when the problem does not occur and that they have coped with similar situations in the past. In Phase 3, facilitators use a systemic, interactionist approach to look at possible theories as to why the problem situation exists. This helps to contextualize the problem and give RTs insights into a range of possible contributory factors they have not thought of prior to the meeting. Promotion of feelings of self-efficacy is also particularly supported at the follow-up meeting e.g.

"Tell me about a change you made since our initial meeting"

The OARS techniques as outlined by Miller & Rollnick (2002) are used throughout the consultation: O = open ended questioning. A = Affirmations. R = Reflective listening. S = Summaries

O- Open-ended questioning

Open-ended and "rich" questioning (Frederickson, 1990) is used to produce a "rich picture" of the problem situation especially at Phases 1 & 2. Again this is done in a solution focused manner. For example:

"What brings you here today?"	(Phase 1)
"How would you like things to be different?"	(Phase 2)
"Tell me what's happened since our last meeting"	(Follow up)

Open-ended questioning encourages RTs to tell their story and then elaborate on it as the process develops.

During the early phase of MI (Phase 1 in the consultation model) it is important for the therapist to establish an atmosphere of acceptance and trust, in which the client can explore his/her problem. The "client" should do most of the talking at this stage, with the "therapist" listening carefully and encouragingly. In the same way, our facilitators encourage other BMT members not to interrupt the RT at this stage –the emphasis is placed on active listening. Not interrupting the RT was a particularly difficult concept for trainee facilitators to grasp: a difficulty that was observed during role play sessions incorporated into the facilitator training. Feedback, on completion of the role plays, from both the outreach teachers and EPs involved, indicated that they realised that when they were in case discussion with teachers prior to the training, they were very prone to "jumping in" and giving advice immediately.

A- Affirmations

Consistent with other approaches to school-based consultation e.g. Kerslake & Roller, 2000, we ask the RT to complete a referral form prior to the consultation meeting. The referral form has a solution-focused bias (after Wagner & Gillies, 2001) and gave the facilitators the opportunity to comment on RT strengths and resources outlined in the referral form. The use of compliments e.g. DeShazer, 1985 or positive affirmations is something that SFBT and MI have in common.

The use of affirmations overlaps with the principle of "Expressing Empathy", described above, in that it helps in the establishment of rapport and building the "therapeutic" relationship between the RT and the BMT.

Affirmations are verbal and non-verbal statements/gestures that indicate recognition of the RTs strengths e.g.

> *"We really appreciate you making the referral and coming to the meeting today".*
>
> > (Phase 1)
>
> *"That's good to hear. Since the referral you've actually started introducing some strategies yourself"*
>
> > (Phase 2)
>
> *"Sounds like you handled that situation really well"*   (Phase 3)
>
> *"That's a really good suggestion."*   (Phase 4)

Facilitators are made aware at training of the possibility of the above coming across as patronising to the RT. Affirmations must sound natural and not contrived or they can become counter-productive and produce possible resistance from the RT.

R- Reflective Listening

Reflective listening is an essential part of MI. We use it particularly at Phases 1 & 2 in our meetings. It encourages the facilitators to listen carefully to the RTs and helps to establish empathy.

Although active and reflective listening techniques use the same principles, Athos & Gabarro (1978) describe how in "reflective listening" greater attention is given by the listener during therapy to the following areas:

- *Reflection of the speakers thoughts and feelings;*
- *Responding to rather than leading the conversion;*
- *Responding to feelings rather than content.*

Miller & Rollnick (2002) highlight how it is important not to assume that professionals involved in therapy are proficient in reflective listening and that *"skillful reflective listening is a difficult skill to master"* (p.190).

We were aware, prior to the intensive 3 day facilitator training, that all the trainees were knowledgeable about "active listening" (Rogers & Farson, 1979). Reflective listening, as described above, was a new concept to many – a skill which was not easily acquired by the trainees during the 3 day course.

Miller & Rollnick (1991) however outline how MI can be used by non-specialists as part of a brief intervention. This was very much the manner in which we anticipated the principles and techniques, including reflective listening, being used in our consultation meetings i.e. in an applied, integrated way.

Our facilitator training therefore only focused on the three basic elements of reflective listening, which we felt would be particularly beneficial during the earlier phases of the meeting. The three elements are:

-   repeating or rephrasing (especially at Phase 1) – *where the listener repeats or slightly amends what the speaker has said*

-   paraphrasing – *where the listener paraphrases or reframes, with meaning inferred, what the speaker has said*

-   reflection of feeling – *where the listener, on responding, focuses on an emotional aspect of what the speaker has said - also known as "emotion labelling"*

We provided a range of set phrases for the facilitators and encouraged them to continue to practice the technique after the training before they started the process with "real cases" in the schools. Examples included:

"You're angry because ...."

"Sounds like ...."

"You seem ...."

"It seems like you are feeling ...."

"Looks like you're feeling sort of ...."

S- Summaries

These are used throughout the process, particularly at each transition point e.g. moving from one phase to the next. The co-facilitator makes notes of the key points on the Summary Record Form and summarises at the end of each phase. The RT is also given a copy of the form at the end of the meeting. Below are examples of the summarising process at the end of Phase 1:

"Are there any other issues/concerns the group would like clarified?"

"Can I sum up what's been said .... Is that a fair reflection of your main concerns?"

Readiness to Change

The Trans-theoretical Model, generally referred to as the Stages of Change Model (Prochaska & DiClemente, 1982), provides a theoretical basis for MI. It was initially used to describe the series of stages people go through when trying to come to terms with problematic behaviour e.g. smoking, additions. Examples of its application within educational settings are found in McNamara (1992), Atkinson & Woods (2002) and Atkinson & Amesu (2007) in relation to their work with pupils evidencing problem behaviour.

In relation to Solution Focused Behaviour Therapy (SFBT) DeShazer (1985) describes the difference between "visitors", "complainants" and "customers" regarding the client's readiness for or willingness to undertake therapy.

The concept of readiness to change or motivation to change was addressed at two levels in our pilot: i) organisational whole school change and ii) individual change.

Organisational Change

Although originally developed to facilitate the promotion of change in individuals, the Stages of Change model has since been adapted for use in organisations e.g. Prochaska et al, 2001(b), Duckworth, chapter 8.

Organisational change is a complex issue. Schools like any organisation are constantly changing and therefore need staff to change with them. Attempting to effect change on a whole-school/systemic basis can be difficult and in many cases unsuccessful. Prochaska et al (2001b) postulate that this could be due to the fact that attempts at systemic change are often carried out without any real understanding or awareness of the psychology of the concept of change.

Prochaska (2000) argues that organisations go through the change process in more or less the same way as individuals. However, a potential difficulty lies in the fact that not all members of the organisation may be prepared to "buy into" the change process, especially if they feel it is imposed upon them.

It is estimated that less than 20% of employees in most organisations are willing to make changes that are imposed on them (Prochaska et al, 2001a). This highlights the importance of systemic change being a process, occurring over a period of time, involving ongoing staff consultation and collaboration.

Although we were aware that not all teaching staff would be willing to become involved in the pilot, from the outset we ensured that all teaching staff were kept informed and that the process was always transparent e.g. the staff briefing at the start of the process, which included a question and answer session. We also encouraged the schools involved to include a representative sample of staff in the membership of the BMT, in order to ensure that it was not seen as an alternative to the SMT. As this was operating within Stage 2 of the Code of Practice, we emphasised the importance of the school staff taking collective responsibility for the "problem situation". This term was used specifically, even on the referral form in order to move staff away from the idea of only referring individual pupils. It was made explicit that a problem with a group of pupils could be the reason for referral. Nonetheless, throughout the pilot RTs still tended to refer individual pupils. We concluded that the move towards an indirect model of service delivery would take time and involve a "cultural change" in schools.

The idea of collective responsibility is important - as managing change in schools inevitably requires staff to work together to achieve a common goal. Collective change is invariably linked with the concepts of collaboration and teamwork, which were objectives identified in the pilot aims. We found this especially significant in relation to the secondary schools involved. The RT in the secondary school was usually a Year Head or Form Teacher, whose role after the meeting would be to further consult and work with relevant school staff after the consultation meeting.

Prochaska at al (2001a) emphasise the importance of sharing knowledge and learning from others in order to become active participants in the change process. We had hoped initially that those RTs who found the consultation process helpful would share their success with colleagues, perhaps informally in the staffroom. We know of one example of a teacher who refused to become involved initially in the process because she felt it hadn't anything to offer her - very much a precontemplator! On hearing very positive feedback from her colleagues she eventually decided to refer to the group. Following the consultation meeting she told the facilitator involved that it had been a very useful meeting and that she felt, for the first time, her colleagues had really listened to her and taken her concerns seriously.

Another concern we had at the beginning of the process was that of "maintenance" i.e. the schools being willing to continue with the approach once the direct involvement of the Board facilitators was withdrawn. Some schools have shown "relapse" behaviour and have decided either to abandon the approach or allow it to just 'died away' through lack of regular use.

Before schools embarked on the pilot programme we emphasised the need for it to be included in the school development plan for the year – so that it was seen as a priority endeavour and so that dates and times for all the meetings were planned well in advance. This was done to indicate and acknowledge at a systemic level the importance of and the need for the school practices, policies and procedures to reflect the existence of and the need for the consultation meetings.

Individual Change

A basic assumption of the referral model was that referrals would be voluntary. Consequently, it was deemed reasonable to assume that the RTs were at least at the "contemplation" stage of the Prochaska & DiClemente model. However, this was not always the case as there were occasions when a RT was "encouraged" to refer by the school SMT or Head Teacher.

The RT's motivation for and readiness to change was something that the facilitators were encouraged to assess both at the time of referral, through analysis of comments on the referral form, and by being primed to listen carefully to what the RT said at each Phase of the consultation e.g.

- Phase 1: The RT's presentation of the problem situation

- Phase 2: The RT's willingness or ability to reflect meaningfully, honestly and positively on the problem situation.

- Phase 3: The type of theory/theories the RT presents, if any

- Phase 4: The RT's willingness to contribute towards strategy generation and/or acceptance of contributions by other group members

In conjunction with the above, the RT's non-verbal communication/body language was continuously assessed as was their reaction to input from other group members.

Each case consultation had its own particular slant and dynamic and its course and outcome depended, at least in part, on how the facilitators assessed the RT's position on the Stages of Change Model. Our intention was that the model would encourage positive change in a supportive environment and help the RT move through the Stages of Change.

The follow-up consultation was a useful monitoring device. Due to the facilitator's understanding of the the Stages of Change model, they were able to assess the RT's ability or willingness to i) put suggestions into action and (ii) maintain the plan implemented. Usually the RTs involved developed and implemented an action plan over the four weeks between initial consultation and the follow-up session.

The scaling question on the original referral form and follow-up was a particularly helpful monitoring device i.e. where the RT had to indicate their level of concern regarding the problem situation on a scale of 0 to 10, where 0 indicated no concern and 10 indicated most concerned.

Some examples of changes in response to the scaling question from the original referral form to follow-up are outlined below:

"On a scaling question where 0 means "no concern" and 10 means "most concerned", where are you regarding your concern?"

	Original Referral		Follow-up
RT1	9	———————→	2
RT2	10	———————→	3

RT1's problem situation involved a Year 6 pupil who was physically and verbally aggressive towards staff and peers. Strategies prior to the consultation tended to be negative and/or reactive.

At the consultation meeting it was suggested that RT1 should consider communicating more positively with the child, focusing on increased rates of approval for appropriate behaviours.

This change in behaviour management style in conjunction with individual social skills work with the pupil had a dramatic positive impact on the child's behaviour.

At follow-up RT1 recognised that the change in her own behaviour in relation to interactions with the child was very effective and reinforcing to her as a teacher. She was keen at follow-up to continue to maintain a more positive communication style with the pupil in future.

RT2's case involved a primary school child who was either refusing to eat in school or when she did would make herself sick. Prior to referral to the BMT, the child's mother was able to confirm that there was no apparent medical or physical reason for her daughter's behaviour. The behaviour was becoming increasingly distressing for the RT, resulting in ever increasing levels of anxiety and frustration about her ability to do anything about it. Prior to the initial consultation, the main intervention focus was to accentuate the child's inappropriate behaviour e.g. taking the child to the headteacher and asking him to speak to her.

Some basic behaviour management strategies were suggested at the initial meeting. These included:

- Use of positive reward programme, with daily and weekly rewards for the child when she at least made an attempt to eat at break and lunch time;

- Meeting with child's mother to encourage use of similar strategies at home;

- Working collaboratively with the Learning Support Assistant (LSA) in relation to the supervision and management of the behaviour, especially at break and lunch times when the problem was most evident.

At follow-up RT2 confirmed that the success of all three strategies had led to overall improvement in the child's willingness to eat in school. The RT recognised that the structured use of a behaviour management programme in conjunction with a more collaborative approach to intervention i.e. actively involving the child's mother and LSA had a significant impact on the child's problem behaviour. As a result RT2 felt less anxious about the child's behaviour. She was therefore able to lower her score considerably on the scaling question, regarding her concern, from the maximum of 10 to 3.

In general it emerged from follow-up sessions that RTs were prepared:

- To reflect more on their classroom practice;

- To acknowledge the interactive nature of problem behaviour in the classroom rather than focusing primarily on "within-child" factors;

- To recognise the impact that a positive change in their behaviour had on pupil behaviour.

RTs also highlighted the importance of effective "peer support" and shared responsibility as critical factors in managing problem pupil behaviour more successfully.

Conclusions/Reflections

In this chapter we have outlined the process of developing and implementing a school-based consultation pilot which draws on aspects of MI and applies it to work with teachers.

At the time of writing a second cohort of schools has been identified and a new group of facilitators trained. We intend to start the interventions with the Cohort 2 schools in September 2008.

We also intend to begin an in-depth, evaluation of the initial cohort (cohort 1). Feedback from cohort 1 participants has helped us considerably in the reflection process with regard to the nature of future training and practical amendments regarding the implementation of the model in schools.

In general, the schools involved have embraced the model and the resultant change wholeheartedly. Timing of the meetings was an issue that most schools commented on – meetings were held at the end of the school day. It was felt that this was not a good time to hold the meetings - teachers being delayed because of after-school duties, "end-of the-day" fatigue and the length of the consultation meetings all being cited as factors. We have addressed this at the initial awareness raising training for potential Cohort 2 schools by alerting Head Teachers to these issues and have encouraged them to think about time-tabling the meetings at a more suitable time

Most Cohort 1 schools indicated that they would have preferred much more information/training at the start of the process on a whole staff basis. We have expanded our briefing session with the whole staff of schools involved to make it more interactive and more informative. We also now place more emphasis on selling the possible benefits of involvement in the process for participants vis a vis

At whole school level:

- Providing professional support for staff;

- Creating an atmosphere of self-evaluation and reflection, assisting schools to become effective learning organisations;

- Developing an evaluative approach to school systems and procedures;

- Adopting a solution oriented outlook.

At a personal level:

- Increased repertoire of skills and interventions;

- Developing skills as a reflective professional;

- Continuing Professional Development and reflective practice including Induction, Early Professional Development and Performance Review and Staff Development

It was encouraging to find that the majority of cohort 1 schools felt confident to continue the process without active ELB facilitator support.

Feedback from ELB facilitators indicated that they found the process useful. Indeed some outreach teachers involved reported that they have started using solution-focused and MI approaches in relation to one-to-to consultations with teachers. Although one of our initial aims was to empower school personnel, facilitators report that they too felt more empowered professionally.

Facilitators also reported how beneficial and enjoyable it was to work collaboratively with a co-facilitator from a different educational discipline and with schools as active partners.

Future

Goals   Pending the outcome of the evaluation, we intend to expand the pilot on a year to year basis with the eventual aim of all schools in the two Education Library Boards being involved.

There is also the potential, on a more formal, structured basis, to extend the methods/techniques used in one-to-one consultation with individual teachers.

We would also like to i) further enhance the facilitation skills of the ELB facilitators e.g. through more specialist training in MI techniques and ii) expand on its usage within our approach.

Challenges   We have a substantial number of small Primary schools in our Education and Library Boards. Some of these are only 2, 3 or 4-teacher schools. We are considering the idea of "clustering". This would bring additional challenges but these can be met cf Dowd & Thorne (2007), who have described how they developed a model of consultation with clusters of schools.

Another challenge is that of schools which are currently unwilling or reluctant to become involved in the process. These schools may well have systemic behaviour management difficulties. Prochasksa and Velicer (1997) in an application of the Stages of Change model to health behaviour change found that the likelihood of success was increased when staged-appropriate change strategies were employed. Likewise, in an educational context, those schools we deem to be at the precontemplation stage will require ongoing "education" on the consultation model, involving the provision of more information on the potential benefits and awareness raising activities with staff. EPs, outreach teachers and BST members who are in regular contact with such schools are in an ideal position to provide this type of support and facilitation. They will be encouraged initially to apply the model to their work with willing, individual teachers in these schools. This strategy is based on the premise, outlined by Prochaska et al (2001a), that *"as individuals gain and share knowledge, learn from others, and become creative problem-solvers, they become active participants in change"* (p.10). Hopefully as groups of individual teachers begin to see the benefits of a move towards a consultative model of support, it is anticipated that they will encourage and influence the wider school staff to initiate steps to become involved at an organisational level.

Ensuring that schools maintain the impetus to continue with the process alone is a further challenge. Again the Stages of Change model could possibly help in this area e.g. by helping schools put in place relapse prevention strategies when they have reached the Maintenance stage - rather than providing reactive support when relapsed has occurred. Such strategies include encouraging schools to self-monitor the process as they continue without the direct ELB support. We also believe that in order to reduce the potential for relapse or dropout, that schools should formally integrate the group consultation framework into already-existing behaviour management policies, practices and procedures.

In conclusion although we have found the process challenging, we feel we have learned a lot as a result and have found that the "change" we are experiencing in relation to our role as educational professionals is both exciting and rewarding. This is particularly true in relation to the joint working involved with other professionals. By working in this collaborative way, sharing psychological theory and practice with our educational colleagues, we hope we have successfully "given another bit of psychology away" (Miller, 1969; Kay, 1972).

Acknowledgements

Special thanks to Mandy Yung, Educational Psychologist, SEELB and to Eithne McGinley, Assistant Advisory Officer, BELB for their significant contribution to the planning, development and implementation of the pilot.

We would also like to thank Dr. Harry Rafferty, Course Director, DECAP Course, School of Psychology, Queen's University, Belfast for his support and advice in preparing this chapter.

References

Arkowitz, H. & Miller, W.R. (2007) "Learning, Applying and Extending Motivational Interviewing" in Arkowitz, H., Westra, H.A., Miller, W.R. & Rollnick, S. (Ed.) *Motivational Interviewing in the Treatment of Psychological Problems.* New York/London: Guildford Publications

Athos, A.G. & Gabarro, J.J. (1978) Interpersonal behaviour: *Communication and understanding in relationships.* Englewood Cliffs, NJ: Prentice-Hall

Atkinson & Amesu (2007) Using Solution-Focused Approaches in Motivational Interviewing with Young People. *Pastoral Care,* June, 31-37

Atkinson & Woods (2003) Motivational Interviewing Strategies for Disaffected Secondary School Students: A Case Example. *Educational Psychology in Practice,* 19, (1), 49-64

Bandura, A. (1997) *Self-Efficacy in Changing Societies.* Cambridge: Cambridge University Press

Bozic, N. & Carter, A. (2002) Consultation Groups: participants' views. *Educational Psychology in Practice,* 18, (3), 189-202

Bundy, (2004) Changing behaviour: using motivational interviewing techniques. *Journal of the Royal Society of medicine,* 44, (7), 43-47

Department of Education for Northern Ireland [DENI] (1998a) *Code of Practice on the Identification and Assessment of Special Educational Needs.* Bangor: DENI

Department of Education for Northern Ireland [DENI] (1998b) *Promoting and sustaining good behaviour: A discipline strategy for schools.* Bangor: DENI.

De Jong, P. & Berg, I. (1998) *Interviewing for Solutions.* Brooks/Cole Publishing Company

De Shazer, S. (1985) Keys to Solutions in Brief Therapy. New York: Norton

Dowd, R. & Thorne, H. (2007) Developing levels of consultation in an Inner London Borough. *Support for Learning,* 22, (1), 31-35

Farouk, S. (2004) Group Work in Schools: A Process Consultation Approach. *Educational Psychology in Practice,* 20, (3), 207-219

Festinger, L. (1957) *A Theory of Cognitive Dissonance.* Evanston, IL: Row, Perterson & Company

Frederickson, N. (Ed.) (1990) *Soft Systems Methodology: Practical Approaches in Work with Schools.* London: Educational Psychology Publishing (UCL)

Gutkin, T.B. (1999) Collaborative versus Directive/Prescriptive/expert School-Based Consultation: Reviewing and Resolving a False dichotomy. *Journal of School Psychology* 37, (2), 161-190

Gutkin, T.B. & Curtis, M. J. (1982) "School Based consultation: Theory and techniques" in Gutkin, T. B. & Reynolds, C. R. (Ed.) *The Handbook of School Psychology* (2nd ed.) New York: Wiley

Hanko, G. (1995) *Special Needs in Ordinary Classrooms: from staff development to staff support.* London: David Fulton

Hanko, G. (1989) After Elton – How to "manage disruption"? *British Journal of Special Education,* 16, (4), 140-143

Harker, M. (2001) *"How to build solutions at meetings."* in Ajmal, Y. & Rees, I. (Ed.) Solutions in Schools. Creating Applications of Solution Focused Brief Thinking with Young People and Adults. London: BT Press

Kay, H. (1972) Psychology Today and Tomorrow. Bulletin of the Births. *Psychological Society,* 25, (88), 177-188

Kerslake, H. & Roller, J. (2000) The Development of "Scripts" in the Practice of Consultation. *Educational Psychology in Practice,* 16, (1), 25-30

Larney, R. (2003) School-Based Consultation in the United Kingdom. *School Psychology International,* 24, (1), 5-19

Lewis, T. F. & Osborn, C.J. (2004) Solution-Focused Counseling and Motivational Interviewing. A Consideration of Confluence. *Journal of Counselling & Development,* 82, (1), 38-49

McLean, A. (2003) *The Motivated School.* London: Paul Chapman Publishing

McNamara, E. (1992) Motivational Interviewing: The Gateway to Pupil Self-Management. *Pastoral Care in Education, 10(2)* 22-28

Miller, G.A. (1969) Psychology as a means of Promoting Human Welfare. *American Psychologist,* 24, 1063-1075

Miller, W.R. (1983) Motivational Interviewing with Problem Drinkers. *Behavioural Psychotherapy,* 11, 147-172

Miller, W.R. & Rollnick, S. (2002) *Motivational Interviewing: Preparing People for Change.* New York: Guildford press

Miller, W.R. & Rollnick, S. (1991) *Motivational Interviewing: Preparing People for Change.* New York: Guildford press

Office of Public Sector Information (OPSI). *The Special Educational Needs and Disability (Northern Ireland Order).* Bangor, UK. Department for Education (2005)

Prochaska, J.M. (2000), A transtheoretical model for assessing organizational change: a study of family service agencies' movement to time-limited therapy, *Families in Society: The Journal of Contemporary Human Services,* 81 (1), 76-84

Prochaska, J. M., Levesque, D.A., Prochaska, J. O., Dewart, S. R. & Wing, G. R. (2001a) Mastering Change: A Core Competency for Employees. *Brief Treatment and Crisis Intervention,* 1, (1), 7-15

Prochaska, J. M., Prochaska, J. O., & Levesque, D.A. (2001b) A transtheoretical approach to changing organisations. *Administration and Policy in Mental Health,* 28, (4), 247-261

Prochaska, J. O. & DiClemente, C.C. (1982) Transtheoretical Therapy: Toward a More Integrative Model of Change. *Psychotherapy: Theory, Research and Practice,* 19, (3), 276-288

Prochaska, J.O. & Velicer, W. F. (1997) The transtheoretical model of health behaviour change. *American Journal of Health promotion,* 12, (1), 38-48

Reinke, W.M. (2006) The classroom check-up: a brief intervention to reduce current and future student problem behaviours through classroom teaching practices. *Dissertation Abstracts International: Section B: The Sciences and Engineering.* 66, (7-B), 3935

Rogers, C. and Farson, R. (1979) "Active Listening" in Kolb, D., Rubin. I. and MacIntyre, J. *Organizational Psychology (third edition),* New Jersey: Prentice Hall

Rollnick, S., Heather, N. & Bell, A. (1992) Negotiating behaviour change in medical settings. The development of brief motivational interviewing. *Journal of Mental Health,* 1, 25-37

Rollnick,S. & Miller,W.R.(1995) What is Motivational Interviewing? *Behavioural and Cognitive Psychotherapy.* 23, 325-334

Rollnick, S., Miller, W.R. & Butler, C.C. (2008) *Motivational Interviewing in Health Care: Helping Patients Change Behavior.* New York/London: Guildford Publications

Schein, E. (1988) *Process Consultation: Its Role in Organisation Development. Vol.1 (2nd Edition)* Workington: Addison-Wesley

Senge, P. (1990) *The Fifth Discipline: The Art and Practice of the Learning Organisation.* London: Century Business

Treasure, J. & Ward, A. (1997) A Practical Guide to the Use of Motivational Interviewing in Anorexia Nervosa. *European Eating Disorders Review,* 5, (2), 102-114

Wagner, P. (2000) Consultation: developing a comprehensive approach to service delivery. *Educational Psychology in Practice,* 16, (1), 9-18

Wagner, P. (1995) School Consultation: frameworks for the practicing educational psychologist – a handbook. Kensington and Chelsea Educational Psychology Service, 108A Lancaster Rd, London W11 1QS

Wagner, P. & Gillies, E. (2001) "Consultation: A solution focused approach" in Ajmal, Y. & Rees, I. (Ed.) *Solutions in Schools. Creating Applications of Solution Focused Brief Thinking with Young People and Adults.* London: BT Press

Chapter 10

Concluding Observations

Eddie McNamara

From its early beginnings in the 1980's motivational interviewing theory and practice has developed considerably. There is no doubt that it will continue to be further refined and developed over the coming years. This publication has attempted to bring together descriptions of some of the work that is being done with children, adolescents and young adults - work stimulated by the theory, practice and ideals of motivational interviewing.

It is probably the case that much more varied work based on MI is being carried out with children, adolescents and young adults than is reflected in this publication, for many innovative practitioners do not have a propensity to publish their work. A second edition of this publication, planned for 2011, will be aimed at reflecting a wider range of applications with this client group.

A significant question that is asked regarding the use of motivational interviewing is "Can it be used effectively when working with young children?"

In part the answer to this question is dependent on the therapist's skills with regard to translating and interpreting the semantic content of MI theory and practice into child friendly language which is understandable and meaningful to the child, and in part on the child's capacity to respond effectively and differentially to what they feel, hear and understand.

Williams, B. (2009, Personal Communication) has worked effectively using MI strategies with children in the 7 years to 11 years age range - see Appendix.

Motivational Interviewing – a Changing Concept?

The definition of motivational Interviewing has evolved over the last quarter of a century. In 1983 Miller (p147) defined motivational interviewing as...

> *".... an approach based upon principles of experimental social psychology, applying processes such as attribution, cognitive dissonance and self efficacy. Motivation is conceptualized as an interpersonal process and the model places heavy emphasis on individual responsibility and internal attribution of change."*

In the years since Miller's 1983 publication change is to be seen with regard to clarifying, refining and specifying the *processes* of motivational interviewing. More recently emphasis has been re-directed from the specification of the *processes* of MI to the specification of the spirit of MI.

In their publication Motivational Interviewing, 1991, Miller and Rollnick emphasized that from its beginning Motivational Interviewing has been *practical* in focus.

In the same publication (p 52), in answer to the question "What is Motivational Interviewing?" they respond with an essentially functional definition, namely

> *"It is a particular way to help people recognize and do something about their present or potential problems".*

They then go on to list five general principles of MI, namely -

> express empathy
> develop discrepancy
> avoid argumentation
> roll with resistance
> support self efficacy

In the 2002 edition of their Motivational Interviewing publication, Miller and Rollnick developed and refined the definition of Motivational interviewing as

> *"MI is a client centred, directive method for enhancing intrinsic motivation to change by exploring and resolving ambivalence".*

In this latter publication they 'drop' *avoid argumentation* as a principle, presumably because if the other principles were being followed arguments would not arise.

Perhaps the biggest change to be seen with regard to Miller and Rollnick's description and definition of motivational interviewing is that whereas initially they emphasized the *practical nature* of the contents of motivational interviewing in the latter publication that emphasize the *spirit* of motivational interviewing.

In the latter of their two publications they describe MI "a way of *'being with people'* " (p 34) and go on to identify its' underlying spirit as being concerned with *"understanding and experiencing the human nature that gives rise to that way of being"*.

Such a move away from a purely functional definition to a more abstract one could give rise to a diversity of interpretations of what constitutes MI and the spirit of MI. Perhaps to counteract this possibility, Millar and Rollnick then go some way towards operationalising the concept of the 'spirit of MI' by describing facets of 'the spirit' eg

Collaboration   – working as an equal partner with the client

Evocation   - not imparting things to the client eg wisdom, insight or
                     reality, but eliciting these things from within the client

Autonomy   - acceptance and respect for the fact that responsibility
                     for change, or no change, lies with the client

In their most recent publication Miller and Rollnick (2009) express a degree of concern that the evolution on MI has, in some instances, produced conceptions and descriptions on MI that depart substantially from how they have understood this method. It is perhaps significant that in this paper, titled *"Ten things that Motivational Interviewing is not"*, they refer to "this method" re. MI, as apposed to making reference to "the spirit" of MI.

Miller and Rollnick's (2009) current definition of MI is

> *"MI is a collaborative, person - centred form of guiding to elicit and strengthen motivation for change".*

While many, if not all, Practitioners of MI believe their practice to be substantially consistent with the tenets of MI as espoused by Miller and Rollnick, some nonetheless use alternative semantics when describing their practice. For example, the terms 'motivational dialogues' and 'motivational conversations' are sometimes used. These alternative semantics circumvent possible sterile debates regarding what constitutes MI in contexts in which helpful practices are being developed to help clients help themselves.

Descriptive Models and Working Models

Duckworth (section 2, chapter 8) describes how he used the TTM to elicit motivation in school staff with regard to systemic behaviour change - a clear example of how many practitioners see MI and TTM as inextricably linked.

In their latest publication (2009) Miller and Rollnick emphasize that MI is not based on the trans-theoretical model (TTM), although they do refer to there being a 'natural fit' between MI and the TTM (p 130). They point out that, while MI and the TTM were both presented at the 3rd International Conference on Treatment of Addictive Behaviours (1984), MI was never based on the TTM . But Miller and Rollnick do then go on to acknowledge that the stages of change model provides a logical way to think about the clinical role of MI, and MI in turn provides a clear example of how clinicians can help people to move from pre-contemplation and contemplation to preparation and action.

Whatever the nuances of definition of MI, there is no doubt that the techniques of Motivational Interviewing have been profoundly influential in helping people change and that the TTM has enabled the practice of Motivational Interviewing to be carried out with a degree of precision which might otherwise have not been the case.

In my opinion, the complementary nature of Motivational interviewing and the TTM is best appreciated within the nomenclature of 'models'. A 'model' is a representation of something.

The TTM is a *descriptive* model in that it describes the phases through which an individual may move in a progression from not being motivated to change their position, be it with reference to belief, behaviour or attitude, to a position of being motivated to change and engaging in change activities. However, the model does not indicate how such movements can either be achieved by the individual in question or be facilitated by a helper.

In contrast to the above, Motivational Interviewing is a *working* model. The unique characteristic of a working model is that it "tells you what to do". In other words, the techniques of Motivational Interviewing facilitate 'the helper' collaborating effectively with 'the helped' in the journey from the pre-contemplative to the active change phase.

Thus there would be few, if any, who would disagree with the conclusion of DiClemente and Velasquez (2002) that the TTM, in particular the stages of change aspect of the model, has played an integral role in the development of Motivational Interviewing and brief interventions using a motivational approach.

No Help for Those Who Don't Want to Be Helped

In the past it has been common practice, which can still be found today, for 'Help Agencies' and individual therapists to strike off clients from their list whom they deem to be 'not motivated' to engage with them in the therapeutic process.

In a way this is a sensible pragmatic approach to take – for it is obviously 'more sensible' to work with clients who want to change than with clients who do not want to change. Nonetheless some would question the ethics of designating some potential clients as 'unreachable'.

Such an individual or Service response to clients deemed to be 'uncooperative' may in fact mask personal feelings on the part of the putative helper. These personal feelings may be of professional inadequacy because of their inability to engage with such hard to reach clients.

Thus, just as the hard to reach client with personal problems may believe that their situation is hopeless in that they do not have the personal capacity to achieve change, so to the professional helper may have similar feelings with regard to their professional situation ie it is hopeless in that they have not the capacity ie therapeutic skills, to engage with the 'hard to reach'.

Viewed in the context of the above two described perspectives, MI as a therapeutic resource both *addresses* the client's feelings of personal hopelessness and personal inadequacy and *redresses* the therapist's professional feelings of professional hopelessness and professional inadequacy.

References

DiClemente, C.C. and Velasquez, M. M. Motivational Interviewing and the Stages of Change in Motivational Interviewing Preparing People for Change WR Miller and S. Rollnick the Guilford press New York 2002

Miller, R.W. (1983) Motivational Interviewing with Problem Drinkers. Behavioural Psychotherapy, 11, 147 - 172

Miller and Rollnick (1991) Motivational Interviewing: Preparing People to Change Addictive Behaviour. The Guilford press New York 2002

Miller and Rollnick (2002) Motivational Interviewing: Preparing People for Change WR Miller and S. Rollnick the Guilford press New York 2002

Miller, W.R. and Rollnick, S. (2009) Ten Things That Motivational Interviewing Is Not. Behaviour and Cognitive Psychotherapy, vol. 37, No. 2 pp129 – 140.

An Invitation

A second edition of this publication is planned for 2011. If you are working with children, adolescents or young adults, either directly or indirectly, using MI/TTM and would like to contribute to this publication contact:

gmcnam7929@aol.com

Appendix

Working with Younger Children

Can MI be used when working with young children?

In the light of the fact that this question has not been addressed in any of the chapters of this publication, it is responded to by way of reporting the substantial content of a personal communication received with regard to this question (Beth Williams,2009). Beth's work identified problems and strategies relevant to working with younger children.

Context

The work was conducted in the context of a Local Education Authority initiative to identify children at risk of entering segregated specialist educational provision for children evidencing SEBD (social, emotional and behavioural difficulties).

This work was carried out by Beth when she was the Psychologist heading a two year BEST (Behaviour and Education Support Team) Primary school initiative.

Three schools were selected for inclusion in the BEST initiative - on the criteria of' 'high incidence' of EBD pupils. The target pupils were identified after all Key Stage 2 pupils (aged 7 to 11 years) had been screened using the BIP (Behaviour in Primary school) Vulnerability Matrix.

Preliminary Work

The first task Beth identified when beginning to work with the selected pupils was to establish if they understood the distinction and links between behaviour, thoughts and feelings.

This was done by discussion with the pupils and engaging them in non problem related activities prior to and separate from consideration of the pupil behaviour that was of concern for their teachers.

The purpose of this was to ensure that, before working with the pupils in an MI context, the pupils understood that the way they thought and felt influenced the way they acted - and similarly the way they acted influenced the way they felt and thought.

Beth identified that a significant number of the selected pupils had not developed the competencies of differentiating thoughts from feelings from behaviour.

This was the major obstacle encountered when working with pupils in this age range.

This obstacle was identified to be substantially semantic rather than developmental ie involved the problems the children encountered with regard to vocabulary. The children, especially the younger ones, did not have a wide enough vocabulary with which to express themselves with regard to thoughts, feelings and behaviour. In particular, they experienced great difficulty separating and expressing their thoughts, which were often judgmental, from their feelings.

First Goal of Intervention

To enable the pupils' to master the distinction between thoughts and feelings was the first task identified, particularly to broaden their vocabulary regarding their feelings.

The SEAL (Social Emotional Aspects of Learning) materials - materials disseminated to all Primary schools by the DfES (Department for Education and Skills) were used to achieve this.

These materials were developed as part of the Government's *Primary Behaviour Strategy.* Included in the resources are comprehensive age related lists of words for the purpose of widening the children's vocabulary with regard to labeling and describing emotions.

The materials also include photographs - which can be used to help children to identify non-verbal behaviour/expressions that help to cue them as to which emotion is being experienced.

An understanding and mastery of a range of appropriate words to describe these emotions was established through the use of flashcards, discussion, matching words and pictures and story telling – the last listed being a particularly effective teaching strategy.

Beth read stories to the group, checking out what they thought a character might be feeling. The children each had a list of words they could use as an aide memoire when they struggled to find the words to communicate how they felt the story character was feeling.

Beth also modeled emotional expression for the children during the story sessions. Beth told them when she was excited, sad, proud as appropriate. Beth made sure that she did not just express positive emotions but negative ones such as feeling ashamed of herself if she had failed to do something she had promised or frustrated if materials or room space was not available as she had expected.

She provided feeling names for children's emotional expression. For example, if a child wanted to use a paint colour that was in use Beth would suggest they might be feeling disappointed that they had to wait until their turn. Similarly, when they did something well Beth would suggest they might be feeling pleased or proud with what they had accomplished. Beth too had a feelings word list as an aide memoire to make sure she did not repeatedly use the same words.

When further work was required around extending the range of emotions that the child could recognise, recall and describe Beth used the Emotional Toolkit.

The story telling and, when appropriate, Emotional Toolkit Activities, were followed by activities which were set up to make explicit the distinction between thoughts and feelings. The first activity was a game Beth created based on naming thoughts, acts and feelings on sort cards. Beth made the cards herself. The activity was then integrated into classroom writing activities. The pupils were asked to produce pieces of persuasive writing. Initially, the children were helped to separate their thoughts and feelings about social issues such as recycling and the banning of football in the playground. The same activities were then used when considering more emotive topics such as bullying and racism.

Second Goal of Intervention

This was *cueing them into the moment.* Often the children were unfocused and 'not present' in the moment under discussion i.e. they couldn't project themselves back to the "problem" situation under discussion and so they could not report about or respond to enquiries about their thoughts and feelings at the time - as they were unaware of them. It appeared that they often tended to respond to situations without any thought as to the nature of their response or its' possible consequences. This was less obvious with the older year 6 group of children (aged 10 to 11 years) than with the year 5 children (aged 9 to 10 years). It is possible that developmental factors played a part in this. It became apparent over time that the children, particularly those who acted out, just responded to an emotional stimulus without any apparent acknowledged thought. This was a feature of their holistic response that made it difficult for them ie the young people, to modify their behaviour.

To encourage reflection on each aspect of the triad of thoughts, feelings and behaviour, Beth encouraged the children to draw pictures representing an incident of concern. Using the picture of the incident as a stimulus, the children were then encouraged to fill in captions of what they were thinking and feeling at the time.

Following on from this, the children were led in a discussion about how a change in one modality of functioning might lead to changes in the other two modalities. For example, if, on hearing a noise in the night, they hid in a wardrobe, it was pointed out to them (or they volunteered the opinion) that they were frightened because they thought that a burglar had entered their house. The children then identified this thought as the explanation as to why they hid in the wardrobe. It was then put to the children that the noise that they heard in the night might be caused by their elder brother coming in late after a night out. The link between this thought and behaviour different from hiding in the wardrobe was then discussed and the children were facilitated to draw a different cause – effect relationship ie that they would feel re-assured and content and that they would go to sleep.

Conclusions

Beth's judgment about the children she worked with was somewhat as follows.

"They did not generally experience specific speech and language difficulties. Rather, their "language difficulties" were limited specifically to

- the reception and understanding of the language of emotion

- the expression of emotion through language.

In addition

- they did not pick up on the emotional content of others' speech through non-verbal signals or tone of voice and

- they were unable to articulate their own emotions as they had no adequate way to label how they felt.

Consequently the children's communications were compromised by frustration. This in turn may have had a negative impact on their self esteem and lowered their feelings of self efficacy. Parents, teachers and other pupils' negative responses to their maladaptive behaviour may have compounded these effects."

Thus the activities engaged in by Beth, when successful, promoted the pupils' self esteem and feelings of self efficacy - two of the goals of MI.

The work engaged in by Beth is of particular significance as it is

- "therapeutically targeted" at the needs of younger children evidencing EBSD

- consistent with achieving the goals of MI (improved self-esteem, knowledge of "problems", concern about "problems, internal attribution style and elevated feelings of self-efficacy and

- is consistent with national educational initiatives – for the National Curriculum guidelines for Primary schools recommend that all pupils should understand the link between thoughts feelings and behaviour before moving on to secondary school.

Historically, interventions with younger children evidencing SEBD have had a behavioural bias and have focused on changing the pupil's observable and recordable behaviour. But over the last decade or so the limitations of a solely behavioural approach have been recognised. The focus of interventions has shifted from being mainly about diminishing behaviour that has been considered unwanted or dysfunctional towards a cognitive behaviour approach – addressing children's thoughts and feelings as well as behaviour.

An important manifestation of cognitive behavioral approaches is the collaborative nature of the endeavour embarked upon between helper and helped.

Such collaboration requires that the person to be helped is actually motivated to engage with the helping endeavour. Motivational interviewing provides the helper with the means of eliciting such engagement. Beth's work identifies some of the problems that are encountered when working with younger children vis-à-vis the children's competencies to engage with motivational interviewing.

Readers interested in working with children within a cognitive-behavioural paradigm are referred to the 2002 Paul Stallard book.

Reference

(Emotional Intelligence Toolkit - available from:
http://www.aquietplace.co.uk/shop.html).

Stallard, P. (2002) Think Good- Feel Good Cognitive Behaviour Therapy Workbook for Children and Young People. John Wiley, Chichester

Also Available from PBM Publications

Pastoral Management Series

1.	On – Report	Eddie McNamara
2.	Pupil Self Management	Eddie McNamara
3.	Behaviour Contracts	Eddie McNamara
4.	Classroom Management	Eddie McNamara
5.	Anxiety Management	Eddie McNamara
6.	Motivational Interviewing	Eddie McNamara
7.	Cognitive Behavioural Management	Mark Fox
8.	Responding to Pupil Bereavement	Leslie Ratcliffe
9.	Pupil Support: a Solution Focused Approach	Ioan Rees
10.	Anger and Its Management	Jackie Lown
11.	Circle of friends: Promoting Social Inclusion	Jackie Lown
12.	Promoting Self Esteem	Jackie Lown
13.	Promoting Emotional Literacy	Gillian Shotton
14.	Changing the Thinking and Feeling to Change Behaviour: Cognitive interventions*	Garry Squires
15.	Preventing and Responding to Bullying in Schools	Val Besag

Pastoral Intervention Series

1.	Therapeutic Stories	Gillian Shotton
2.	Accelerated Learning	Peter Lloyd Bennett
3.	Coaching in Schools*	Zoe Stephens, Jacqueline Lee and Elinor Wilde

All publications £7.99 except* which are £9.99

10% discount when ordering full set.

Behaviour Checklist for Primary Schools

Description The Behaviour Checklist consists of

1. seven classes of behaviour each consisting of 10 items -- each item is a description of pupil behaviour which could be a cause of concern.

The classes of behaviour are:-

i) *Academic behaviours* ii) *In seat/out of seat* iii) *Behaviours concerned with rules and routines* iv) *Verbal' noisy behaviours* v) *Aggression (towards pupils)* vi) *Aggression (towards teachers)* vii) *Social/Emotional behaviours*

2. A Checklist of factors in the classroom environment which may be associated with disruptive pupil behaviour.

The Checklist is also designed for the pupil's teachers to describe the pupil's positive attributes.

Purpose

To structure teacher information in order to answer the following questions about pupil behaviour and the circumstances in which it occurs.

i)   What does the pupil do to disrupt lessons?
ii) To what extent is the teacher concerned about the behaviours?
iii) Are the behaviours associated with specific circumstances?
iv) Can the specific circumstances be changed?

The *manual* describes how a baseline assessment of pupil behaviour can be made and how the information can be used to formulate an individual behaviour plan (IBP). Methods of evaluating the effectiveness of the IBP are also described.

Price £29.99 incl. postage. All material can be photocopied.

Towards Better Behaviour: a CD Secondary School Resource

Part I   The Behaviour Survey Checklist*

Purpose

The behaviour survey checklist and summary chart is a schedule designed for secondary teachers to

i)   identify in the problematic behaviour of a pupil who disrupts lessons
ii)   provide a profile of the lessons in which disruptive behaviour occurs
iii) identify the circumstances which are associated with disruptive behaviour
iv)   provide a profile of the nature of the disruptive behaviour
v)   describe the pupils academic ability and social skills in the context of his class

Part II   Assessment

This consists of four checklists/observation schedules, an assessment model for pupil motivation and an assessment strategy for pupil compliance, and 83 page manual.

1. *The Pupil Management Checklist.* This is designed to assess   i) if appropriate in-school responses to pupil problem behaviour have been implemented and   ii) the effectiveness of in-school responses in promoting appropriate pupil behaviour

2. *The Pupil Behaviour Schedule.* This is designed to provide answers to the following questions   i) **what amount of time** does the referred pupil spend on-task and off – task?   ii) what is the **nature** of the off-task behaviour?   ii) how does the referred pupil's **behaviour compare** with that of other class members?   what **quantitative** and **qualitative** behaviour change occurred as a result of changes in classroom management?

3. *The Classroom Situation* This Checklist this is designed to assess **factors in the classroom** which may be associated with appropriate and inappropriate behaviour

4. The *off Task Behaviour Analysis* This Schedule is designed for the detailed observation and analysis on an individual pupil's behaviour.
(Includes 98 page manual).

Part III   Intervention

This resource consists of a wide range of protocols, templates, contracts, teacher monitored on report protocols, pupil/teacher conjoint on report protocols, and pupil self-management materials. Purchase of this resource includes photocopying rights and development rights of the contents for use in the purchaser's service. (Includes 92 page manual).

Cost, including p & p. Part I £59.99, Part II £59.99, Part III £59.99. Full set £149.99